THE AUTHOR AND HIS BOOK

David Northcroft spent the earlier part of his boyhood in Worcestershire and Susse father became exciseman at Cragganmore Distillery, Ballindalloch, Banffshire, he was moved up to the North-east. He has seen no reason to live anywhere else ever since.

He attended Aberlour High School, followed by degrees at the Universities of Aberdeen, Cambridge and a doctorate at Stirling. His career has been in education, firstly as a teacher of English at Aberdeen Grammar School, then as a member of staff at Aberdeen College of Education (later Northern College). By the time of his early retirement he was Vice Principal.

He has divided the happy years since then between helping to look after granddaughters and researching in, first, Scottish school education and latterly in oral history, where he has concentrated on building up an archive of personal reminisce from North-east folk. In November 2010, he brought out what is planned to be the first of four volumes which draw upon these recollections: *Grampian Lives, 1900-1950* (Leopard Press), followed three years later by *Grampian Lives, 1950-2000*. The present volume, *Aberdeen Lives Volume 1: Aberdeen at Work and Play* is their follow up. He also is responsible for two earlier books: *Scots at School* (Edinburgh University Press, 2003) and *North-east Identities and Scottish Schooling* (Aberdeen University Press, 2005).

He has lived in Muchalls for nearly fifty years. He is married to Kathleen and they have two sons: Jonathan, who as Football Correspondent to the Sunday Times is based in the south where he is forced to watch Man U and Chelsea rather than the Dons, and then Mat, who is both a Primary school teacher and a Grade 1 referee. Mat, Elaine and his three North-east granddaughters – Erin, Abby and Rachael – also live round the corner in Muchalls and together with the more recently arrived offspring of Jonathan and Jan – Ishbel and Cora – are, all five of them, a constant source of wonderment and delight.

While the bulk of the interviews which fill this volume were conducted by David Northcroft, some dozen of them were the work of **Ken McHardy** who describes himself as the son of a 'toonser' and a 'teuchter'. He was born in Fonthill Maternity Home in 1955, first lived in a tenement in Causewayend and then grew up in Kincorth, starting school there. He moved on to Aberdeen Grammar School at the age of nine where, in 1967, he first met his young English teacher, David Northcroft. Ken went on to study medicine at Aberdeen University and a career as a diabetes specialist in Aberdeen with a major interest in teaching and training.

Aberdeen Lives: Work and Play purports to offer a collective portrait of the shape and texture of daily life in the city of Aberdeen, as experienced by folk who have spent formative years there. The personal recollections which appear in this book are extracted from the recorded words of some of the 500 people David Northcroft has interviewed over the last 16 years. Usually these interviews have been made in the subjects' own homes and been conducted in an informal, conversational style. The selection of witnesses – commonly derived from word-of-mouth recommendation or newspaper letters and stories – has been guided by the wish to cover a representative range of places, social backgrounds and occupations.

This present work focuses on both the working and the recreational and sporting life of Aberdeen during the twentieth century. In that respect it acts as a complement volume to the author's earlier pair of Grampian Lives books in that, while they concentrated on the region's rural and coastal experiences, Aberdeen Lives: Work and Play is devoted to the city itself

It is intended that this volume will be followed by one more: *Aberdeen Lives: War and Peace* which will include such aspects as family and community life, school, church and the arts, and so complete a four-part rounded portrait of daily life in our own North-east of Scotland.

Readers are invited to get in touch with observations and further memories. They may do so at **davidjnorthcroft@gmail.com** or telephone 01569 730621.

Published in October, 2017

A catalogue record for this book is available from the British Library

ISBN 978-0-9570999-8-2

Design and typesetting by Leopard Press
LePress@btconnect.com

Printed and bound in Scotland by
Robertsons, Forfar

Published by Leopard Press
Auld Logie, Pitcaple, Inverurie, Aberdeenshire AB51 5EE

ABERDEEN LIVES

Aberdeen at Work and Play

Volume 1: 1901–2000

David Northcroft

Dedication

To the memory of Roderick Lakin, 1949-2015. Born and bred in Aberdeen but one who went forth to share his generous talents with the wider world of music and the arts.

Acknowledgements

No book can ever be produced without the assistance and support of others- in the case of *Aberdeen Lives* that has been especially so.

While the great majority of the photographs which illustrate the reminiscences in the pages that follow have been provided by the speakers themselves - people who have trustingly allowed me access to precious family collections - I must thank a number of other helpers. Some ten images have been purchased from Aberdeen Journals and here I must thank Duncan Smith for effecting this business in such a friendly and helpful manner. Similarly David Oswald of the City Library's Silver Vault collection has facilitated the acquisition of the four photographs which are attributed to Aberdeen City Libraries and has done so in a most speedy and supportive way.

A number of individuals have been helpful in a variety of ways, either by establishing contacts with likely interviewees or by readily answering specific queries. They are Chris Anstock; David Brown; Irene Bryce; Janet Byth; Ron Caie; Bob Cooper; John Dunn; Mike Forbes; Bill Gordon; David Hartley; Ian Lakin; Graham Law of the Scottish Rugby Union; Betty Lawrie; Rosy Long; Moira Mapley; Bob Meconi; Jennifer Meek; Irene Milne; Sylvia Petty; Rod Ramsay; Alistair Ritchie; Dennis Scott; Alison Sharman of the University's Elphinstone Institute; Bill Sleigh; Howard Smith; Carol Strang; Gwen Topp; Brian Watt; the families of Frances Garden and Bill Anderson; Midstocket Church Men's Group; the Torry Heritage Society.

Even more important has been the enthusiastic and collaborative help unstintingly offered me by my old Aberdeen Grammar School pupil and Balmoral Cricket Club team mate (and occasional run out partner), Ken McHardy. His contribution is explained in the 'About the Author' section but I would wish here to add the extent to which it has been a real pleasure to have enlisted his assistance in the composition of *Aberdeen Lives*: not only has he uncovered some dozen valued interviewees but he has also proved to be a ferociously vigilant proof reader. Many, many thanks, Ken.

Once more I must also offer up hearty thanks to Lindy Cheyne and to Ian Hamilton of the Leopard Press, whose genial and inspiring co-operation has exceeded the normal bounds of professional assistance. Not only have they performed their customary skilled and creative task in editing and laying out the presentation of *Aberdeen Lives*, they have been fine folk to have worked with.

I would dearly like to thank my family for being just that - my family, an unfailing source of life-giving support. The names of this incomparable set of North-east and North-east related people are Kathleen, Jonathan, Mat, Elaine, Jan, and young Erin, Abby, Rachael, Ishbel and Cora.

But above all else, my gratitude belongs to all the City and North-east folk who have opened up their memories to me. Once I had exhausted the circle of my own relatives and friends I became dependent upon the willingness of complete strangers to welcome me into both their homes and their lives, there to ply me with fly cups, home bakes and their own very human stories. The names which appear in this book confirm the truth that the city of Aberdeen and its rural and coastal hinterland contain some of the finest people you could hope to meet anywhere. I hope that they will accept this further volume as my repeated tribute to them.

Cover Photograph

This shot depicts the fitting team which worked on an order at Hall Russell's shipyard in the 1890s. It has been supplied by Norma Reid whose own story as a Fittie girl and the daughter of an engine driver appears in Chapters 3 and 7 of this book. Her Granda Kelly, a skilled cabinet maker, is shown second left, back row.

Notes

The words which appear in this book are taken from transcripts of recordings of the recollections offered by the named contributors to it. In each case, scripts were sent back to the speakers for their amendments before an agreed version was arrived at. The accounts set out in *Aberdeen Lives* are selected extracts: the typical interview lasted some 90 minutes and generated over 4,000 words. Editing has been kept to the minimum necessary to smooth out repetitions and hesitations and also to produce a narrative flow.

Witnesses spoke in their own accents and dialect. As these ranged along a continuum of usage rather than falling into any distinct 'Standard English'/ 'Doric'/ 'City Spik' category – often within the one interview – the decision has been made to render their words in the one Standard form, excepting emphatic instances of reported direct speech.

The place names which appear after each speaker's name refer to the locations focussed on in their recollections, not birth or current living places. The names of interviewees appear as given to me which in the case of women has usually been their married rather than their maiden forms.

Many more interviewees have given of themselves than I have been able to squeeze into either this present volume or the companion *Aberdeen Lives; at War and Peace* which is planned to come out in the autumn of 2018. I hope they will not take their omission as being enforced by anything other than the exigencies of space. My great discovery in researching this book is that everyone – and especially in the North-east – has a worthwhile story to tell whether I have found the room for it or not.

Sadly, but inevitably, given their age range, some of my witnesses have subsequently died. As, however, it has been difficult to ascertain exact dates and occurrences, the decision has been made to give the date of birth only.

Every effort has been made to trace the provenance of the photographs reproduced in this book. If, however, any outstanding examples are found then the copyright holder is invited to contact the author.

CONTENTS

ABERDEEN LIVES, GRAMPIAN LIVES
Town and Country, City and Shire

The North-east contains some of the finest types of the true Scot. They smell of their soil; the smoke of the peat is about them
W.S. Bruce: *The Nor-east.* 1922

There's this work ethic; if you can't afford something then you just can't have it. No shortcuts, no loans. This springs from the morality of the North-east. I can't imagine this applies to the same extent elsewhere, not in Aberdeen. But by the time you get to Dunecht, going out towards Alford, most people will have this mind-set.
Norman Harper: *North-east Identities and Scottish Schooling.* 2005

I loved dealing with North-east patients, especially those from the country. They were, and are, so stoical, so forgiving and so anxious to help you help them, an attitude that seems to be common in a region where climate, the nature of the land, and the attitudes inherited from a farming or a fishing background have grown people with a firm grip of reality.
Audrey Dawson: interviewed 2014

So there you have it: we might group together the entities of Aberdeenshire, Kincardine, Banffshire and Moray, alongside the city of Aberdeen itself, as comprising the one regional identity of Grampian or the 'North-east' but in practice we would rather think of it as falling into two distinct entities – town and country, city and shire, town people and country folk. A branding of identities which is sometimes – and in a not altogether complimentary way – fixed as 'toonser' and 'teuchter'.

More than this, we often turn the separation into a judgement. Although the city of Aberdeen holds fully one half of its population, the 'real' North-east, in character and essence, is, we instinctively respond, to be found, not on its bustling streets, its stony tenements or its quiet West End bungalows and mansions, still less in its ever sprawling suburbs, but somewhere out there, within the hard-won acres, the fishing ports, the proudly self-sufficient villages and small towns which make up its vast rural hinterland.

The smoke of the peat may be long gone but the flavour of its homely warmth lingers in the memory to suggest an earthy reality that no coal-fired grate or factory stack could ever rival.

The comments of Audrey Dawson, reflections born of a career tending the region's sick at its central hospital at Foresterhill, point to the underlying reasons. What we like to think of as the essential North-east character –

its stoicism, the uncomplaining acceptance of all that life can throw at you – is a quality born as the legacy of generations who have had to contend with the unremitting vagaries of soil, of weather, of tides and running seas. Life on the land or out on the North Sea is more elemental, more character forming, than any easier existence among the protective comforts of the city can ever be. It is this which has given North-east folk their 'firm grip upon reality'.

Such an approving evaluation naturally merges into moral approbation – as Norman Harper's comment shows. The traditional virtues of the North-east – thrift, common sense, a canny distrust of extravagance, a work ethic which teaches that an acquisition has to be earned, not anticipated – are at their most evident, not in the city's show but out of it, to be reached along the roads and the by-ways which stretch beyond its boundaries.

Aberdeen, it would seem, might be in the North-east but cannot truly be considered to be of the North-east. It is a place apart, the lives of its population necessarily less rooted, more distant from the human realities of existence than those led by its country cousins. The city might have its own range of places – Ferryhill, Kincorth, Woodside, Ruthrieston, Gilcomston and the like – but their names quite lack the evocative power of such as Buchan, Garioch, the Mearns, Laurencekirk, Glenlivet and the Howe of Alford.

Such, at least, has been the received viewpoint. There are, however, a number of arguments by which to counter such invidious claims. One could point to the extent to which the assumption of a rural superiority reflects that Romantic strain in Northern European thought which grew up during the dislocations of the Industrial Revolution, that time when people began to yearn for the settled order of the village as opposed to the noise and din of the urban slum – a sense of loss that has taken on the colouring of myth. The North-east, after all, has had its full share of people who migrated into the city, not in order to lead an inferior existence but to better themselves socially as well as economically. A considerable proportion of the witnesses that make up *Aberdeen Lives* can trace their ancestry back to rural forebears who made exactly that journey and who never regretted it.

There is no doubt, too, that such views, still being held onto in the 21st century, are as much nostalgia as current reality. The old demarcation between 'City' and 'Shire' has, in the years since the war, become increasingly blurred as the number of those earning their living by agriculture has sharply declined at the same time as the rise of car ownership has generated a way of life that frees individuals from the necessity of seeking their homes within a bike ride of their place of work. The results are to be seen in the steady suburbanisation of the countryside, in the way that the edges of the town intrude further and further into its green sanctuaries and the ancient villages swell into featureless dormitory settlements.

And in any case, the rural – town divide ignores the extent to which the daily interactions of commerce and sociability have bound their fates together. In a large region, which has only contained the one really big centre, it is inevitable that even the remotest Grampian inhabitants have come to regard Aberdeen as 'their' city, a necessary amenity to be depended upon for at least the occasional visit in order to carry out a transaction, to study, to consult its medical specialists, to undertake a big shop, to go to the theatre or to follow the Dons.

These are general arguments. For me, the most convincing advocacy for the virtues of an Aberdeen life is to be encountered in the actual testimony of those who have grown up under its formative influences and who sought their living within its environs. What has struck me – a life-long rural resident by preference – is the warmth with which the interviewees, those whose stories make up this and its succeeding volume, talk of their own city experiences. Listen to the fond detail with which people like Bob Erridge and Dennis Scott recount the teeming, companiable street life of their Roslin and their Bedford Road boyhoods or the way in which Carol Strang and Marjory Rose look back with gratitude upon the Mastrick and the Hilton of their youths.

What is striking is the way in which their memories carry such a strong sense of place and local identity. Read the pride with which Wilma Gillanders and Charlie Allan dip back into their Torry childhoods, as do Mike Forbes and Sandy Gallacher theirs in Ruthrieston Circle and Nellfield Place. To them Aberdeen is no amorphous, anonymous sprawl but a collection of vivid neighbourhoods, of urban villages where the street and the tenement possess the communal vitality of the village

Beryl Mackenzie, growing up in a cramped city centre back street, could nevertheless experience her Aberdeen as a wonderland of amusement and of enlightenment. To her it was a daily invitation to savour its libraries, its shops, its markets, Miss Auchinachie's choir and the weekly sing-song at the Salvation Army, the cinema, the baths and the church – an enrichening liberty to be summed up as her birthright to enjoy the 'freedom of the city'.

To city dwellers like these their surroundings loom in the memory as vividly as any village, the topography of small tradesmen, the back street workshops, the corner shops, the abandoned air – raid shelters and the twopenny tram rides fill their pasts with just as great a sense of adventure as any recall of field or wood or harbour.

Nor will it do to consider the work ethic of the North-east the preserve of the farm servant or the trawler deckhand, not when you listen to David Allan sniff in his memory the wood of his joiner's apprenticeship or Sandy Curle explain how he couldn't wait to get to John Lewis's each working day, so captivated was he by the drama of shipbuilding, or how Michael Main would take his children to marvel at the craftsmanship of their granite-carving grandfather. Consider too the boyhood of Ian Leask where the example set by the numerous trades and busy little shops that surrounded his home in Great Western Road set him off on a life of unremitting and satisfying toil. Then there is the formidable dedication of the self-made, of men such as Jimmy Milne, Ian Lakin, the Donald brothers and Stewart Spence: all people who left school with little in the way of academic qualifications but who went on to build up businesses from next to nothing into centres of excellence in their respective fields, each guided by a fierce desire to rival the best to be found elsewhere.

Shipbuilding, paper, granite, textiles, fish – these are the old established products of Aberdeen and were made so by men and by women who were prepared to devote their working lives to mastering the skills required to turn out the high quality products which made Aberdeen a famous centre of expertise and devoted industry.

To these may be added medicine. At such centres as Foresterhill the city has developed a coming together of medical skills which have served the whole of the North-east, sufficiently well to attract the skills of a nationally recognised bacteriologist like Hugh Pennington or the haematologist Audrey Dawson. The expertise of such names is obvious but what is as striking is the way in which they see themselves as serving people, an attitude echoed in the words of the nurse Isobel Corrigall. To them and to the police and the firemen such as Alistair Ritchie, Ken Raitt and Jim Butler who have safeguarded the streets, the city means people, the place where the country and the town join together in a common quest for health and for social wellbeing.

Such a devotion to service is also to be seen in the reminiscences of those numerous shopkeepers and office staff like Moira Mapley's butcher dad, a man who would deny his own family the best cuts of meat so that they could go to his customers, or like Jim Leslie, the plumber who went out at all hours to ensure his customers received the best of care and of attention.

This volume, however, isn't only focussed on 'Work'. Its sections on Sport recognise that the city acts as a centre for high level accomplishment in a way that the country never can. The accounts of Ian McCrae, of John Fitzpatrick, Colin Smith, Alan Freeland, Muriel Thomson, Jimmy Wood, Mel Edwards and the rest demonstrate that Aberdeen has produced its share of top-class performers. But these are exponents who have risen to the top by more than inborn ability. The lonely early morning miles in Hazlehead, the hours spent hitting bucket after bucket of golf balls, the modestly borne will-power of a Bill Anderson, the fitness of the tennis veteran, Jimmy Wood, the grit of Colin Smith bravely squaring up to the world's fastest bowler, all exemplify a dedication to achieving excellence as strong as any North-east cattle breeder or trawler skipper

The Aberdonians whose stories are captured in *Aberdeen Lives: Work and Play,* to which will be added those to appear in its successor volume *War and Peace,* have as great a right to be considered authentic sons and daughters of the North-east as any rural dweller. The city which they recall is set before us as a vibrant and intensely human congregation of North-east folk, a centre whose activities and attitudes have been an integral part of the richness of the North-east experience. They have complemented, not been in opposition to each other, each as essential to the wellbeing and wholeness of the region as the other.

At the conclusion of the Kincardineshire novelist Ian Macpherson's *Shepherd's Calendar* (1931), the central character, young John Grant, is now coming of age and is about to set off from the Mearns family farm for university in, to him, the strange and distant world of Aberdeen:

'He knew his days would pass in discontent, were he divorced from the valley. His heart ached for the companionship of living things, his own and the land which was his and his forefathers'. His body ached for the labour of the fields.'

He is reluctant to go; the age-old pull of the land is too strong upon him and the city seems artificial and alien in comparison. He protests as much to his mother who, though loath to lose him, knows that the town represents a fullness of opportunity their howe can never offer him. To all his arguments she makes the one simple but conclusive counter and it is this: 'There's so many things in a town.'

Indeed: and that is especially so when that town is Aberdeen.

THE WORLD OF WORK
Manufacturing & Heavy Industry

A traditional Aberdeen granite yard such as the one Alec Milne worked in.
[COURTESY OF ABERDEEN LIBRARY SERVICES]

THE SHIPYARDS Hall Russell and John Lewis

Hall Russell: I wouldn't describe myself as a natural

After the war as a trained joiner I got early release from the Army. I still had my tool kit – canvas tool bag, Stanley hammer, saws, oil can, turn screw, marking gauge – some 30 items all for the total price of £3.4.11d. That would be worth over £400 nowadays because it was all good quality stuff.

'In 1947 I married and it was then that I started to pick myself up.' David Allan marries his Verna, accompanied by brother Jimmy and his wife Jean.

But I was traumatised by my war experiences and found it very hard to settle down again. I got a job but didn't have a clue as to what I should be doing. I was only there for a month or two before I got my jotters.

I must admit I did have something of a chip on my shoulder. It just didn't seem fair, that I had given all those war years and got through all that danger for my country, yet afterwards I was left stranded, my know-how forgotten, my mind still in a turmoil. But then in 1947 I got married and it was then that I started to pick myself up. I realised that there was nothing else for it but to get on with things and learn my trade. I went down to the shipyards, to John Lewis's but there was nothing for me.

I walked out of the yard downhearted but then I saw a bus passing which had 'Footdee' as its destination. 'Hold on a minute – isn't there another shipyard over there?' So I jumped on the bus and off I went to Hall Russell's. I was directed to the joiners' office and went up to the head joiner there. I'll never forget his name – it was Bob Findlay – and he was to prove to be my guardian angel. He was about to retire so he decided to take a chance on me. 'You can start tomorrow.'

I was there for three years and that's where I really learned my trade. One thing about working in a shipyard in those days and that was the priority given to high quality work.

Hall Russell's over a century ago. Picture supplied by Norma Reid whose Granda Kelly, a skilled cabinet maker, is shown second left back row.

Hall Russell's was making ships for clients all over the world, anything from trawlers to luxury liners. I was given free rein to fit out cabins and staircases, using the finest wood and working to the highest specifications.

I found I could take as long as I liked to make the very best job I could. I could spend six months just working on the captain's cabin and bathroom suite and this gave me the time to work out any problems I came up against and to gather the experience I needed to develop into a top class carpenter.

We did six cruise liners for Fred Olsen, where the emphasis was on good finish. 'Made at Hall Russell' was the sign of real quality and the yard had a high reputation to maintain.

But I wouldn't describe myself as a shipyard natural. I didn't really take to the working environment. You'd be working away inside the cabins and outside there would be this constant din of the riveters – 'Bang! Bang! Bang!' – or of the caulkers up on deck drilling off any loose bits of metal. I'd go home after an eight-hour shift with my ears still ringing from this infernal racket. No-one thought of protective gear in those days, so no ear muffs or anything like that.

But there was a good spirit among the workforce. Hall Russell in the late 1940s was employing 4,000 men. Back in those days of full employment the shipyard would find room for some very odd characters, the kind who would never have got a position anywhere else. There was one guy who went around all day long, sweeping, and who had ribbons tied to his broom handle – Liberace, we called him. Then there was another who never did any actual work on the ships but who acted as a sort of solicitor. He'd come in with a briefcase full of books and documents and spend the day passing out advice to any of us who needed it – all at Hall Russell's expense.

David Allan, b.1919. Hall Russell & Co. Ltd, Interviewed 2014

Sandy Curle in mid-career.

The shipbuilder: I couldn't wait to get to the yard

I enjoyed my time at Robert Gordon's College but it wasn't to be for long. In 1941, my life changed for ever. There was this woman, Emma Beaton, who worked in the office of A.B. Hutchison, the bakery firm my father worked for. Her father was a plater at John Lewis the shipbuilders. One day she asked my father whether his boys would like to be shown round the yard.

I'll always remember that visit. It was in the early years of the war. John Lewis was building minesweepers and Flower class corvettes for the Navy. We were shown round and that was that: from that moment on I knew I just had to get into that yard. It was something I've been gripped with all my life; even now I have it.

There was no way now I was going to stay on at school when I could be going to the yard each day for my living. Not long after, Miss Beaton was telling my father there was a vacancy for an office boy in the yard. I went down for an interview, got the job and began my life's work at John Lewis shipyard.

On Monday, 9 June 1941, I entered the 'commercial' office, with the prospect of an apprenticeship as a marine draughtsman. Ten months later I went upstairs to become the drawing office boy. These were the days of the blueprints, when the tracings would be put through a machine which had arc lights travelling through it; the print would come up blue under the lights – 'blue prints' – although they would print out white.

In June 1951 I was picked out of the drawing office by Andrew Lewis, to become Assistant to the legendary Isaac Beaton, shipyard manager. He was the absolute God in the yard: men would be so terrified of him they would dodge out of the way if they saw him coming. He could reduce grown men to nothing, so brutal was he with his tongue. He was a very formal man, dressed always in collar and tie and a dark blue suit; he wore a bowler hat wherever he went. In all the years I knew him I never ever addressed him as anything but 'Mr Beaton'.

I was now one of the two under managers. My responsibility was the fitting out of the ships – getting them ready between the time just before their launching and being finally handed over. I really loved my job; I couldn't wait to get into the yard each morning and that's the way it remained. You would start off with a space in the yard, a completely empty space with nothing in it. Then logs would be laid down – the standing ways – and gradually a ship would emerge from it all. The keel blocks would be put in position, the form would take shape.

John Lewis drawing office, 1949. Sandy Curle is second right.

Then there were the smells: hot steel, various timber smells – teak, oak, pine, oakum, marine glue, pitch, anti-fouling paint, varnish, French polish, the welding flux, the tallow etc. And the sounds: the steam hammers in the blacksmith's shop, the riveting, caulking, the hiss of oxy acetylene cutting and so on. Memories are evoked just thinking of them all.

The ship would be made water tight and ready for its launching – which was a big event with guests – and then the space you had started with was there again, ready to be filled up with another John Lewis-built ship.

The din and the noise went on non-stop. Each riveting squad consisted of four men – hammer boy, holder-on, catcher and riveter. They had to heat the rivet up to a white heat and then hammer it in hard; they did this with pneumatic hammers that would flatten the heads; on the other side there would be the 'holder on', who would hold it and batter it so as to make sure the rivet was absolutely tight. It was hellishly noisy. I never tired of the excitement of it all: the lights flashing, the sparks, the hammer of the white hot rivets going in.

It was very demanding work. The yard would get an order and with it an agreed date for the launch. This had to be adhered to: the launch would be a big event with lots of invited guests so it could never be changed. There was the added difficulty of having to read the tides accurately. This was because we had to launch our vessels straight down into the Dee, which is very tidal at that point. We would time the launch for half an hour before high tide – a few minutes later, the waters might be running in from the sea so strongly that we wouldn't be able to control the situation; a few minutes earlier then we might not have enough water for an effective launch. We were at the mercy of the weather and of the tides.

We built all sorts but mostly concentrated on trawlers and cargo vessels. At our peak we would complete 14 vessels or so in the year. This was the work I gave my life to, a life I never for one moment regretted. Each day I would get up and find I couldn't wait to get to the yard. When the hooter went at half past seven I would be already out, watching the men gather, ready to go off on another day.

Sandy Curle flanked by Superintendent Engineer Morrison and Chief Engineer Campbell.

To begin with I had been reluctant to take the step out of the drawing office; I felt I knew little about the practical side of shipbuilding but Andrew Lewis had invited me into his office and persuaded me to go for it. The foremen under me were a great set of men and they taught me all that I needed to know about fitting-out.

From June 1951, at each launch I was in charge of the 'on board' squad. It was not lost on me that, on these occasions, the vessels travelled faster than they'd ever do again. The

'We built all sorts': Sandy Curle overlooking the setting of one of the masts on 'Malcolm Miller', a three-mast schooner built for the Sail Training Association in 1967/68.

average time from start to finish was about 30 seconds. Down below, Isaac Beaton shouted out his instructions and after many bangs, clatters and shudders, he blew his whistle, the triggers were knocked in and Andrew Lewis, on the launch platform with the owners, dignitaries and guests, told the lady to swing the bottle and christen the ship. Looking down on Isaac Beaton's bowler hat in 1951, little did I think I'd be shouting the orders and blowing the whistle some 17 years later – but without the bowler.

During those 17 years (1951-68) I was gradually introduced to, and schooled up in, the intricacies of practical ship construction and repair work, by Isaac Beaton and the foremen, who were the real backbone of management. I owe them a tremendous debt, especially for the early days, when they kept me right, and always in the nicest and most respectful possible way. To put it briefly, they knew everything about something – the something being every facet of the trade they supervised – and thus it was only necessary for me to know something about everything.

And the men in the yard, well, what they didn't know about the practical side of the business wasn't worth knowing. Yet some of them were scarcely literate and would have to get the foreman to fill in their time sheets for them. But as craftsmen they were fantastic and could make anything out a piece of steel. They had learned on the job; in many cases the craft had been in the family for a couple of generations. These were men who had been brought up with a feel for the job. Nowadays they probably couldn't have worked in the trade at all: they would be required to go to Technical College and pass exams and learn up the theory; that would have been quite beyond some of them.

Seven days a week we worked; Saturdays and Sundays would be half days. It was a basic 44-hour week – but the hours were never too long for me. We built all sorts. While our staple work was the trawlers and the cargo vessels, we also built Flower and Castle class corvettes, boom defence vessels, minesweepers, tank landing craft, tugs, cargo vessels, a lightship, a floating dock, countless conventional trawlers, stern trawlers, a factory trawler, an inter-island ferry, deep sea salvage vessels, a shrimp catcher and fleet tenders for the Ministry of Defence.

There was always some new challenge to meet. But gradually through the '60s shipbuilding was in decline, as it was for all the British yards. In 1972 Lewis & Co. was taken over by the Wood Group and the type of work we did had to change. At its peak the yard had employed 350; now it was being converted into an oilrig supply yard.

I had been given the shipyard manager's job when I was 41. Five years after the Wood Group takeover, a month before my fiftieth birthday, I was given Executive Director status, in which capacity I served for 15 years till retirement at 65.

But I can't pretend that I wasn't broken hearted at the way the yard had changed. Instead of being John Lewis, ship builders to the world, we were now 'John Wood Group Repairing', building only the odd trawler; the rest of the time it was the repair and refitting of oilrigs. Ian Wood was developing other oil-related ventures elsewhere in the harbour and he would take away our best men. Not that I will hear a word against Sir Ian: he had vision and was very astute.

And I have to admit that the changes away from shipbuilding were inevitable; indeed it was the initiative of men like Sir Ian Wood that kept Aberdeen harbour going. But I'm old fashioned; for me there was nothing like the old shipbuilding days when John Lewis was at its peak and had a reputation second to none.

And the characters that we had about the yard! The work was hard and it was their humour that kept them going; the banter and the spirit were fabulous. One example: it was a hell of an evening with the rain pouring down and we were doing evening overtime. We wanted to shift this old steam trawler away from the Torry Dock quayside so as to get the ship we were fitting-out alongside. Now, the last thing the firm would do was to pay for the hire of a tug to pull the ship out of the way so what we would do was to get a gang of men, line them up with a rope over each shoulder and get them to advance step by step, pulling on it all the while. That way the boat would begin to move – slowly.

The youthful crew of the 'Malcolm Miller' going through their paces.

Well, the rain was hammering down on the men; in those days they had no protective clothing, not even helmets or oilskins. So there they were, pulling in step, the boat slowly shifting and the water pouring down their backs and literally running out of their trouser legs. Just as the soaking was getting hold and the rain coming down harder than ever, this voice suddenly broke into song and the words of 'This is a lovely way to spend an evening' – a very popular love song of the late Forties – began to ring out. It was a worker named Bartlett: he had a lousy voice but he was making his own comment on the situation. The scene was unbelievably dreich but he could still find the humour to rise above it.

Shipyard humour… it was said that if you worked in the shipyard and didn't have a sense of humour, then the best thing you could do was jump into the dock.

Sandy Curle, b.1927. John Lewis & Sons Ltd. Interviewed 2006

One of the big cranes was hoisting a load just as he was coming round the corner of the slipway. The load hit a cable and broke free. It all came down on top of him and flattened him.

The shipyard: I found life in the yard so exciting

I started off with John Lewis in June 1953. My first job was as a rivet catcher. You'd stand with a basket while the rivet heater heated up the rivets; when they were red hot he'd drop them so that you could catch them in the basket; then you had to run like hell over to where the riveter was working. You would stick them into the holes on the plate for him to complete the job. If they had cooled down too much he would moan like hell and send you back for more. Sometimes you had to dash a whole distance and crawl along to get to him if he was working in the hull, at the bottom of the boat.

Health & Safety didn't really come into it. I once saw a bloke killed right before my eyes. One of the big mobile cranes was hoisting up a load just as he was coming round the corner of the slipway where the boats were hauled up for repair. The load hit a cable and broke free. It all came down on top of him and flattened him into a pancake. He was killed outright, a man in his 30s.

I found it an exciting life in the yard. There was always something going on. At lunchtime there'd be games of football. If we were working overtime we'd rush over to Max's café up on the Esplanade – 'Dirty Max.' We'd phone up our order: '30 boys coming up in an hour – get it all ready.' We only had half an hour so we would run up there like hell. When we got there the eggs and bacon would be all laid out. The 30 cups would be set out on a tray and Max would go up and down them with this huge kettle and fill them up with tea. It was like watering the garden, up and down with no break.

There was always a good spirit in the yard, always a laugh and a carry on. There would be strength contests where the men would try to lift up the 56-pound weights above their heads. We'd also hold stretching competitions where the idea was to pick up a matchbox from off the ground with one hand behind your back, using only your teeth.

John Lewis had such a high reputation for quality. We once built a luxury yacht for Barbara Hutton. It was the foreign cut-price competition that killed the Aberdeen yards off. Now it's all prefabrication. There's no call for the kind of craftsmanship we specialised in. If you go on a ferry now the last thing you will see is wood; it's all metal and fold-down stuff.

Dennis Nicoll, b.1938. John Lewis & Sons Ltd. Interviewed 2006

The shipyard electrician: I thought I'd had walked straight into Hell

I left Ruthrieston School at 14. I got a bursary to stay on for another year – all of 10 shillings. I didn't take advantage of it. I was good at art and wanted to go to Gray's School of Art but my father said: 'No, none of that – you must get a trade.' For him that would be a safeguard for life. In those days men still tended to be defined by the skill they had acquired by serving their time and it was regarded as important to have one

Top left: 'I met some wonderful men there…' Jim Wyness, back row extreme left, among fellow sparkies on their night out.

Top right: Ex-sparkies' night out, over half a century on. Jim Wyness is fourth right.

rather than risk being a mere 'unskilled' labourer.

Mr Smith, at the school, fixed me up with a position as a trainee electrician at John Lewis's shipyard. I left school on the Friday and started there on the Monday. I was fortunate at the shipyards. There were some wonderful men there. I can say that some of the brightest and most able people I have ever met worked in that shipyard.

The first time I was in the shipyard, I thought I had gone straight into Hell. I found myself walking down through this long, narrow place along duckboards, with benches on either side and dirty-looking men all hammering away and staring at you. I was straight from the school and still in my short trousers. It seemed to be still dark and there were sparks and flares all around you. There was an infernal din. I finally made my way to the foreman's 'buckie' to meet Jim Reid, who would be my boss. He was a nice man, one who prided himself on looking after 'his loons'. 'Oh yes, you can start on Monday,' he told me, and that was that.

That's where I really started my education. I went to evening classes at Ruthrieston but I got little in the way of practical electrical instruction there. It was the journeymen who taught you back at the yard.

It was a long working week. You'd work Saturday mornings till 12.30, and all for the wage as an apprentice of 19s 9d per week. But Lewis's was a good firm. They specialised in making and repairing small cargo boats and trawlers. We all took a lot of pride in our work. Some of the owners began to take their work down to Appledore, in Devon, for the cheaper quotes there, but the standard of workmanship was quite shocking compared to what we did in Aberdeen. If you were to look beneath the skins – that's what we called the internal coverings in the ship – you'd find that the Appledore boys had left wiring all over the place; we would have neatly routed all the various wires so that they didn't get tangled up. The wiring would be hidden beneath the skins but we simply couldn't leave it in such a mess; our pride in our work wouldn't allow us to. We had a very strong work ethic, and I'm sure that held good for most other firms in Aberdeen at that time.

The journeymen would look after the apprentices but they would also beat you if you failed to measure up in some way. Once one of them grabbed me and nailed me to the deck because I had been giving him cheek. I couldn't get up or escape and had to lie there all over my dinnertime. I was left until he returned and released me in the afternoon.

Then they might 'mega' you. The magabox had two wires and was driven by a generator. If the wires touched you would get a sharp electric shock. To 'mega' an apprentice meant to attach the wires to his genitals and make the victim hop about and scream. Another thing they did was if you were standing around too long in the one spot,

Sparkies football team, 1951. Jim, kneeling, second left.

they would weld your tackety boots to the floor; or they might red-lead your arms and legs.

The shipyard was where I learned about people, about life. The trade union helped me in that respect. Some exceptionally bright men were involved in the movement. They had good values too. They might like a drink but you would never see them the worse for it. They took pride in the way they were dressed, how they were turned out.

Good family men. Only one man in the whole yard was a divorcee. They didn't believe in violence; no fighting was the rule. Some of them kept very fit with boxing and weight lifting but they wouldn't use it against you. They were also honest. They would steal from the employer, of course, but not from anyone else and never from a workmate. When one of them died, his toolbox contents would be auctioned off and the proceeds handed over to the widow. We always made sure that they fetched a good price and that the bidding was high. We'd also do jobs for each other and never look for payment. I would go round to a joiner mate's house and put in some plugs for him; he might return the compliment by coming round to me and fixing a cupboard.

Good family men. They didn't believe in violence; no fighting was the rule. They were also honest. They would steal from the employer, of course, but not from anyone else – and never from a workmate.

There was a high level of political consciousness among us. During the election campaigns after the war we would all be gathering round the wireless listening out for the results as they came in. Politicians like Judith Hart would come to the yard to address us all; these events were well attended and quite lively. The shop stewards were men who were crystal clear in their honesty, some to the point of stupidity. This made them a target for management and if there was any slump they would be the first to be dismissed. The management could be tough on us. If you were a few minutes late you'd find the gates locked against you and that you'd be docked half a day's pay.

James (Jim) Wyness, b.1933. John Lewis & Sons Ltd. Interviewed 2005

After 20 years in the shipyards, James suffered a serious work related accident and had to retire. He then took a degree in History at Aberdeen University and became a teacher at Summerhill, then Hazlehead. In 1980 he was elected to the city council as a Labour party representative. He occupied that position for 23 years including a spell as Lord Provost.

PAPER and PRINTING

The Paper Mill: I was the one who had to walk through that door

There I was, going through the gate of Robert Gordon's College with only a Junior Leaving Certificate, but I was sure something would turn up. This was the 1950s and academic qualifications were not then regarded as the sole criteria for future career success. After all, the college had given me important social experiences – I had been class captain for each year I was there, I had played for the First Rugby team and had enjoyed the social life of the school and developed my communicative skills. Besides, this was still the era of British manufacturing pre-eminence so even though it was clear that I wasn't destined for any of the traditional professions I felt there was a huge world out

Robert Gordon's College Colts XV 1956/57. Ian Lakin is front row seated first right. The captain is (Sir) Ian Wood.

'I left school with only a Junior Leaving Certificate – but with some great social experiences.'

As General Manager, Donside Paper Mills, 1991.

there waiting to be seized.

My father told me he had sent away 80 applications on my behalf and had received 80 rejections but still I didn't worry. Then he told me: 'Look, I've pulled a string or two – I've landed you an interview at Stoneywood Paper Mill. It's for the position of production manager trainee – now it's up to you.' I went along to see Commander Wilson who was in charge of Personnel and got my grilling. He was a very aloof figure, no nonsense about him, a real naval officer type.

I was offered the post. I'll admit that connections assisted me on my way, that you could call it the Old Boys' network in action. But I would say this: my father had shown me where the door was but I was the one who had to walk through it and make a success of what I found on the other side. I knew I was arriving at this hugely important employer, one that had 1,700 workers; I was being asked to get myself through a tough five-year long course and to accept everything that was thrown at me. I had to start off on the floor along with the rest. The very first thing any of the workers said to me was: 'Hello, you Tory-faced bastard.'

The production manager trainee is expected to get experience of all the departments and prove proficiency in each of them – machines, engineering, instrumentation, sales, accounts, the lot. I got through by treating it as sport: I would understand the rules and all the skills and then I would make sure I won my way through. This meant willingly submitting to a work regime that entailed 12-hour shifts and seven-day weeks, on top of attending evening classes three times weekly. The mill worked as a 24-hour operation and I had to engage fully with that. And all this on £4 a week, rising to £5 after two years.

My part time studies were a success – I could now see the relevance and worked my way to qualifications in Paper Technology and awards by the Business Management Institute. At school I had hardly passed one examination; after, I never failed any. I was

The Donside Board 1993: Back row left to right: Bruce Stuart, Alistair Dinnie, Cliff Kirk, Tom Speirs. Seated: Jim O'Connor, Ian Lakin (Managing Director), Andrew Finlay.

When the future still seemed set: Donside Paper Mills early 1990s.

driven on by the thought that I had to prove myself, that I mustn't let my parents down.

But I also had to win the acceptance of the workers. The conditions we worked in were very harsh in those days. After all, paper is 99% water to start off with and has to be turned into 96% substance. The machines were noisy and the atmosphere was humid – in summer unbearably so – as the paper had to dry off. Back then there was no heat extraction process so a lot of the moisture just went into the air you breathed. And these machines were dangerous too. So many of the workers had lost a finger or two, even an arm, that no-one remarked on it. Indeed, there was the odd fatality as workers were sucked into the machinery and this too was accepted as an occupational hazard.

It was demanding, both physically and mentally. It took me three years before I was finally accepted on the shop floor. You just had to keep at it and show them all you could do whatever they had to do, and without complaint or seeking any favours or putting on any airs and graces. Unlike the typical foreman figure I made a point of being open and approachable; of not standing on my dignity. I never forgot those lessons I imbibed from my contacts with the shop floor workers – I owe them a lot.

Stoneywod Paper Mills was a great business then. The Don gave us our power and our water; we had the largest watermill in the UK at that time. We had 150 employed on research and development alone; we were at the forefront of the industry. We were skilled in utilising the latest techniques in converting raw materials into products – watermarks, laundry labels, battery separators, stamp paper, cheque paper, cardboard, writing paper: we

State of the art: the 'Super Calendar', capable of exerting pressure of one tonne per paper width inch.

did it all. There was great pride among the workforce in being at the top of their tree.

At the end of my five years, I considered myself to be thoroughly grounded in the life of the paper mill, and had now caught up with any graduate entrants. Yet all that I was guaranteed was a superintendent's post. But now I got the luckiest break of my life. The mill at Fort William had just been opened; they were looking for bright young supervisors and I landed a post there. My salary now leapt from £250 a year to the heady heights of £1,750 – for some time to come, I kept the letter of acceptance by my bedside and would stare at it in wonderment.

Fort William made me. It was a brand new plant, kitted out with some of the most advanced equipment in Europe, and the field was open to innovation and fresh techniques. At Stoneywood I'd had the problem that when I suggested any new approach I'd get a 'Na, na laddie – we tried that 10 years ago and it didna work.' But I knew the world was moving on and that more precise instrumentation was now available. In particular, computerisation was transforming the work. In the past it had all been done manually – the sizing up of properties such as weight, colour, moisture content – but now the computer was there to do it all for us, and to a much greater level of precision.

Then, less than three years later, the Donside job came up – as Production Manager. It was smaller than Fort William but more complex; it was undergoing a refit and the way was open for an enthusiastic young manager. Then came another lucky break: when I was 34 the General Manager decided to move south and I got the vacant position. I was in it for a further 17 years. We became a world leader in the manufacture of high quality coated papers; the future seemed assured.

During those years papermaking in Aberdeen was still a thriving industry; now it has more or less gone. Yet when I left Donside in 1993 it was still a profitable enterprise. The reasons for this sudden fall tells us a lot about the way the economy now works in the modern world and our country's inability to keep up with it. If you look at the traditional industries of Aberdeen and the way they have suffered in recent times, you can see a pattern. The granite ran out just as one day the oil will, and that is obvious enough. But paper is another matter; like so much of our industry it has suffered from short sighted management decisions, external take-overs and an inability to match the scale of operations being developed elsewhere. The old prosperity was built on a tight and experienced workforce. But in a globalised age that kind of work can be done much more cheaply in the Third World

Again it's a failure to move with the needs of the times. With papermaking the problem has been that a once leading industry has been caught up in the demands of a rapidly changing and highly competitive scene. And now the mill itself is closed, this very year. Production is to shift to China; it has become a victim in the globalised market of high domestic costs – the high price of gas and fuel, the high exchange rates of the pound against the Euro and the dollar.

Yet papermaking is hardly a dying trade: the demand is there and the equipment and the workforce are there. In the past the closure of a well-established, highly reputed

North-east business would have raised such a hue and cry that the politicians would have been stung into action. But – and this is the final tragedy – after 30 years of closures and the disappearance of all sorts of British industries that once would have seemed an immovable part of the national landscape, people in this country now seem to have become fatalistic about it all. The workers get their £15,000 redundancy cash; the land gets sold off for yet more housing and people switch their attention back to the oil and the whisky – and quite soon the whole matter is forgotten. Papermaking is becoming simply another casualty in the long line of retreat from the time when the North-east was a thriving industrial scene.

Ian Lakin, b.1942. Stoneywood and Donside Paper Mills. Interviewed 2009

The printer:
Every bit of paper had to be accounted for

After I left school I had no clear idea as to what I wanted to do. But one of our neighbours worked as a compositor and he seemed to be in a steady and reasonably well paid job. His example set me in mind of a career in the printing trade so I began to do a tour of the various workshops in the city, enquiring as to whether they had any openings. Aberdeen University Press and Cornwall at the Castlegate both offered me an apprenticeship but the director at the University Press, Dr Harold Watt, couldn't bring himself to give me a firm date to start so I decided to opt for Cornwall's.

Ironically later, Cornwall's was to be bought over by Aberdeen University Press so finally I did end up working for them. It was there, as union representative, that I was to have one or two encounters with the notorious Robert Maxwell. As it later emerged, the man was a complete fraud but I have to confess that he had a great presence about him and when he addressed us all he could soon have us eating out of his hand.

G. Cornwall & Sons was a very high-class lithographers, printers and book binding firm, just about the largest and most prestigious of its type in Aberdeen. It carried out a whole range of commissions, ones which ranged from bank cheque printing and passport printing for Trinidad and Tobago, to the Koran in Arabic. We even printed bank notes for the North of Scotland Bank though because of the high security involved we only did part of each note, the rest being shared out with two other firms. Even at that the bank sent its own representative

TEL. NO. 20299
J. B. CAMPBELL
D. CAMPBELL
W. CAMPBELL
G. M. CAMPBELL
A. C. FARQUHARSON (MANAGING)
W. RENNIE

ESTABLISHED 1830.

TEL. ADDRES
'CORNWAL
ABERDEE

G. CORNWALL & SONS

LITHOGRAPHERS · PRINTERS · BOOKBINDERS

DESIGNERS
DRAUGHTSMEN

RAILWAY PRINTERS

BANK CHEQUE PRINTERS

ACCOUNT BOOK MANUFACTURERS

CONTRACTORS TO MUNICIPAL, COUNTY COUNCIL AND OTHER PUBLIC BODIES

PARLIAMENTARY MAP & PLAN DRAUGHTSMEN

COLOUR PRINTING A SPECIALITY

ESTIMATES ON APPLICATION.

LAW & COMMERCIAL STATIONERS

DIE STAMPERS

CALENDAR MANUFACTURERS

CONTRACTORS TO H. M. STATIONERY OFFICE.

42-45, CASTLE STREET.
ABERDEEN

JBC/HP/358

3rd March, 1964.

'The largest and most prestigious in Aberdeen': 1964 letter heading for G.Cornwall & Sons.

The Artists' Department

first thing each morning to sit and to observe at every stage of the operation – and every single piece of paper had to be accounted for: if you mangled a piece it couldn't be disposed of in the bucket in the usual way; it had to be presented to the bank representative along with the completed sheets.

Of course, printing has changed tremendously even in the time I have been retired. In my young day it was still very much a heavy manual operation. I concentrated on the lithographic side of things. Here we were, still using heavy limestone slabs, each about three feet square and requiring three men to shift them about onto the machine. The whole process was dependent on the fact that water and grease don't mix. What happens is that the desired image for printing out is transferred onto the stone by chemical means so that a greasy image is imprinted onto it which, being limestone, is water receptive. The result is that when a greasy roller is run over the stone the ink sticks to the image that you wish to print.

This is the traditional lithographic method and one that is still in use at a specialist printer like Peacock's. But it is a very laborious business and has been largely superseded. First of all a system was adopted using metal plates rather than the stones and this had the advantage that you could bend the metal around a roller and so produce a faster output – 10,000 copies an hour could be achieved and 7,000 was quite normal. Now in most printing works the process has become very high tech with computerisation and laser printing doing the work. I know that if I were called in to do a job I would have to learn the trade all over again.

At Cornwall's I worked in the stone and plate preparation room in a small team; then

Lithographer staff, 1940. Extreme left, seated, is William Watt – 'Wattie' – a weel kent Castlegate character.

Stone and Plate Preparation Room

there was the printing room itself where a team of six or seven was engaged and then came the binding room which was usually occupied by a mostly female team. We did everything from letters and invoices right the way up to high-class catalogues. For example, we handled the catalogues for Anderson's Roses where, of course, a high standard of colour reproduction was essential.

I enjoyed my work. It could be a bit noisy and back then there was no regard for Health & Safety issues. The power was generated in the basement by a steam engine and was conveyed through a system of leather belts so you'd be working with these belts flying past just inches from your body. Then there was the cold. The rooms were quite large and the sole heating was by a small, thin, hot water pipe. It was common to go in on a Monday morning to find that the water bucket was full of ice which you then had to break. The firm took care to heat the equipment so that everything ran smoothly but not us workers.

Ian Mann, b.1936. G. Cornwall & Sons. Interviewed 2014

The Machine Room: each printer had allocated a female assistant to feed the paper into the machines.

If Caxton had walked in he could easily have produced a book

I'd tried an exam for the printing trade in the old Aberdeen Academy in Belmont Street and when the results came back I was offered a job with the University Press at the top of Upperkirkgate, next to the Students' Union. The University Press was the premier place in Aberdeen and my father said: 'That's a great trade to be in.' It seemed a tremendous opportunity so I started with them.

I remember the exam was on a Saturday morning. There was a guy sitting next to me and he whispered to me: 'The Eiffel Tower, that's Blackpool isn't it?' and I nodded: 'That's right.' Even then I was devious because I thought, well, that's one of them out of the way. There were lots of people trying that exam; I don't know how many they took – it must have been the top half-dozen or something like that.

I ended up with three different options: bookbinder, printer and compositor; I chose compositor.

There were a lot of talented people at Aberdeen University Press: folk interested in photography, botany, geology and things like that. They were all voracious readers. We used to discuss books and plays and left-wing politics, and we had some amazing arguments. We were going to overthrow the world at one stage.

Being at the University Press was brilliant. It was in a truly ancient building, on Upperkirkgate. The stone façade is still there. You went in a courtyard and there were plaques all round it. In at the door there were various flights of stairs. It was a great place – you could hide for days. There were people there that I never knew exactly what they did. The reading department was great, in an old house that was incorporated into the building. These guys used to sit in what must have once been bedrooms and living rooms. It was so ancient. If Caxton had walked into the University Press at that time he could easily have produced a book.

Compositors in Aberdeen University Press, Upperkirkgate, around 1960. From left: Mike Smith, unknown, Derek Pyper. [PICTURE: CHARLES COUTTS]

Then Aberdeen University Press bought new premises in Farmers Hall Lane and moved up there. My pal, Alec Cormack, and I were the only two apprentices left behind in Upperkirgate for six weeks to facilitate the move. We got all the things ready for the vans coming. It was fantastic, six weeks on your own in a near empty building. It's a wonder we weren't shot, the things we got up to. We used to let off fire extinguishers and the like.

The University Press used to rent rooms to an undertaker where there were coffins and shrouds, but no bodies.

At the end, there was just a skeleton staff left and they had a machine room and one of the huge printing machines, that had been there for God knows how long, was so old that it wasn't going to be taken up to Rosemount. Everything to be left was being rouped and the auctioneer set up his stall in front of this ancient machine. Just before he got it sold for scrap, it fell through the floor, down through two stories – at the very moment the auctioneer got to it. It had been a tragedy waiting to happen and at the last minute it did, crashing through the floor that had been rotted over years with all the paraffin, printing ink and linseed oil.

I finished my apprenticeship in Farmers Hall Lane. The apprenticeship wasn't all done on the job. We got a day off every week to go to the college at the printing college in what had been the old Marywell Street School.

I think, in some respects, we maybe had a healthy respect for authority but in the other aspects young people nowadays just wouldn't put up with the way we were treated. I mean, when going to classes, the guy that owned University Press was that greedy that he was the only print master in the town that made his apprentices go to work from half-past seven to quarter to nine before walking down to Marywell Street for your classes. Then we were there until eight o'clock at night, because we had our three hours evening class as well, which we didn't get paid for. You just had to do it.

I remember every year you got lined up and told your exam results. 'You'll have to try harder'; 'This isn't very good.' The next one would be told: 'You've done very well.' God, you were feart that the boy would say: 'You're not doing very great, are you?' I remember I had gone out from the AUP for a drink – everybody had gone for a drink in the Kirkgate Bar. But the gaffer came round and everybody that had a few pints got warned, and us younger ones got put home. I hadn't actually done anything because I was too young to drink but the gaffer said he was going to write to my father and I was absolutely terrified, that I'd have my apprenticeship stopped. I thought he was serious and I would never have dared ask if he was kidding.

Apprentice AUP compositors at Farmers Hall, mid 1970s. Ian Stephen front, John Walker behind.
[PICTURE: CHARLES COUTTS]

The funniest thing that happened to me while serving my apprenticeship was typical of things that happened in Aberdeen at that time. The University Press used to rent rooms to an undertaker where there were coffins and shrouds, but no bodies. They made and prepared coffins there and when you went down the back stairs you had to go

'The Bouncing Czech': Robert Maxwell, owner of Aberdeen University Press, in his pomp.

through this bit that they called 'the coffins'.

At half past nine every morning, the younger apprentices used to get sent out, with everybody's money and notes of their orders, to the baker's shop across in St. Paul Street for rowies and sausage rolls. You'd sneak up the back stairs and into the canteen with all this stuff before the gaffer saw you, terrified you might get caught.

One day, Alec Cormack and I were sent out through the coffins with the orders. We were coming back up the stairs, all in darkness and unaware that one of the guys had got into a coffin. As we passed, he sat up. Well, there were rowies and sausage rolls all down the back stairs. We ran back down into St. Paul's Street. We were feart to come in until we heard all this laughter and then saw the older apprentices at the top of the stairs. They claimed that we were shouting 'Mummy. Mummy.' While I hoped that wasn't true, it might have been.

I had a very good life in the printing trade. The characters I met were wonderful; that made the job. They were a great bunch of people in the printing trade in Aberdeen. It had a great history as well. The University Press did lots of books, mostly technical manuals.

One of the biggest customers was the Faraday Society. When Robert Maxwell bought the University Press for his Pergamon empire, the Faraday Society wouldn't go with him. That was the death-knell for the University Press because the Society was the backbone of their work. We did the Chemical Society, the Faraday Society, and all these different societies because we had specialist readers in maths and science; they were highly educated people, these guys that read the proofs.

But the Faraday Society wouldn't have anything to do with Maxwell. He was going to make us the richest printers in Britain; that was his little speech when he spoke to us on the Friday – and 30 folk were paid off on the Monday. Mr Watt, who had owned the place called him 'the Bouncing Czech.' Anyway, I was coming up to be married and I thought 'I'm out of here.' I'd had 20 good years there. It was time to move on.

Alexander (Alex) Rae, b.1947. Aberdeen University Press. Interviewed 2016

BALMORAL GROUP

The Jimmy Milne Phenomenon

Balmoral Group Managing Director Jimmy Milne.

I can't wait for the next challenge

I grew up on a farm at Tullos where Greenbank Road is now. Back then everything south of the railway line was fields and my father farmed the land from the Bay of Nigg to Kincorth. So you could say I haven't moved very far in my long life: just from the bottom of the hill to the top of the hill.

There were nine of us in the family: five boys and four girls. I was the youngest of those boys. The expectation was that as we grew up we would be working on the farm under my father. In fact, that's what my other brothers did. But I was different: I determined right from the start that the last thing I wanted to do was to work on that farm; my ambition was to strike out on my own, to be my own boss, to get on in life.

One reason for this was that farm work just sickened me. It was hard, cold and non-stop. My father was quite a hard man and he demanded every effort from us all. I'd be shaken awake at two in the morning to be told that 'the coo was calving an ye've got to help oot.' So you'd stumble out to the byre and the calf would stick halfway out and you'd be half asleep and freezing cold. Then there was the work in the fields, what with the kale and the neeps, and you'd be out there picking the stuff with cold water pouring down your neck and the ground all hard with a frost.

So it's not surprising that from the age of no more than 10 I made up my mind I would be working for myself; I didn't know what, where or when but it was just a fact in my life, simple as that.

I used to work with my brother Sandy; he had a little mushroom business and also grew cabbages and lettuce. He was always good to me and I would get up at 4.30 of a morning to help out and then do the same after school. But he got married when I was 16 and ran a small holding over at Balmedie. So I decided to carry on his business at the farm.

When I was 17 I had up to 10 guys working for me, usually policemen or electricity board workers, guys who were on shift work and could be with me part time. I would also pick big old cars, do them up and hire them out. I was working round the clock –

but it was never a question of the money: it was the drive to succeed, to make the very best of my abilities and any opportunity that came my way.

I did, of course, go to school – but only untiI I could leave at the earliest opportunity, when I was 14. I attended Walker Road, then Torry, which is situated at the top of a hill – so I could always claim that that was my High School. Neither of these establishments enthused me with a love of academic learning. I liked the practical stuff, the Technical, the Woodwork, the Crafts, but as for History or Geography or English, forget about it. I found the school a tiresome place right from the start – to sit at a desk all day when you could be out and doing something.

So my education has been the university of life. What has been of great benefit to me have been those early years when I was working all hours on the farm and then getting my mushroom business off the ground in that old shed. Being close to the land – even though I hated much of it – taught me about the realities of life, about the value of hard work and sticking at it. That and the great virtue of common sense.

'For services to industry': Jimmy Milne receives the CBE, at Buckingham Place 1995, with daughters Sarah-Jane and Caroline.

I had left school at 14 without a qualification to my name. However, I was good with my hands and was always fascinated by how mechanical things worked and how to improve them. Because of my background I assumed that my employment was likely to be in agriculture, so at 14 I got a job as message boy with the North-east's biggest manufacturer of agricultural machinery, Barclay, Ross & Hutchison.

Then when I was 16 I took on an apprenticeship as an agricultural engineer. I was 10 years on the shop floor and loved every minute of it. Then I went into the drawing office and became involved in development. What began to strike me as I examined the machinery designs which came across my desk were the huge problems caused by corrosion. I thought that there must be some way round this issue, that there must be a material which wouldn't be subject to rusting. I did some research; the problem excited me. I came upon a solution: the future must lie with composites, with glass-fibre.

By now I was 25 and I was beginning to feel that it was time to make a move. So,

Balmoral Group HQ, 2017.

armed with my new knowledge concerning glass-fibre, I went up to my boss and asked for a raise. As I expected, the answer was 'no', and my reply was ready: 'Oh, well then I'll be off at the end of the week and start out on my own.'

I conducted three years of self-funded research. I like to know the A to Z of anything I'm involved in so I went round Europe visiting raw material and glass-fibre manufacturers. By 1968 I sold my first product – a compressor cover for a customer in Peterhead.

I never doubted I would make progress. Quite where all this will to succeed comes from I can't say for sure. But, obviously, my upbringing on the farm has stood me in good stead. My father was a hard taskmaster but he was also a strong Christian who drove the virtues of respect, of integrity and the work ethic into us. I'm a great believer in the power of positive thinking; with that you can move mountains. Never take 'no' for an answer and never settle for second best.

Tenacity is the key, that and team work. Look, Balmoral is not just about Jimmy Milne; I have taken care to respect my work force, to think of their loyalty as something you have to earn – respect them and they will respect you. I've had a terrific set of people, people who've seen the firm through thick and thin.

In that time I've had ups and downs and suffered some terrible reversals. The worst was losing my wife to cancer when she was only 40. For years she had been taking Rennies for what she thought was no more than persistent heartburn. But when they finally operated all they could do was sew her up again and send her home to die. It was stomach cancer. We had two wee girls, aged three and eight.

At the time I couldn't see beyond my loss but time passes and I have got remarried, to Gillian, a Fifer and 30 years younger than me. Twice that wee nickum has taken

I spring out of my bed each morning, take my shower and then I'm ready to go. I'm still buzzing with ideas.

advantage of me and so we have two sons; my girls are now 25 and 29 and the boys are 12 and 13. I have been blessed.

I've also suffered some real business disasters. By the late 1970s I had built up a thriving business, providing mouldings for a whole range of industries and making container tanks. We had also developed a construction arm and soon we had the largest property building company in Aberdeen. I named the overall business 'Aberglen' and at its peak we were employing 1,000. We had opened up export markets and were doing big business in Iran and Nigeria. But we began to run into problems. The Nigerian economy collapsed and the Shah was overthrown in Iran. At the same time interest rates were soaring and we were overdue with VAT payments – not by more than a couple of months but that was enough for the taxman to demand instant payment.

His ultimatum infuriated me. On an impulse I put the company into receivership, went home and had a good cry, thinking of all those good creditors we had let down. However, six months later I read an article in the 'P&J' stating that the Aberglen receiver had not managed to find a buyer for the glass-fibre division of the company; I had been getting all sorts of enquires from old customers as to whether I was going to start up again. So I bought back this side of the business and set up 'Balmoral'.

That was in 1980. We got going with five employees, designing glass-reinforced plastic products such as storage tanks and modular buildings. The reformed business went from strength to strength. By the end of the century Balmoral had a payroll of 600. But now came my second big business disaster. We were developing a range of products for the deep sea oil industry but the gas and oil projects were being postponed and I felt we needed to do something about it. I had spent millions in research and development on hybrid buoyancy insulation modules and knew we should be in a strong position to advance with what I considered to be a world-leading product.

Round about the same time, we were selected to use a new rotational moulding material for Balmoral Tank domestic fuel oil tank range. The new material, named Borocene, had been developed by a company that was believed to be the best in the business.

Everything seemed set fair: to be linked with such a prestigious company was a dream. But our suppliers, Borealis, had not done their homework thoroughly enough and, after a couple of years, reports were coming in that our tanks were developing leaks. At one point I had over 20 people manning the phones, having to handle the complaints and claims that were coming in against us. The tanks had carried a 10-year guarantee and I was determined to honour it. We were paying out half a million pounds a month on compensation.

It was an absolute nightmare. Obviously, we had a strong claim against Borealis and took them to court. For 11 weeks we were down in London waiting for the High Court to make its decision. We were very confident but we lost on a technicality. This huge multi-billion company had well and truly screwed our small Aberdeen one.

I had to take steps to stay in business. I was forced to sell our Marine Division which was providing moorings for the North Sea oil industry. I sold it for £18,000,000 to the Management Team; two years later it was sold on for 10 times that sum. But I don't regret anything; that sale had kept Balmoral going. We then did a Joint Venture in our subsea division and that was a disaster.

That was nine years ago and since then Balmoral has made a great recovery. We had to start again with a clean sheet, no money but lots of determination, great people and with lessons well learned from our disasters. Never again would I take anything on trust, however prestigious the messenger. Now if we are handling a new material we will test and test it to destruction before we use it.

My fear was that our reputation was in tatters. But we decided to focus on deep water projects because that is where the real future for oil development lay. We had hardly started when we got a call from a major operating company that was involved with a big project in the Gulf of Mexico. They were asking for a quote. I thought that this must be to act as a lever to bring the price down and that some bigger guy would get the job. But I could also see that this was an opportunity so we threw everything at it. We did the design and engineering work and prepared a highly detailed proposal. We got the contract.

Ever ready to reflect and to learn: a recent photograph of Jimmy Milne.

That was us up and running again. By now we are involved in virtually every deep seas project worldwide – Brazil, India, Angola, China, Norway and so on. It just shows how much the industry thought of us and were prepared to regard our Borealis disaster as a mere hiccup.

And that brings me to another great reason for success: never think of a reversal as the end but rather as an opportunity to learn valuable lessons. That and the importance of conducting matters with honesty and respect. These are the qualities which I imbibed during my growing up on that family farm.

And now the North Sea industry is going through a real depression. We are facing a double whammy; the oil is expensive to extract, the fields are becoming ever more marginal and this at the time when the price of the barrel has plummeted. Fortunately for Balmoral we have become a truly international enterprise and are not dependent on the local fields.

But you have to keep motoring on: if you stop then you might as well retire. I spring out of my bed each morning, take my shower and then I'm ready to go. I'm still buzzing with ideas. The Lord has blessed me with health and providing I can keep everyone else happy, I'll work on and on until the Lord comes for me or I fall off my perch.

Balmoral has been an incredible adventure; each step taken is a story in itself. But don't get me wrong – although I am intensely proud of what it has achieved, Balmoral is far from being a one man band. I have a strong and loyal management team, one which shares the same progressive philosophy. I employ dozens of graduates – just because I left school with nothing doesn't mean I don't appreciate what people with proven brains can offer. I tell them: 'Look, you are far cleverer than me – what I've got that you haven't yet got is lots of experience. So let's work together and pool our resources'.

You need to look ahead all the time. The oil industry is constantly evolving and you must never assume that where you are today will guarantee tomorrow's success. What you have to do is treat each project as a step towards learning about the next one. We began in the North Sea and have been successful in supplying the industry with what it has needed. But the North Sea only runs to depths of 150 metres. What you have to realise is that it's a pond compared to some of the newer areas of development such as the Gulf of Mexico, Brazil, China, Australia and the rest. That is why we have drawn upon our North Sea experience to develop buoyancy products that can be used in depths down to 7,000 metres. We do this by testing, testing, testing, taking readings and then by extrapolation, getting tolerance levels up to higher and higher degrees – we aim to be within two percent loss of buoyancy requirements and for our products to have a life span of 25 years.

So the fire in the belly still burns bright. I mean, what would I do with retirement? Play golf? No, I subscribe to my father's philosophy that to spend a day chasing a wee ball around a big field with a stick is no way for a grown man to use his time.

How do I spend my spare time? Well, I do sleep at night – but this is to recharge my energy for the next day. I'm involved in a number of charities, especially the Friends of Anchor, where my daughter Sarah is prominent. I'm the Deputy Chair at the local SCDI branch.

But I must admit that it's work which occupies me for the most part; I would estimate that I work a 12- to 14-hour day. I expect my workforce to share my devotion to the Balmoral cause but I also realise that you have a duty of care to your workforce. I am a committed Christian and I strive to apply its values to my business. That must come first, the business second. But, in fact, I find that consideration for the workers also makes good business sense in that it inspires loyalty.

Of course, the city is going through some testing times. But then life has always been a series of challenges. Something you try goes well, that's a valuable lesson to take with you into the future. Something goes badly, well that is also a lesson. As for me I can't wait for the next challenge…

James (Jimmy) Milne, b.1940. Balmoral Group. Interviewed 2015

WOMEN at WORK

I would travel back home on the bus and open up my pay packet and count the cash inside. One week it amounted to £9. I remember the conductress looking wide-eyed and asking: 'How much?'

Largest envelope manufacturer in Britain

After school I took a job with a bookshop and stationer in George Street – George Adam's. I was there till I was 16 but when I heard about the big wages on offer at Pirie Appleton's envelope factory I decided to make a move there. 'On your own head be it,' my granny told me but I never had cause to regret it.

I worked in the cutting department up on the first floor. We had to take the reams of paper off the racks and feed them into the cutting machine, where they went back and forwards for shaping. It was a non-stop operation and our hours were 8AM till 6PM. But the load was lightened by the banter and chat with the other girls. We could also open the window and look out into the lane and over to the railway. People would shout up at us and the train drivers would give us a wave.

Pirie Appleton's did prove to offer good pay and with bonuses too. In those days it was the biggest manufacturer of envelopes in the whole of Britain. For the first two years there I would hand over my pay packet to my mother but then I moved on to a board and lodging system with her. I would travel back home on the bus and open up my packet and count out the cash inside. One week it amounted to £9. I remember the conductress looking wide-eyed and asking: 'How much?'

The workforce in my department was all female; when you got married you had to leave or reapply for your job. I met my husband in 1959 and married in 1961 but the firm had looked after us well.

Frances Garden, b.1938 Pire Appleton's.

The canning factory choir

My mother left school aged 14. During her working life she was employed for a time as a machinist in Marshall's Canning Factory. The job was pretty repetitive but then all the girls on the shop floor would break into song. They achieved a high standard of harmonisation in their performances, their repertoire being the hits of the Roaring 1920s and 1930s. Apparently they became so good that passers-by would stop

I used to wonder why the glue man always seemed to have a big grin on his face and went about singing.

and listen to the 'Marshall's Choir'. People at that time didn't need TV – they made their own entertainment.

Irene Milne, b.1936. Marshall's Canning Factory

No wonder he had a big grin on his face

I left school at 14 and got a job in a factory down in Union Glen. This was a glove factory and my job was to sew up the holes that were left after the machine had put the gloves together. For this I got paid all of five shillings a week out of which threepence had to be kept back for the insurance stamp. This meant I had four shillings and ninepence to hand over to my mother at the end of each week. In those days you automatically handed over your wage packet to your mother, however small.

After a time I decided to leave and went to talk to the Floor Manager, a very bossy woman. She got angry for my leaving, 'After all I've taught you.' As if sewing holes in gloves was not something that a monkey could do.

Then I got a job in the Torry sawmill – Patterson's it was – which was situated where Tesco is now. My job was to hold up the planks of wood for the sawyer to put through the cutting machine. It was a job which had its dangers – I couldn't help noticing that the sawyer had a finger missing. We specialised in making boxes for fish to be put in and this required gluing together. These were the days long before anyone talked about glue sniffing – but I used to wonder why the glue man who had to keep the pots of the stuff always seemed to have a big grin on his face and went about singing.

Staff of Patterson's sawmill, 1940: Gina Gove is back row, left. The glueman is seated extreme left – grinning.

Gina Gove, b.1923. Torry Sawmill

Ready for the Comb works Dance, 1951: Betty McHardy is right, with sisters Mary and Mina on her right.

The Comb Factory: Just like a herd of bloody elephants

I started work at 14, in the Comb Factory, the packing department. We had this older supervisor and she could be a bit strict but the girls themselves were great fun to work with. When she came in we all fell quiet; she didn't approve of us talking while we worked, but as soon as she left again there would be non-stop chatter. My job was to pack combs. The combs would come through in boxes and what we had to do was to put them into paper, working in batches of a dozen. I could do a gross by a gross in one shift.

The factory didn't just make combs. There would be lovely brooches and statuettes of monks: 'Brother Martins.' We had to pack them too, as a special order. You'd be at your work, which was like a desk in front of you, and you had a run of elasticised string wound round a nail which you would pull on for tying up in bows. My hands could just fly through the work. But oh, the toilets. I hated using them, they were so filthy. At home when mother offered me some pudding I would say: 'No thanks – I might be needing a pee and I couldn't face those toilets.'

Because we were on piecework we would keep going. We were a happy crew. The other girls were all young and happy-go-lucky, just like myself. The hours were long: 8 in

Publicity for British Industries Fair 1947.

You'd hear this rumbling noise and then we'd all cheer out because that meant that the heating was coming on.

the morning till 5.45 in the evening, with an hour in the middle for your dinner. I would go home for that – but no pudding. It could be tiring: my shoulder would swell up and go all red with the repetition of it all. But we had great laughs. We would have what we called these 'endings': these were the odd bits of plastic left over where the machine had come to the end of a row of combs. They would drop off onto the ground around us; by the end of a shift there might be a whole heap of them lying at our feet. One of us would get a brush to them and then the fun would start. We'd be sitting at the table working away when you'd feel this tickle up your leg. 'Moose. There's a moose under the table.' But it would be the brush coming up your leg. You should have heard the screams!

The manager's office was next door and he would complain about the noise: 'Just like a herd of bloody elephants, you girls are,' he would tell us. Then there would be the singing. We'd all be going at it and then when we reached the end of a song we'd round it off with a loud: 'Da-da-da-da-di-dum.' and Mary Gordon would stand up and conduct us all. She was aye in a turban so as to keep the curlers in as she'd be going out that night and her hair had to be at its best.

Aberdeen Comb Works on its site on Hutcheon Street.

The Comb Works were quite large. They said that when the doors opened at night to let the workers out anyone passing by in Hutcheon Street would get knocked over in the rush. The spirit in our packing department was great. But the pay wasn't: just 23 shillings for the week when I started, later rising to £2. There was no holiday pay either. We could take any spare combs home with us, but there's only so many of them that you can use.

The conditions were pretty basic; it was such an old-fashioned place and run on old-fashioned lines. You had to lift up the boxes and these were great wooden ones; they were heavy enough on their own but filled with four gross of combs they were murder. You'd be lifting 100 or so of these boxes during the day so as to carry them into the warehouse. And it could get so cold. You'd hear this rumbling noise and then we'd all cheer out because that meant that the heating was coming on – which wasn't so very often, and it was through this big old pipe. But we were all in it together and there was always something going on. People would be coming and going all day long through to the office next door and there would be banter and crying out at each other.

Elizabeth (Betty) McHardy, b.1930. Aberdeen Comb Works. Interviewed 2004

GRANITE
The Yards and The Quarry

Joe had lost an eye while he was serving his time; that's a common hazard for the mason. Not that any of us wore goggles; you just assumed it would never happen to you.

The granite yard:
Take it or leave it

In 1934, I started work at the granite quarry. The work was heavy but I was young and fit and I took to it well enough. My first job was to sort out the stones. But I was anxious to get proper qualifications so I went into Kittybrewster and entered the yard being worked by the famous Joe Sherriff to serve my time under him.

It has all now been built over and turned into another block of flats but in those days it was reckoned to be just about the most modern yard in town. I had to learn how to dress a stone, to fit it into all the shapes and forms for its use in a building.

Joe had lost an eye while he was serving his time; that's a common hazard for the mason, the way a chip from the chisel could enter the eye and penetrate the iris and leave you without sight. Not that any of us wore goggles; you just assumed it would never happen to you.

He ran a good yard though he had his favourites: some he would stop and chat to, the next time he would pass by without a word. I just got on with things.

You'd start at eight, go hard at it till 12, without any break, take your piece and then back till five. You see, then the bosses were on top and there was no point in asking for any better conditions.

I remember when I was at the quarry at Cults I went up to old Hendry who was running it and asked for a halfpenny an hour more. 'Laddie,' he told me, 'ye're nae doot worth a hapenny mair bit if ah gie it tae ye aa' the rest wid need it.'

That was it: take it or leave it. At Kittybrewster Joe Sherriff kept a book and if you were a minute late it would go down into it and he would make sure you made up the time later on. I swear that there were some who never did manage to finish serving their time because they were always behind what he reckoned they should be doing to complete their five years.

Alexander (Alec) Milne, b.1914. Kittybrewster granite yard. Interviewed 2009

'Still a role as a centre of high skilled work'. The Lockerbie memorial of the 1988 air disaster, all made at Robertson's of Aberdeen .

The granite yard director: Modernise or die

When I started in the trade in the early 1960s I was shocked at how ramshackle your average Aberdeen granite yard was. Men had to work in open sheds with no protection against the elements. In winter the snow would blow in on them and it was freezing. One single bucket of cinders was supplied to give them a small amount of heat but sometimes a workman would pick up his chisel and find his hand frozen to its shaft. It was positively medieval.

Things had to change and a lot of the smaller yards soon went under. In those days there had been more than 30 yards dotted about the city; now we are down to only Robertson's plus Fyfe at Oldmeldrum and another yard at Persley.

The nature of the work has changed drastically. When I started it was mostly large-scale building, now it is landscaping, headstones, fireplaces. Small scale ornamental work, really, but one that requires a high level of skill. When I began, however, there was great demand for prestigious building work, especially in London where public buildings such as the big banks wanted granite facings. Rubislaw quarry was still on the go and for the rest we imported slabs from India, Cornwall, Scandinavia, Italy and so on. These imports would arrive as huge blocks and we would saw them down into the required slabs.

I became a director at Robertson's. I knew we had to modernise and luckily I had landed with the most enterprising granite firm in the city. The really big advance was our investing in the new cutting and polishing machines which were being manufactured in Germany. Before they came on the scene, cutting had been a primitive and long drawn-out affair. It was done by saw boys using chain saws with a syrup tin at each end. These tins contained masses of steel ball shot which had to be regularly applied to maintain a smooth action. Polishing was a similar process, hour after hour of hard grinding work.

But now we had these modern diamond saws which could zip through a block of any thickness. A whole block can be got through in four hours whereas in the past it would have taken weeks. You can program in the exact requirements by computer and it will be done for you at the push of a button. Once it took five years to train up a cutter; now a couple of weeks learning how to push the correct buttons is all that's needed.

All this has revolutionised the industry. When I entered, it was a big employer, with hundreds of men required. The average granite yard required a whole team of workers who ranged from blacksmiths, crane men, and saw boys to the polishers, the box makers and the machine operators. And there was no notion of Health & Safety either – no goggles, no gloves, no helmets supplied. It was the practice to take the rubber inner tube from a bike and snip off lengths to give some protection for the fingers. The dust was overpowering; you'd see men trooping up King Street after a shift smothered from head to toe in dust. No masks were worn and lung diseases were regarded as an occupational hazard. Nobody inspected for working conditions and accidents were an everyday fact of life.

The bosses wielded absolute power. Men could be sacked just like that. Once at

Hogg's this guy on the polishing machine left it for a minute or two; the boss himself came by, and sacked him on the spot. When times were slack 10 men could be laid off without notice.

The old building work died away but we managed to specialise in fine memorial and ornamental work and thrived. Robertson's expanded and developed branches all over the UK, from Shetland down to London.

Although the old extensive building work has now withered away there is still scope for a continuation of the old granite industry by exploiting Aberdeen's historical reputation as a centre of highly skilled work. For the big stuff we cannot compete with the likes of India where the wage costs are less than a quarter of ours. But what we can do is offer fine inscription and design work.

So much of the work can now be programed. We have machines which can inscribe whole portraits and scenes on a gravestone. But the letters themselves will always have to be carved out by hand, by hammer, chisel and a lot of highly trained skill. And although there has been a move towards cremation there are still large pockets of the population who demand burial, marked by a finely finished stone, to keep us in work. Some sections, such as the Jewish community or many within the Roman Catholic one, favour interment still. We also have a continuing trade with the North-east fishing communities where a top notch memorial stone is regarded as a must; often there's a sense of competition here with a request to ensure that the stone is at least two inches higher than those around it.

Eddie Masson, b.1940. A & J Robertson Granite. Interviewed 2016

Robertson's Pittodrie Street yard before it took it over, when derrick cranes still did all the lifting.

A pair of Aberdeen lads with their new acquisition. Hugh Black and the late Sandy Whyte, above Rubislaw Quarry.

There's only one true Granite City!

By 2012 I had completely retired from my ownership of New Style Products, a firm which specialised in advanced building materials. It was then that out of the blue I received a phone call that was to take me on the next step in my life journey. It was an old friend, Sandy Whyte, asking me, quite amazingly: 'Rubislaw Quarry's for sale. Do you fancy joining me in buying it?'

Now, like anybody growing up in Aberdeen, I was, of course, aware of Rubislaw Quarry. Moreover, I was now living in Queen's Road just 100 yards or so from its site. I passed it daily and had noted the 'For Sale' signs but had given the matter no thought. As a young lad I had once or twice on my walks home from Hazlehead Academy popped in to take a look, to stare down into this great hole now filling up with water, and been impressed at the size and spectacle of it all. But buying it? That was a whole new ball game.

But I got thinking and the more I dwelt on the notion the more it appealed. Imagine, two Aberdeen lads, born and bred, from straightforward backgrounds actually becoming the owners of such an iconic city landmark. So we decided to give it a go, not really expecting that our bid could get anywhere. We knew that several property developers were in for it and that they would probably comfortably outbid us. Indeed, as we later discovered, ours proved to be the lowest bid – but one by one the competition dropped out, deterred by all the planning obstacles that would be encountered. We were different: we had no intention of using the site as a development opportunity; our ambition was to act as stewards of what was an historic piece of Aberdeen heritage.

That was just the start: as we found out more about what we were now the owners of, the more and more we realised just how special Rubislaw Quarry really was.

That got us thinking and soon enough we began to receive stories and recollections from people who had been associated with the quarry in its working life and so to build up a picture not only of its history but also of its huge significance in the social and industrial life of Aberdeen. We became aware of it as the place which had stood at the very centre of what was a global industry and of Aberdeen's position as the world leader in producing quality granite.

'A real asset for the city': The Heritage Centre planned for the Quarry.

Everyone was telling us that half of Aberdeen had come out of our hole in the ground; what we discovered was that, in fact, 75 percent of Aberdeen's pre-war built heritage had actually originated as raw stone from this one quarry. We began to appreciate that this hole of ours had produced materials and skills which had reached around the world. For example, when Sydney Harbour Bridge was being constructed, the

The Blondin wires at work for student Bill Jenkins, 435 feet up, planting a toga-attired effigy for a Charities Week stunt, 1951.

New South Wales government sent out for Rubislaw Quarry granite and for Aberdeen stone masons to do the job. Rubislaw had developed a technology and the craftsmen to go with it that had been exported all over the globe.

Our researches also showed us that Rubislaw Quarry had acted as a focus for industrial innovation. The usual approach as a quarry goes deeper and deeper is to cut out broad terraces so that vehicles can get at the raw material. There are terraces along the sides of the quarry but they are comparatively narrow. Access to the granite was solved by using a system of wires and pulleys which were called the Blondin wires – after the famous French tightrope walker. This was unique to Rubislaw and was an ingenious innovation

Hugh Black at his 'hidden gem', autumn 2016.

which deserves to be commemorated.

The quarry finally closed in 1969. That's when the water pumps were turned off and that's when it began to fill up with water. For all the world it now looks like some sort of inshore lake, a wild and neglected place, surrounded by thickets of trees, bushes and grassy banks. But once it was a real place of wonder, a tourist attraction and a staging post on the Aberdeen City and Suburbs bus tours. There was an observation platform and a small stall where you could purchase little granite mementoes in the shape of figurines.

Rubislaw Quarry has been allowed to lie dormant and forgotten for far too long. My hope is that we can do something to remind the world of just how much the city's granite industry has given to it and of the huge role our hole in the ground has played in it. What we plan is a well-designed futuristic visitors' centre which will open up this hidden gem, both to the city and to the wider world. We now have detailed planning permission and are moving through the various legal requirements. The intention is to commence building in 2017 and to be up and running the year after. We are confident that the centre will prove to be a great attraction; after all, no other city has anything quite like it.

Since our ideas have become more widely known we have begun to attract stories relating to its history. One of the most amazing ones is the tale of the hidden Crown Jewels. We got this from Edna Sharp whose father used to be a manager at the quarry. Apparently, during the war, he was one day hurrying to his home in Union Grove because the German bombers were sweeping over the city and he was fearful for his family. It was a bad raid and he wanted to tell young Edna a secret story so as to take her mind off the dangers. What he told her was this: during the war the Government was anxious to find safe hiding places for the sort of treasures that would normally be housed in London. The Crown Jewels had to be kept secure, well away from the capital. And the place they hit upon was none other than a vault buried deep down in Rubislaw Quarry. We are looking forward to lowering the water levels down far enough for us to reclaim this vault. Then we will send them back to the Tower of London and replace the obviously fake replicas which are presently on display there!

So one of our aims is to build up an archive of recollections like these. At its peak the Quarry employed 200 men working at the bottom, blasting and cutting the granite, and a further 600 at the surface, making sets for use on the roads. It was a workplace which touched many lives and it would be good to remind the world of that fact.

We also reckon the quarry could act as a valuable ecological refuge. At the moment there is little wild life there; the water is too deep and too cold to attract native fish such as trout but we have researched the matter and have come across a species called the Arctic char salmon that could survive and even flourish. Presently they are an endangered species because of global warming so Rubislaw Quarry could become an important sanctuary for them. As the water level drops we would also hope to see the peregrine falcons coming back.

The neglect of the quarry has harmed wild life in other ways. The rise of the water has destroyed the trees which used to grow on the terraces; our plans will restore the

'A hole filling up with water'. The Quarry as it is now.

natural woodland of the area. We hope to make Rubislaw Quarry into a living celebration of Aberdeen's past.

Rubislaw Quarry has an aura about it. The site which was once such a hive of industry and swarming with hundreds of workers now lies still and dark and secret. One of the first things Sandy and I did was to get hold of a boat and row out into the middle. We just sat there drinking it all in. Our very own piece of Aberdeen history. But as we sat there staring around us we both felt a strange sensation of vertigo; it was as if we could sense the 600 feet of dark and mysterious depths below us.

At that moment we both realised that we were not simply owners of this place but its custodians. We were determined to create of it a legacy that would be prized by future generations. We know the city is behind us and we have been assured that the Heritage Lottery Fund will back us. We are also confident that once fellow Aberdonians come to appreciate what we are doing then they will also rally round with crowd funding.

Very sadly Sandy died in the summer of 2015, of cancer. It was good that he lived long enough to see our ideas well down the planning route; we will certainly ensure that there will be a memorial to him when those plans are brought to a conclusion.

I am also confident that once the Rubislaw Quarry visitors' centre is opened to the public then it will prove itself as a true asset to the city. In recent years Aberdeen has allowed itself to underperform as a tourist centre. The preoccupation with oil and gas has meant that it is now known primarily as a business destination. But the oil is in decline and with the arrival of the AWPR there is an even greater danger that the traveller will simply by-pass the city in favour of driving on to the castles, the distilleries, the golf courses and the Highlands. Aberdeen badly needs more attractions to reward the city break visitors and we believe that Rubislaw Quarry will provide a unique and dramatic contribution to that effort. After all, as Sandy Robertson, the manager of a still flourishing city granite business always says: 'There are many cities around the world that are built out of granite – but there is only the one true Granite City.'

Hugh Black, b.1958. Rubislaw Quarry. Interviewed 2016

'You can still see his work today': The two pillars Michael Main's father refashioned on the Chanonry.

The stonemason:
He loved working with granite

My father was a stonemason. He took great pride in his skills and loved working with granite. For him brick work could not be considered a real job. It was granite which presented the real challenge for a skilled stonemason. If you take a real look at the old granite buildings in the city you can see what he meant. The skill involved was amazing – the joints which had to be so thin and so precise, yet the stones themselves so large and so heavy. Even to manipulate them was an art; they were so heavy and big that to balance them right and then manoeuvre them into the correct position required real skill. Many of those blocks weighed over a hundredweight, impossible to lift up but he would know how to roll and jig them into position quite effortlessly.

In the post-war era the demand for granite building dropped away but he was always in demand on account of his skills, which became more and more rare. To see the way he knew where to drill the holes into a rough-hewn block, then hammer in the metal feathers so that the stone would split easily and cleanly, well, that required great judgement and a real feel for the grain and the nature of the stone.

Many times I would go out and see what my dad was doing at his work. He did a lot of work for Aberdeen University. He dressed stones for an extension to the King's Library. You'd watch him busy at his work with chisel and hammer in his hands but, as was the norm back then, with no regard for Health and Safety – no goggles, no earplugs, no hard hat. He wore glasses and many a time they came back shattered from a flying piece of chipping. But he was a precise and careful worker so never really came to much harm.

You can still see some of his handiwork today. I used to take my children down to the Chanonry and into the lane next to St Machar's Cathedral. That's where two large pillars stand. And the fact that they are doing so is thanks to my father. He was given the job of rescuing them when they were subsiding; he had to take the stones down, chalk them up with a number and replace them exactly as they had been.

Michael Main, b.1948. Old Aberdeen. Interviewed 2016

TEXTILES
The Rise and Fall of Richards

The Broadford works: at its peak, it was the city's largest employer.

Richards – a job for life...

I took to Richards straight anyway. At that time it was regarded as a world leader in the provision of canvas and hosepipe materials. In 1957 I joined the office as a statistician and stock controller – my title was 'Records Clerk/Statistician', being responsible for monitoring the flow of sales and stock around the various agents out in the field.

Once Richards had a near monopoly in supplying flax mail bags to the Post Office.

The workforce contained some lovely people – hard working and reliable. Yet these were people who often came from the poorest parts of town – Kilgour Avenue, Sandilands Drive, Northfield. Many of them were women. I sometimes had to go to their homes and always I would be greeted by immaculate interiors and well-kept stairways. One spectacle used to upset me. On Thursdays the men would be paid and then you'd find their womenfolk lining up at the gate as they came out so as to make sure they would get their hands on the wages to pay necessary bills before the men sloped off to the pub to spend it.

The working conditions were hard though a great improvement on the old days. I once came across a rules and regulations notice stuck up on the inside door of a toilet and they were positively draconian, containing threats of instant dismissal for quite minor transgressions. Apparently, all an employee had to do to ensure a disciplinary action against a fellow worker was to go up to a foreman and utter: 'Mrs Smith – Rule 45' – or whatever.

There are some revealing accounts handed down from those days. Before the war the firm had been owned by a Mr Hepburn, a rich property owner who appeared to own half of Aberdeen back then. He had lost part of an arm during World War 1. He used to rule Richards with a rod of iron; he loved to demonstrate the absolute power he wielded over the workers. For example, he would decide exactly when he deigned to dole out the wages even though they should have been paid out at the end of the month without fail – a few days late, too bad.

There were some great stories of the old days at Richards, stories which have passed down into its folklore. When I was a trainee manager one of my duties was to go in to ensure that the switch-over from the evening to the night shift was going smoothly. Now, there was this old workman, a country lad he was, who did his 12-hour shift in the boiler room, usually without passing a word to anyone around him. But one night he came rushing up, blurting out that 'twa workers were haeing sex ahin the boiler. 'Are you sure that's what they're doing?' 'Oh aye – I seen them an they were fairly ginging at it.' He named the male involved – a well-known lady's man – but when he was asked as to the identity of his partner in crime he had to confess ignorance. But, he added: 'if aiver ah see her airse agin ah'll be sure to recognise her.'

Richards was reckoned to be a good firm which could offer you a job for life. Many workers had been there for 50 years, the whole of their working lives. In the 1930s and '40s school kids of 14 would approach us asking to be given the chance to learn to spin so as to give them a better chance of landing a job. Once they had mastered the art then they knew that as soon as they left school they were set up for a job for life. The females were generally more dextrous and could adapt better. Indeed, women proved to be the hardest workers – a good working female was better than any man.

This work was arduous in the extreme. I just don't know how they could do it hour after hour. Whenever I tried it I found that the maximum time I could keep a frame going was little more than a quarter of an hour before the ends started to come down and

The Queen visits Richards Broadford Works in 1955.

I had to turn the thing off. You had to catch the weft at the point where the yarn goes through and that was where a spindle was going round. You had to thread a wire down and tweak it onto this wire and then pull it back down again from the bobbin that was spinning. Only then could you let it go. But the spinners were so close together that you'd often get whacked nastily on the hand from one of them and then – when that happened to me – I had to rush off to the washroom to run the hand under cold water. But these women were doing it hour after hour and treated the odd whack on the hand as a simple occupational hazard.

Quite often people would get their hands caught in the machinery and suffer serious injuries as a result. But they rarely reported such incidents. The general work culture was just to accept a few hard knocks as part of the working day and get on with it.

Until conditions improved in the 1970s, the work was dirty and injurious to health. Flax creates clouds of dust yet no-one thought to provide protective masks. Before extraction devices were installed you couldn't see from one side of the place to the other. The result was that many workers later succumbed to respiratory diseases. The din of machinery was constant and deafening but, again, no ear muffs. As a result most workers suffered a degree of hearing loss. But the attitude was this is our job and we just have to get on with it. There was a robotic pattern to the weaving work; if you found yourself following a weaver up the street after work then, as often as not, you'd see her walking along with her hands still going – winding imaginary bobbins as if they were still at the frames.

So the work was hard and hazardous but Richards had been built up in the era when labour was plentiful and cheap; in the early years most of our workforce had come to us straight from school without academic qualifications at the age of 14 and were happy to secure a position at such a big employer and with every prospect they had landed a job for life. It was a hard and unforgiving atmosphere. One of the managers would not hesitate to dismiss you on the spot if, for example, you were having to repeat the work. 'Git yer jacket. Doon the road wi ye.' is what he would tell them. He knew that in those pre-oil industry days there would be no shortage of replacements.

But Broadford did create a sense of community. The regular newsletters which came

There was a lot of inertia about the place, a matter of doing things simply because that was the way they had always been done.

out in the 1970s onwards show the range of activities on offer: angling clubs, football teams, bowling, hillwalking, badminton, a Social Club, the annual election of the 'Richards Personality Girl.' Parties were held for ex-employees and there was a handing out of food parcels to them at their homes. A real sense of loyalty was generated.

My attitude was that you earned respect by showing a willingness to muck in and prove you could put your hand to anything. If something needed cleaning up then I would grab a brush and do it myself. As far as I was concerned we were one united workforce. I enjoyed the work and relished the various challenges it threw up. There was a lot of inertia about the place, a matter of doing things simply because that was the way they had always been done so I could spot a number of ways to improve the flow of output.

Things worked out well for me. I ended up as Senior Manager, having gone through a series of departments – Commercial, Spinning, Development. But after resting on its peak in the 1970s and 1980s things began to go downhill for Richards. At that period the money was rolling in, we had the security of big contracts with the Post Office and were a huge provider of canvas materials to lorries and to shipping. But we weren't quick enough to move with the times. For example, while our tarpaulin products were second to none, they had the disadvantage of holding the moisture when it was wet and were then difficult to fold. It was the newer light-weight synthetic materials that began to take over.

Richards was on a slippery slope and nobody spotted it till it was too late. I tried to persuade the company to work with the oil industry but the attitude was: 'Oil will be a seven-day wonder. But the world will always need textile goods.' Yet we had everything that any oil company could need: buildings, storage space, engineers, medical centres. Ironically we later lost much of our skilled workers to that very same oil industry.

The general attitude seemed to be that we were a highly successful outfit, one with a worldwide reputation so why change? People were unwilling to move out of their comfort zone. So instead of investing our profits in new machinery and in developing our systems we entered into the current mania for take-overs and buying up other companies so as to create an empire. But most of the new acquisitions were lacking in efficiency and so we began to lose money.

The Broadford works had been a splendid example of Victorian industrial expansion back in their day but by the end of the 20th century the plant was feeling its age. The firm would have been better employed investing in a thorough modernisation of its internal communication and transportation systems than in chasing glory by buying up other, often quite dubious, plants while it had the cash to spare. When labour had been cheap and plentiful it hadn't mattered that stuff had to be pushed around on barrows by muscle power rather than by conveyor belts but in a later period this inefficiency began to let us down.

I was at Richards for 37 years, mostly very happy and satisfying ones. I left the firm in 1996 just as it was sliding down into oblivion. I can recall the days when at lunch times

the trams would be queuing up by Hutcheon Street to take hundreds of workers back and forth to their homes in Woodside. And now the trams are gone, the streets are silent and all those crowds of workers have vanished. Nowadays I try to avoid passing by those locked gates and that decaying site at Broadford. Once we employed 3,000 to 4,000, and Richards was the biggest private employer in Aberdeen. Now the place is inhabited by seagulls and rats, a place where vagrants break in to find shelter and fireraisers do their work. Once that site was an object of pride; scaffies were employed to go round ensuring everything was spick and span. And now the place is falling into rack and ruin. Sad, very sad.

Norman Burt, b.1939. Richards Ltd. Interviewed 2015

'A sense of community': Arthur Wyllie, second front left, skipper of the 'Four Tops', a member of the Broadford works flourishing ten-pin bowling league, 1970s/80s.

Richards Ltd – not quite a job for life

After I left Aberdeen Grammar School I became an 'Apprentice Clerk' at Richards Ltd. As such, I was given fairly basic copying and recording jobs to do. I found myself in the big office along with about a dozen other clerks, the cashier, accounts and short hand typists. We worked at old-fashioned desks with big flat tops.

The work never became too repetitive as I was moved around the departments quite a bit. After a few months I was shifted to the Finishing Department. This was where the canvas and hose were baled up ready for despatch. Orders were being sent all over Britain and also to Australia, South Africa and New Zealand, where the firm also had agents. The

'Once a centre of industry...' A shot taken at a derelict Broadford Works, 2016.

Post Office was a big customer, buying the canvas that we sent to prisons to be made into mail bags.

By 1966 I landed in the Hose Department. Again there was a lot of entering data into big ledgers involved only this time no biros were permitted. Everything had to be carefully written onto waxed parchment and by a fountain pen. Any errors meant a row. This was an absolute pest; any mistake had to be painstakingly scratched out with a razor blade and then written over. I could see no real reason for all this; it seemed to be a matter of tradition, pure and simple.

Altogether I was with the company for 20 years, only broken by a boring year at the Torry Marine Laboratory. By 1972 I had risen to the post of Production Control Manager. This was a new department and I found myself responsible for getting in the orders from the Sales Department and then working them into production schedules, at the same time ensuring that all the components would be available at the correct time.

By this time I had acquired a fair overview of the administrative side of things at Richards. The struggle to ensure that everything was ready on time so that the order date could be met meant that my Production job was a challenging one, but all the more satisfying because of that. I remember sitting in my office seeing fleets of lorries leaving the premises loaded with orders, many of which I had been responsible for seeing through and thinking to myself: 'That's my orders in all those lorries.' I felt a great sense of pride.

That was the period when you could still feel great confidence in the future of Richards. It had developed into a firm with an international reach and a worldwide reputation. Those lorries were embarking on journeys that would take our goods all over the world. The old flax industry had declined but we had branched out into yarns and synthetic materials, into knitwear and carpets, and were seemingly in a powerful position.

But as it turned out those days proved to be the final ones of the good days; from that high point of the mid 1980s, Richards began to go into a decline. Part of the problem was increased competition from overseas. Another difficulty was the appointment as General Manager of an outsider who came from an engineering background and who proved to be out of his depth. Then there was the outdated layout of the plant. We were going 24 hours a day, five days a week but full automation came late. In my day men were still pushing barrows of goods from one side of the plant to the other and in all weathers too; only later did forklifts and trailers come into play. There were a lot of demeaning labouring jobs like that. The workshops were still noisy, dusty places with machinery clanking away; the dust led to a lot of absences due to respiratory problems.

From my point of view as Production Control Manager, I was coming under pressure to promise earlier and earlier order completion dates, ones that I knew we could never meet. I would quote something like a 12-week delivery and Sales would change this back to eight weeks and I knew that was now an impossible deadline. The aim was to attract customers but inevitably our failure to deliver on the promised date simply alienated them.

I have lived next door to Richards in Maberly Street for many years now. This means

I am in a prime position to witness the fate of the old factory site since it finally closed its doors in 2003. It is a sad, sad sight, the old plant which had once been such as centre of industry now lying derelict. There are plans to convert it into housing but work has yet to start. Meanwhile, the place lies open to vandals and gangs of kids who enter it and roam all over the place, throwing things about and starting fires. I've lost count of the number of times I've been on the phone to the Police and the Fire Brigade. I live in constant fear that one day a fire will break out in the old office block where I started my work as a young lad all those years ago.

In February 2016, a demolition company took control of the site and have been busy pulling down the unwanted buildings – all the listed ones are to be saved. In March of this year I was given permission to have a last look at the place where I spent so many years. It was even worse than I had feared. The buildings were just full of rubbish and debris; you could see blackened spots where the fire raisers had been at work. When I joined it, Richards seemed to offer a job for life; there were some people who had left school at 14 and who were still there in their 60s. No-one ever thought that it would one day collapse and have to turn its loyal workers out onto the streets.

Arthur Wyllie, b.1948. Richards Ltd. Interviewed 2016

I was given permission to have a last look at the place where I spent so many years. It was even worse than I had feared.

EVERYDAY PLEASURES
The Urban Playground

Tucking into a 'sair hand' – (two slices of bread spread – in this case with rhubarb jam) – Michael Forbes, Ruthrieston Circle.

The URBAN PLAYGROUND

The four-year old Ralph Dutch as a somewhat reluctant kilt-wearer.

There were plenty of kids to play with

Life in our tenement was good – a warm and secure childhood. There were always plenty of other kids to play with in the street. We had a sort of cricket; someone had painted a set of stumps on the gable end of a house and we used this as our wicket. Then there was the football. But we also played a variety of other games, some of which we had improvised ourselves. One great one was 'Walk the Plank or Join the Crew.' Here, you'd elect a couple to stand in the middle of the road while the rest of us would line up on the pavement. At a signal, the pavement people would attempt to dash across the street while the pair in the middle would try to catch them. If you were caught you'd be presented with the choice: 'Do you want to join the crew – or do you want to walk the plank?' Then you'd be tortured – a bit of arm twisting or some nettles across the bare flesh of your legs (we all wore short trousers, of course) until you finally submitted and agreed to join up. It's only years later that I realised that the smart thing would have been to agree to join the crew immediately but as the torture was regarded as a test of your courage, it was important to hold out for as long as possible.

Seven years old and in the Duthie Park with sister Eileen.

We always played separately from the girls. Games had their seasons but by whom or how the start of a new season was declared, none of us ever found out. One day it would be decided that today marked the commencement of the marbles season and out would come our marbles. If you were lucky your father would have fashioned a sort of little bridge structure for you which had archways built into it and here the test was to fire your prize marbles through

the gaps. If you did that successfully you'd be given three marbles from your challenger; if you failed then you had to hand over the marble.

Ralph Dutch, b.1929. King Street. Interviewed 2014

'They're not heavy at all – they're ma family!' Ralph Dutch many years later and now a fond grandfather.

We went out to play

When we moved to Garthdee it was just fields. There was a farm – we just had to go up to the end of the road to see the lambs and the sheep – but then they started building more houses. Kids being kids, we used to go up to the houses and run across the rafters. How none of us fell, I don't know. The watchman used to start shouting so we just used to stand quiet until he was past and then run across these rafters again. I think that, when we were kids, we had more freedom because we went out to play.

Martha Alexander, b.1937. Garthdee. Interviewed 2015

Maybe not PC nowadays, but fun at the time. Jim Duffus riding the Hazlehead tiger. Watch out for this tiger's reappearance in Chapter 3.

Smells give lasting memories

There were other kids in the tenement. We were on the third floor and I can remember just how highly polished the linoleum and banisters were and how everything else was very well kept. More recently, when I've gone to look for student flats and the like, what a state an Aberdeen tenement is now compared to the highly polished status of ours when I was little. The smell of polish was certainly memorable.

I think smells give lasting memories. I remember the shops at the top end of Union Street with their smell of coffee beans from little grocers' shops. You had the big department stores in George Street and Union Street. You went to a particular shop for your school tie and your school uniform.

We were also well-placed at the front window for watching the Torcher parade go by because at that time it came down Union Grove, then wheeled up to Holburn Junction and down Union Street. I remember the sparks from the tarry torches.

Duthie Park had paddle-boats in the pond and from Hazlehead I have photographs of me taken – not politically correct now – by photographers who would have stuffed tigers and zebras in the parks; you were propped on one of these and had your picture taken.

Growing up in the city centre, there were still several big-screen cinemas; the cinema was a big thing in entertainment. Swimming baths – we had one just across from us at Holburn Junction and the old, heated salt water pool at the beach; I used to go to them a lot. The Timmer Market was still on the go, down at the bottom of Union Street; I remember pea shooters – so you'd get hit with a pea and a bit of spit on the back of your head, once a year.

Jim Duffus, b.1954 Union Grove. Interviewed 2016

Everything you needed was no more than a 10-minute walk away

My first family home was at 19 Nellfield Place, in a top floor flat in the Holburn area – mother, father, two sisters and myself in a tiny two-room and box room flat with an outside toilet. This was shared with the residents of the other attic flat and had to be accessed by going down an outside stone stair, crossing the 'backie' and then up a second short flight of steps. Try that on a cold dark winter's night.

I was introduced to inside facilities in 1951 when we moved into a council house in Kincorth. At that time there were no shops or schools there. But I did have a bedroom of my own and a lovely view over the Dee. What more could a young boy want? Answer: Nellfield Place.

I must have worn out countless pairs of shoes and bicycle tyres over the next 14 years as I kept returning to my boyhood haunts. I understood my parents' pleasure in bringing up their children in a house which had a kitchen, bathroom, living room and three bedrooms, our own front and back doors and a garden, so I never once expressed my

thoughts on what I had left behind at Nellfield.

The description by John Lennon of a housing scheme he once lived in best describes my Kincorth as I look back on the 14 years I had to live there: 'a cemetery with street lights'.

By moving to Kincorth they had improved their standard of living in a manner that they would not even have thought possible when they married in 1937. In their position I would have done the same. But I consider myself very fortunate to have been able to experience my early years in that small tenement flat in 'Nellies Pies', as we affectionately called Nellfield Place.

Believe me, that tenement and that street were great places to be brought up in the 1940s and '50s. The happiest of homes and of neighbourhoods with everything a wee boy could want and in walking distance from Holburn Central Church, Holburn Street

A hot day at Nellfield Place. June 1947 and Sandy Gallagher (extreme left) entertains friends on his sixth birthday. From left, Sheila Grant, sister Margaret, Sandra Pirie and Peter Kerr.

At the beach, 1947 with father and sister Margaret.

A babe in arms. Sandy Gallagher along with, from left, May Fiddes, Ron Fiddes, Elizabeth Grant, Irene Shepherd, sister Margaret.

Primary school, Fonthill Road Public Library, the Uptown Baths, the Odeon, Playhouse and Capitol cinemas, the Duthie Park and, most importantly, Harlaw football playing field. A street where only one resident had a car and where we could play football, rounders and cricket at all times.

Almost every Friday night from age seven to 16 I attended the Life Boys and 15th Company Boys' Brigade at Holburn Central Church in the McClymont Hall at Holburn Junction and the BBs also meant summer camps at Finzean and membership of our company's football and cricket teams.

My parents were both very keen readers and encouraged us to use the local Fonthill library where I very quickly got to know the whereabouts of all the 'Just William' books. Thereafter any boys' adventure stories, graduating to John Buchan and then, in my teens, a lot of political stuff. I'm still a member and regular user of the public library. Defend our libraries!

The front bedroom window of our flat looked over the Nellfield Cemetery where I'm almost afraid to admit that a group of us would play war games and hide and seek during the long summer evenings. We gained access by means of crossing the road, going up a

Entertaining friends and neighbours in the back garden at Nellfield Place, 1947. Sandy Gallagher is front left along with Peter Kerr.

close to what was known as the haunted house, climbing onto the roof of an air raid shelter, clambering on to the top of the cemetery wall and then dropping down via the top of the grave stones which were positioned against the cemetery wall. I don't remember us causing any damage although on one occasion one of my pals did manage to half fall through the wooden boards laid over a grave which had been excavated, awaiting its new tenant. Needless to say this caused much hilarity.

Care had to be taken at the outset of any cemetery adventure not to attract the attention of and thereby upsetting the old woman who lived in the 'haunted house' as this encouraged her to get in a bit of stone throwing practice using us as her target. Once she even chased us, brandishing a poker.

With the exception of this stone throwing lady and of perhaps a rather eccentric old man at number 17 who had the nasty habit of trying to stick a knife in our football if it went over the wall between our backie and his place, Nellfield was a neighbourhood where homeliness and common sense prevailed.

Alexander (Sandy) Gallacher, b.1941. Nellfield Place. Interviewed 2015.

A group of us would play war games and hide and seek in Nellfield Cemetery during the long summer evenings.

Playing outside was just what you did

When we went down to 37 View Terrace I was very fortunate because we had lots of families round about so there were always lots of kids to play with. That's a big difference between then and now because we played out in the street. There weren't lots of cars about. There's a photograph of me aged about 10 on my bike and I think there are about two cars parked, one on either side of the street. You could play freely without fear of being knocked down or of bashing into anybody's car and damaging it.

Maybe children still play in their back gardens but they don't have the freedom of running around the neighbourhood. There was a lady, who lived next to us – she was quite elderly – and she used to get really annoyed at the noise we made in the summer time. She used to bang on the window and I remember being quite scared of her. She came round one night to complain to my mum about the noise we were all making outside. She didn't have a telephone and she asked my mum if she could use our telephone to phone the Police to complain about our noise. So Mum invited her in – but then she didn't know how to use the telephone so she turned and stomped out.

Dianne Morrison in front of the family's first ever car – and she still remembers the number – KRG 506F.

Dianne Morrison, b.1967. Rosemount. Interviewed 2015

With brother Bruce
at the Carnival.

I learned as much outside school as in it

I was an inner city child brought up in the 1950s and living in an environment where space was limited and amenities lacking. We had no indoor toilet, bathroom, proper cooker or washing machine until I was 10 years old. But my parents were a loving, caring couple who set great store by our development; they were never content to leave our education to the school and were anxious to provide us with all the rich experiences that the city and its surrounding countryside could offer.

We were within walking distance of the beach, lovely parks, museums, markets. We might have been short of money but they were selfless in the ways in which they gave us every opportunity possible. My father took extra jobs and his entire wage packet was handed over to my mother. He never smoked nor frequented the pub. But he would always find the money for piano lessons, trips to the country or the attractions of the city.

By the time I went to secondary school I had already been on excursions to Bannockburn, to Culloden, to Celtic crosses and to stone circles, to the Robert Burns cottage, the Scott Monument and to all the Deeside castles. A special treat was the Marischal Museum with its vast array of random, exotic objects like Egyptian mummies, a pickled Chinese lady's foot, Beaker People remains, scalped heads and shrunken heads – and then the highlight: the threepenny climb up to the top of the tower and the view all over the city.

We also had a car, with models ranging from an Austin 7 to a Truimph Mayflower, and in it we would tour all over Scotland, staying in youth hostels.

Another joy was the Art Gallery where my special favourite was the great Landseer's rendition of the flood in the Highlands. And we also enjoyed popping into the old

Pause for a picnic
on one of many trips
around Scotland.

market with its wonderful first floor gallery of quirky specialized shops which sold foreign stamps, second hand books and old coins. It had an atmosphere of its own underneath that marvellous ironwork and glass roofing. But to get to it you first had to brave the filthy Market Street entrance which led onto a gauntlet of blood soaked sawdust and dripping hanging beef carcasses. Get through that lot and you were onto the spicy perfumed area where there were all sorts of exotic fruits and nuts on display in open brimming hessian sacks.

When I was seven I had the choice of going to the baths, to the ice-rink in Spring Gardens, to Miss Auchinachie's choir for children; Saturday morning meant the cinema – 6d downstairs, 9d up. Every day there was something. One evening would be devoted to the Salvation Army's Temperance Society where we all sang songs like 'Deep and Wide.' Every week we'd take a little trip to the antique shop down the road. There I'd go round the shop and look at wonderful things like shell bracelets and little delicate boxes; often the stallholders simply gave me them. Nor did I lack for books. The Public Library was just a 10 minutes walk away. I joined up when I was seven. I remember the first book I took out – 'Teddy Bear Robertson' and it was a plain hardback book with these black and white illustrations. Magical.

I also learned to play the piano. I went to Mrs Edwards for lessons, over on the other

'We would tour all over Scotland in our car.' With parents and brother Bruce, 1950s.

1952 and a flower girl: (Beryl is right) for neighbour's wedding at St Nicolas Church – but note the various costume lengths. Hers was simply a converted party dress – no new matching costumes in those austerity days.

A place of spices and exotic fruits: The old 'New Market' which was a source of delight for the young. [PHOTO: ABERDEEN LIBRARY SERVICES]

side of George Street. No, I would say that I was deprived of nothing in my childhood; not in terms of being cared for or having experiences. We were truly the rich children of the inner city for we had the 'Freedom of the City' – unlike the more affluent but spiritually impoverished children of today, who seem to be timetabled for everything.

Beryl Mackenzie, b.1946. Baker Street. Interviewed 2004

To me it was a magical place

I was born in October 1938, in Roslin Street at our tenement home there. I still think of it as my true home. To me it was a magical and warm place, one which I've never quite managed to replicate anywhere else. Roslin Street in the '40s was a stable and neighbourly community. We lived in what was termed a good tenement where people took pride in the cleanliness and orderliness of their homes. A great sign of our aspirations was the energy put in by the women into getting out the Cardinal polish and making the stairs gleaming and also ensuring that the bowls of flowers were kept in proper order.

Nearby, on King Street, there was the wonderful ice creamer kept by the Italian ice cream makers, Marcini. The great Sunday afternoon treat was to go there for a Knickerbocker Glory. And when you were walking back after an evening at the BBs you could go into Tortolano's for a poke of fritters – really fingers of tatties fried in deep batter; horribly greasy but what a treat!

I lived in Roslin Street throughout the war. After the war the shelters became another place for us to play in. The children would make up a concert and invite others to be our audience while they sat there – and we erected a curtain across the entrance. Only six or seven would gather to watch us but we went through a whole routine: 'Item 1': 'Item 2' and so on. I had my own party piece which was the current hit song: 'I tot I taw a puddy cat a-cweeping up on me'

The streets were lit by gas lamps and each nightfall the lamp lighter would make his tour of them. We would pester him: 'Gie's a shottie mister!'

It was a city East-end tenement but on the edge of the open spaces of the Links and the Beach. From our window you could look out onto the Broad Hill – but we always referred to it as the 'Broader'.

Roof top boys: With fellow senior pupils at the Academy building in Belmont Street, 1955.

Stalwarts of the 34th: Bob Erridge, left, with fellow BB members.

The Roslin Street gang: Bob extreme left, 1950.

Along Seaforth Road you came to what was known locally as the Piggery. This was an area of small huts which housed various workshops where bikes were mended and other odd jobs done. Then onto the Broader and then the Beach – and freedom. On the way you passed the Rocket pitch – now where the King's Links driving range is but then the home to a six-hole golf course. Round about here there were tunnels into the earth and you could crawl into them – I shudder to think what would have happened if the roof had ever fallen in – but we were free and fearless in those days. Along the Beach itself there were still the vestiges of the war so that you could enter a number of abandoned pill boxes; an inviting hide – except that they always seemed to stink of stale urine.

We would spend hours at the Beach and did swim in the sea. I used to wait for the tide to go out and that's when you could leap and whoop into the pools left in the hollows of the sand and take advantage of the way in which the water had been warmed up by the sun – which, in those days seemed to shine more readily than it has ever done since.

We played in the street too in those more or less traffic-free days. 'Kick the cannie' was one favourite as was 'Walk the Plank' or 'Join the Crew.' Then we would play with a tennis ball, throwing it up to catch it as it came down from the gable end. And, of course, we played bools, which we referred to as dazzies.

Our district was full of wonders to our young imaginations. Nearby was the City Hospital where it was rumoured they experimented on monkeys and we would plot various cunning ways of liberating them.

Learning the arts of the javelin. Under the instruction of Dr Graham Morrice, Barmuckity camp, 1955.

Pittodrie was only a few steps away and you could work out how the match was going by the roars of the crowd. I was present at that midweek cup replay which held the record crowd of over 45,000. I biked down, abandoned my bike and got in – but couldn't see a thing.

Trams were a great feature of Aberdeen life then. We would place coins on the rails so as to see what sort of shape and markings would emerge after being run over. Being a passenger and travelling all the way up to Hazlehead was something of a real voyage; you would climb upstairs, go through the doors to the front and then stand there as if you were on the prow of some great ocean liner.

The Boys' Brigade was also an important part of my life. I was a member of the 34th Company. I did tinker with the idea of joining the Scouts but on the whole I considered that organisation to be a bit too nancy for me. I mean, just compare the two mottos: 'Be Prepared' against the BB's 'Sure and Steadfast', with its ring of moral strength and sense of

Memorable summer days at the BB camp at Barmuckity Farm, 1955.

forthright purpose.

We met weekly at the Gallowgate Porthill Church – now gone beneath later developments of car parks and high rise flats but then a place to be reached up the steep Seamount Steps, which I would almost bound up each Friday evening. A great event was always the summer camp held at Barmuckity Farm near Elgin. I enjoyed it all; the emphasis on physical activity was just what I wanted – the formation marching, the high jumping in the hall, the football.

I was 15 years living there and when the time came to move I was heart-sick to leave it all. It had given me such a secure and safe start to my life.

Robert (Bob) Erridge, b.1938. Roslin Street. Interviewed 2016

An interesting area for a boy back then

My father had been a panel beater for a firm in Dee Street but when I was five he went out to Canada; the intention was that he would get a job, settle in and then take us all out to join him in a new life. We had our passports and our medical cards all ready. But he actually disappeared, never to be heard of again, so leaving my mother to bring us all up single-handed. She had to take any cleaning job she could get hold of, often working early in the morning and then at night.

So life was very frugal. Quite often by the end of the week we were running out of food and had to make do with sugary pieces – a slice of bread with sugar sprinkled on it.

The first time they had met. Dennis Grattan with Sandra, his future wife at the Arts Ball, 1966.

And that was for a main meal mind, not just a snack.

Crown Street was an interesting area to be a boy in back in the '50s. We were right in the centre of city life with shops, cinemas and pubs all around us. We indulged in lots of money-making little scams. There were then a fair number of old buildings being pulled down and redeveloped in the centre of town and that gave us the opportunity to enter them at night after the workmen had gone and to scavenge for anything useful. We were particularly on the lookout for copper and lead which we would then take to the scrap merchant. You'd come across a section of the roofing that hadn't been properly cleared, you'd rip the lead off, roll it up and then get a few quid for it, no questions asked.

Another ruse was to search the area for old lemonade bottles for which a two-penny deposit was due back. The Beach was an especially fertile hunting ground and I would spend my summer holiday days scouring the sands and collecting them up in my bag. The real bonanza was to come across a soda syphon because the deposit for that was five shillings.

Then there was the telephone box scam. In those days the caller had to put coins into a box, press button A and make the call. But if there was no answer or the call ended sooner than anticipated he could then press button B and get some of the coins back. There was a whole row of phone boxes outside the Crown Street PO and rich pickings to be had from any caller who had neglected to press B. And we had a way of helping the process. What you did was to insert a hairpin into the mechanism and this held back the coins. The caller would assume that – as was quite common – the B mechanism wasn't working properly so after a failure to get his money back would simply walk off. That left us to go in, remove the hairpin and so release the coins. On a good day you might net as much as six or seven bob.

I would also visit the municipal rubbish collecting depot at Poynernook Road and get bits and pieces, old wheels and pedals and so construct my own bicycles. Security in those pre Health & Safety days was pretty lax. But we had our limits as to what we would get up to. Poverty drove us, not mere greed, and we knew only to take what other people had discarded or no longer wanted. It was really the urban equivalent of a spot of poaching – maybe not altogether legal but harmless in its impact on others.

Dennis Grattan, b.1946. Crown Street. Interviewed 2016

Bedford Road was a sheer delight

Growing up in the tenement environment of Bedford Road was sheer delight. The area around us made for the ideal urban playground: there were the cleared bomb sites and abandoned air raid shelters. Across the road was a selection of garages, and lock-ups along with commercial properties such as the Cruden Bay Brick & Tile Company, Briggs, Newstyle Products, the Regent Oil depot, Bon Accord Taxis, Jimmy Gall's garage with its large Esso sign that creaked as it swung on a windy day.

When Sunnyside Farm was still semi-rural and another of the young Dennis's haunts.

It was among these that we loved to race around, pretending we were cops and robbers or Brits versus Germans. This area today forms the Kittybrewster Retail Park.

Another area we made use of was behind the shops in Bedford Avenue with its huge trees left over from the era of the policies of Powis House. Our favourite initial play area was 'Wullie Weir's – overgrown fields surrounding the defunct Sunnyside Farm, a reminder that this used to be a semi-rural district. And at the bottom of this huge area was an open burn called the Gibberie which ran from the bottom of Bedford Road beside the University Officers' Training Corps camp until it disappeared through a weir into the grounds leading to King's College. This whole terrain was our very own happy hunting ground where we could let our imaginations run riot. Our mothers knew exactly where we were but never had to worry because they realised we would always return home when hunger got the better of us.

As we grew older and more adventurous, the vast Kittybrewster railway goods yards became our next target, despite – or maybe because of – the repeated warnings from our parents to stay away from them. There was a pair of gates just off the road so we could walk in at any time. Of course, the railway staff were on the lookout but although they would shout at us and give chase they were content just to make that gesture as they knew we were never going to cause serious harm. As far as we were concerned their efforts were simply another way of testing our speed and ingenuity. We were never caught.

In the sidings there were always a few carriages parked and they made for a happy hunting ground. We would climb up into them and use them as a secret gang hut. And because of the proximity of the marts, trains were always bringing in cattle so we could watch them being prodded and coaxed along. Some of them were headed for the abattoir at the bottom of Hutcheon Street and whether they realised their fate or no, some of them would be sufficiently spooked to break away and run amok. Then they might gallop down the road and end up in people's gardens. We would chase after them, keen to help – or was it rather to enjoy the drama of our quiet streets being invaded by these crazed beasts? Best of all was the time of the year when the circus came to town; this was

Butter wouldn't melt in his mouth: a young Dennis Scott in his Bedford Road days.

held at the bottom of King Street near the bridge over the Don so Kittybrewster was where the animals and the equipment were unloaded. This gave us the spectacle of elephants and horses and caged tigers being marched down the road.

Another huge attraction was the three marts themselves across the Great Northern Road from the station. We would help unload the trucks as they came in, especially when there were any sheep that needed to be kept in line. In the Central Mart there was some old equipment which had been abandoned – tractors, binders and the like – and we would swarm over them and sit in the cabs and make out we were driving them along.,

Bramble hunting was another ploy. In those days there were still any number of semi-wild spots in the city and among the best of them was the single track line which followed the old canal route down to the harbour. We would clamber over the old sleeper railway fence on Elmbank Terrace and raid the bushes on the banks, always keeping a look out for the odd goods train which would come trundling along.

We would scramble over 10-foot high walls, balance our way along the tops and think nothing of the drop on the other side. The old air raid shelters acted as our gang huts. We would crawl into them and light up candles. Sometimes we'd get hold of torches and flash signals at each other in a sort of made up Morse code. We'd break into gardens, help ourselves to apples, plums and pears and pinch the canes holding up the flowers and fashion them into bows and arrows.

We'd go down to the railway lines and place halfpenny coins on the lines; after the train had passed over them they would have been flattened out into the size of pennies. But we usually had no money at all, not that that stopped us from wandering up and down George Street, all the way to 'Little Woolies' and gazing into the goods in the windows.

So the town for us was a huge playground, a place where there was never any shortage of sights and discoveries and things to do. We were happy to make our own entertainment and almost anything would serve to feed our imaginations.

But there was no devilment in us, just a wee bit of childish mischief. Vandalism was an unknown concept for us.

Dennis Scott, b.1946. Bedford Road. Interviewed 2015

Going doon toon was a real adventure

Going doon the toon was a regular adventure. The great place was the Co-opie in Loch Street. There was the Arcade, with its wonderful split balcony. Going to spend the divi was a big, big event. You would stand there up on that balcony, gazing down on all the others milling around, out spending their divi too. And the shops! They had these marvellous cylinder tubes into which they would pop your money; it would whiz off somewhere and then return with your change and your receipt. It was just about the only time in the year when I could get to visit a restaurant and enjoy a

drink and a fancy piece. What a treat that was, the Co-opie tea-room.

As a child, you'd be dragged along and herded into these crowded shops, there to stand for hours. Queuing could be a tricky business: in the Co-op there was a butter queue and a sugar queue and if you forgot something from the other side then you would just have to queue up all over again. As a child, down there among the legs and the bags, you could become overlooked. Then you always had to remember the Co-op number to ensure the purchase was counted against your divi. My mother's was '57164' – I can always remember that though I've quite forgotten the number of the last car I bought.

Douglas Young, b.1940. Broomhill Road. Interviewed 2004

A great adventure: the Loch Street Co-op Arcade and the Mecca for a young Douglas Young. [PHOTO: ABERDEEN JOURNALS]

We played a lot of street games like 'kick the can' or 'leevieo'; the quines were good at beddies, skipping and bouncing balls and singing rhyming songs in time to each bounce of the ball.

The summer days back then felt sunnier

As a school-age 'Torry Loon', living in Menzies Road was great: the whole area by the River Dee was just like a large adventure park. The steep, tree-clad river bank (known to us kids as 'The Livers') ran from the Chain Bridge to just under Craiginches Prison, (now demolished). It was here many a Cowboys and Indians film was re-enacted. It was also an ideal place for hide and seek and swashbuckling adventures; an old washing rope strung from a branch and we kids would become Tarzan. Much swimming took place in the river during school summer holidays, or helping out at Alex Ogilvie's boat hire shed near the Chain Bridge, now long gone. There was a small council playground with a chute slide, swings and a small roundabout. We played football in our 'jimmies' (gym shoes) on a rough cinder area.

The only organized football was to play for your school, or for one of the amateur football clubs. I played for the Walker Road Primary School team, and also the 20th Company Boys Brigade team. Walker Road School had access to Walker Park at the base of Girdleness lighthouse. To get there we had to walk across the Nigg Bay golf course which still had many bunkers, shelters and gun emplacements as this whole area had been taken over by the Army during the war. Access to football pitches then was very poor, and the school league matches were played at Harlaw playing fields, which meant taking two buses. The BB matches were played on football pitches at Hazlehead Park, also a very long hike.

The summer days back then felt sunnier, and I suppose longer, as so much energy was crammed into every spare minute of time. Daily during the school holidays, when I was armed with a jam piece and a bottle of Hay's lemonade, my mother would ask: 'Where are you off to?', and the usual response was 'Doon the Dee', to start a new adventure. It was only a greater hunger which drove each of us loons and quines home for something to eat at 'denner time', and then back 'doon the Dee'.

We also played a lot of street games, a lot safer then, like 'kick the can 'or 'leevieo'; the quines were good at beddies (hopscotch), and skipping and bouncing balls and singing rhyming songs in time to each bounce of the ball. For us loons the summer craze was playing 'bools' (marbles). One game was called Kypie: the Kypie was a small hole made in the soil using the heel of your shoe, then each player from an agreed line about six feet from the Kypie would throw or roll his bool at it. The player nearest to it would take his position at the Kypie and then could aim his bool at each of the bools of the other players; each player would stand behind their bool with their heels together forming a V shape; this was known as a 'Fainey'; a good player could clean up using his favourite bool, called a dazzie or a peesie.

One of the other games was known as 'Ringie'. Here each player put a marble in the ring marked in the soil, at an agreed distance from the ring, about six feet; each player could aim at the ring to hit the marbles and those hit out of the ring became their marbles. Now kids play on computers or tablets. It's a whole new generation.

Kenneth (Ken) Watmough, b.1935. Menzies Road, Torry. Interviewed 2016

A family orientated scheme

When I was no more than nine months old we moved into a brand new house in a brand new housing scheme up at Mastrick, a couple of miles to the north-west of the city centre.

For us and for the other families who were making the move, Mastrick meant a new fresh start, the opportunity in most cases to escape some poky tenement flat for homes with their own front door, a bathroom and a fitted kitchen.

But my default place was always the outdoors. Like most kids of that era I would go outside in almost all weathers and not reappear till mealtime. The grownups trusted us to look after ourselves and each other – there was none of the fears of heavy traffic and of stranger danger that there is now.

Quarryhill School was opposite our house and that became our playground. We would go in and use the school walls to bounce our balls against. I became very adept at a two-ball game in which you had to throw balls up against the wall and catch them as they came back – first forward, then behind the back, then between the legs, then turn around, and so on through a series of variations.

We also did a lot of skipping, sometimes with one rope, sometimes using two at a time – 'Lundies' or London ropes. You'd line up and wait your turn while two girls were turning the ropes round and round. The important thing was to get into the rhythm of the ropes and to keep going while the rhyme or chant was being sung out.

Another great favourite for me was my bike. I'd cycle off for hours on end, with no sense of fear at all.

One place we would make for was a disused quarry, the Dancing Cairns, between the city and Bucksburn. The old quarry had filled up with water but that didn't stop us from climbing down its sides and hunting for tadpoles. I would go home with my latest batch, complete with the necessary chickweed.

And there were always plenty of other kids to play with; Mastrick was very much a family orientated housing scheme then. So life out in the suburbs was good; but that didn't stop me from enjoying regular forays into town; the Number 9 or 10 would take you there.

I used to get half a crown as pocket money and that was enough to feed my growing enthusiasm for the popular music of the day. A record would cost 6/8d so three weeks pocket money had to be saved up and then down to Bruce Miller's in Loch Street to listen in to the latest numbers in one of their beautiful wooden booths. The very first record I purchased with my own money was Bobby Darin's 'You must have been a beautiful baby'.

Another haunt was Woolies. The bus fare down was twopence so this left me with 2/2d to buy hair clips or sweeties. But I just loved wandering round the store, which prided itself on selling just about everything, and just looking.

Carol Strang, b.1952. Mastrick. Interviewed 2015

I became very adept at a two-ball game in which you had to throw balls up against the wall and catch them as they came back

Not always up to mischief: Alistair was a faithful member of the BB's 58th Woodside South company. Alistair is middle row, third from right

I got up to all sorts with my mates

I enjoyed plenty of freedom as a boy to roam around and get up to all sorts with my mates. Pictures at the Astoria, Kittybrewster, were a great treat; I loved the all-action, sword brandishing, gun-toting films featuring Errol Flynn and all those cowboy heroes such as Roy Rodgers and the Lone Ranger.

But we had lots of outdoor adventures of our own. We'd play for hours in the Stewart Park or pop down the road to the Westburn. A favourite ploy was to make our way to Persley and walk along the banks of the Don. The bridge at Grandhome carried pipes on its underside and once we crawled along holding onto them beneath the bridge, hanging over the water, so as to make our crossing that way. There were a number of lades in the area to feed the paper and the textile mills and we would put a plank across them and show our strength by lugging a big boulder from one side to the other. Once one of my brother's pals fell in doing this and, as he was wearing a big heavy coat, he was soon dragged under the water and swept downstream. Fortunately he was pulled out – still clutching the boulder – and then had to make his way home with a trail of water dripping behind him.

As boys we would take old bits of linoleum and poke a hole through a square of them and carry out sword fights, using bamboo canes, and with the lino acting as a guard. We would also use bamboo canes to fashion bows and arrows. We would get the stalks of Michaelmas daisies, loaded with chicken wire so as to give them weight, and then fire them off over the neighbouring roof tops into the back gardens.

Guy Fawkes' Night was another great occasion for us. We'd get hold of some Brock's 'Cannons', which were four old pence a go, and tie them to our arrows, light the fuse, and, at the right moment when we reckoned they would explode in mid-air, we'd fire them off. This required some nerve and some luck – not to mention considerable stupidity – since you had to stand there with the fuse fizzing away, knowing that if your timing was out they could go off in your face. We also stuck rockets in milk bottles and launched them up into the sky. We would search out old clothes and make up a guy whom we would then push around the streets in an old cartie in the hope of collecting 'pennies for the Guy.' before setting it on our bonfire.

Alistair Brown, b.1940. Hilton Drive. Interviewed 2015

We were never short of games to play

We lived in Ruthrieston Circle, in a block where it was two up, two down. Heating was by an open coal fire and the water by a back boiler. There was no regulator so the water was forever overheating so that the fire would start roaring away and you would have to dash into the kitchen to turn the taps on and cool things down again. But chimneys in the Circle were always going on fire and the Fire Brigade was a frequent visitor. The real problem was that cash was tight and nobody was willing to pay out for getting the sweep in twice a year.

The women in those days always seemed to have tartan legs through the winter – mottled red marks caused by sitting too close and too long up against the fire. No central heating in those days.

In the centre of Ruthrieston Circle there was something of a children's playground with swings, a chute and a maypole; we would rub candle grease onto the chute so as to make it more slidey. There were also three air-raid shelters and we would light bonfires at their entrance, put on gasmasks and pretend we were at the front, fighting the Germans.

There were three air-raid shelters and we would light bonfires at their entrance, put on gasmasks and pretend we were at the front, fighting the Germans.

We did so many dangerous things in those far off days but never came to much harm. We were warned about 'dirty old men' but nobody ever explained what they would do to you or what their 'dirtiness' consisted of. And there were plenty of them around, too. One who did catch me and molested me later went to gaol. I had no idea what he was trying to do to me; all I know is that he gave me a half crown for my trouble – and that was a lot of money to a young lad back then.

Being taken for a ride in Ruthrieston Circle. Michael in his sister Gloria's boyfriend's car.

So we were never short of games to play and little adventures to get up to. One of our favourite pastimes was 'to rake the buckets', that is to go round all the rubbish bins in the Circle and rummage through them for any little treasure we might be able to come across. Those were the days when people were throwing out their Wally dogs and we would break them up and make chalk. A rag and bone man would also come round regularly, pushing his cart and giving out balloons and windmills in return for discarded old clothes and the like.

We would steal apples from gardens. We always seemed to be hungry and we'd gobble down anything. The usual was bread, jam and a smear of margarine. We'd grow blackcurrants in the back garden; another treat was an HP Sauce sandwich.

We played conkers and bools – 'tattie mashers' and 'KPs.' Then there were games of Cowboys and Indians and Japs and Jerries. Down by the Dee there's a small clump of trees and in them is this manhole cover – nowadays overgrown by grass – but we'd lift it up, drop down inside and walk through under Riverside Drive to the Ruthrieston Burn. If there'd been a flash flood we'd have been swept away.

We'd swim in the river and often you could pick out old machine gun bullets which we would hand over to the police at the Bridge of Dee. Nobody seemed to worry about the way in which we would wander freely all over the area. We'd go and help the salmon fishers in the Dee. We'd assist with the pulling up of the boats from the Dee by holding onto the rope which was wound round a big mangle type contraption.

Michael Forbes, b.1945. Ruthrieston Circle. Interviewed 2014

What, no central heating?

Marjory as Dux of Woodend Primary School, 1949.

Hilton proved to be a good place to grow up in. I was aware of certain values, chief among which is what I would term the work ethic and the sense of a social responsibility that was the result of the strong feelings of aspiration within a community which was predominantly working class. The general drive was to get on – to create a better life than their own parents had been able to enjoy and to ensure that the next generation would have a better life still.

There was rationing on the go, but we were used to that. Goods had to be bought by coupons and to mislay or lose your ration book was a serious matter. Sweeties were strictly rationed but there was always 'Andy McKessock's Little Wonder.' If you ran across Great Northern Road you would come to a little shop, not much more than a shack really. Inside was its proprietor, Andy McKessock himself, a big man who more or less filled the whole store with his bulk. But he sold sherbet dabs, which weren't covered by the rationing, and that's where we'd go and get our treats.

Another local shop was Bremner's Grocery store. Every autumn the rumour would go around: 'Bremner's is getting in a stock of tinned fruit!' and I would be dispatched to join the queue, which quickly stretched along the road outside. When you got to the head you would find that you would only be entitled to a tin of pears and a half-size tin of fruit cocktail. I would run home with our tins and my mother wouldn't open them immediately; no, the tins would be placed on the sideboard like some sort of trophy to be sampled only at Christmas and I would stand there staring at them and thinking to myself: 'How I wish it was Christmas.'

A vivid memory is the arrival of the' tarry boiler', come to make repairs to the road. It was thought that the smell of the tar had strong medicinal properties, especially for cases of whooping cough. Mothers would take their bairns up to the boiler and command them to breathe deeply in.

Then there was the funfair at the Central Park. I loved the dodgems; then there were the flying chair planes; my mother took me on them but I soon felt sick so that we had to rush home on foot – to risk the bus in that state could lead to something quite shameful.

I was also a voracious reader. Just across the road from the Woodside Primary School was the Sir John Anderson Library and I soon became a regular user. The librarian was Miss Boyd and she came to think of me as her star reader; I was there just about every day changing my books.

I devoured most of the normal children's books – Enid Blyton, Arthur Ransome and the rest – but my special favourites were the school stories of Angela Brazil and, above all, the 'Chalet School' series. These were set in the Alps in either Switzerland or Austria and I remember how fascinated I was to encounter the exclamation, 'Gruss Gott!' Later I moved onto historical romances – Georgette Heyer and Jane Austen. The scenes depicted in these books were remote from my own Aberdeen, of course, but I loved the escapism, the chance to lose myself in a completely exotic world.

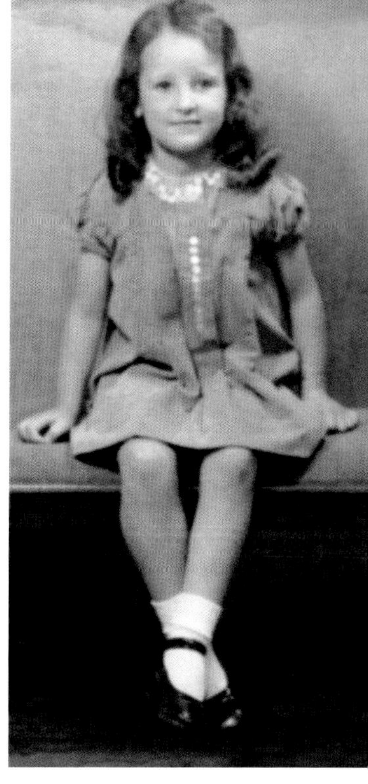
Marjory aged three.

I listened to the wireless, especially Children's Hour, and also took Arthur Mee's 'Children's Newspaper.' I also read the 'Girls' Crystal' as well as the inevitable 'Dandy' and 'Beano'. I was a 1940s and 1950s child. Looking back it's obvious that we were being brought up to conform to the acceptable norms as laid down by adults but I thrived on it and don't regret having been too old to participate in the upheavals of the Rock and Roll, the pop music and the youth fashions of the next generation.

Our way of life at the time seemed to us to be just fine but whenever I tell stories of my childhood to my grandchildren they simply cannot countenance how we could possibly have survived such primitive conditions. What no central heating? No wall-to-wall fitted carpets and only rugs and lino? No daily showers and having to dress underneath the blankets on a cold winter's morning!

...and 10 years later as a History graduate at Aberdeen University.

Marjory Rose, b.1937. Middlefield Crescent, Hilton. Interviewed 2015

Taken on a Torry doorstep. Charlie with older brother Jim and sister Liz., 1962.

Torry – a magical time

Balnagask Road was a great street with a good community spirit. I loved it there as a kid. There was some open ground behind the tenement and that is where we made our football ground. We laid out a whole pitch, complete with goals. There was this old woman, Ma Lumsden, who stayed in the flat beneath us and her job was to make nets for the trawlers. She made some into goal netting for us. Then some of the fathers and older brothers got hold of chunks of wood and put up goalposts for us.

So we ran our own little stadium there. We'd play hour after hour.

Other escapades I remember from those days are the way we would play at the 'Man from Uncle', as seen on TV, and at Batman and Robin. We'd do this in the old washhouses, which in those days each tenement block had at the back of them; they made great gang huts and hiding places. I would use my mother's black silk blouse as my batman cape and would put my pants over a pair of her tights for the leggings.

The neighbourhood also sported a number of shops and characters. There were institutions like Sandy's Sale Shop in Victoria Road where cheap tellys were to be had. Then, in Balnagask Road, there was Sherrat's Shop and Billy Wood's shop, where they were quite happy to cash the weekly family allowance so as to clear off the debt my mother would build up. The son of the owner was John Sherrat and he would give me comics and toys. Then there was Jim the Chipper, who would sell you cheap batter and tattie fritters. I also remember the ragman with his horse-drawn cart; he would give out plastic soldiers and even the odd goldfish in exchange for old clothes.

Really, I see my Torry boyhood as a magical time. It was a great area. There were still open spaces around at the back and we could wander the fields. We would pinch tatties and go into the huts of the workmen, who were putting up all those houses which now cover the district, and make chips to ourselves. We would go down to what we called Torry Beach, the small strip of sand at Nigg Bay, and play there for hours.

Coming of age. An 18th birthday celebration at Flamingo's night club.

Charles (Charlie) Allan, b.1958. Balnagask Road, Torry. Interviewed 2007

The WORLD of WORK

The Commercial Sector

All ready for the Christmas rush. The staff of G. Caldwell's outside the Holburn Street shop, 1946.

Apprenticeship completed – but the Army beckons. A 1939 photo taken pre – enlistment and five years of heroic service.

TRADES PEOPLE

The joiner: It's all theory and computers nowadays

After a few years working for others I reckoned I had gathered sufficient experience to run the show myself. All you needed was a small hut as your office, the architect's drawings laid out before you and a scale rule to get the measurements right. I would think nothing of sending off orders for a thousand pounds worth of timber, quite sure I had got all the sizes absolutely correct. Nowadays, the computer will do it all for you and most houses are made from prepared kits. The result is what I would call matchstick houses for matchstick people. Not nearly as satisfying as when I was having to take the responsibility of measuring and planning and placing orders myself.

I had started my apprenticeship when I was 16. I joined the firm of Clark & Donaldson. You never see a real joiners' workshop these days, not like that one. You'd go in and come across a real hive of industry with more than a dozen men at their benches, building up window frames or planing down doors. On the floor there would be strips of timber laid out, each with a space around it so that the air could circulate and make it dry out and become properly seasoned.

I've loved being a joiner. It's so satisfying to work with wood, to take the raw product and then shape it into something that will not only be of use but which will give pleasure to people. After I retired I would go down to Littlejohn Street and pop into the cabinet-makers' workshop there just to be able to feel the smell of the wood in my nostrils. Everyone needs shelter, a home, and I have helped to meet that basic need. It's wonderful to be able to put up a house and know that it's going to be there for years to come. I've left monuments all over the city.

My kinds of skills have now fallen out of favour. It's all theory and computers these days. When I was a young man it was a proud thing to serve an apprenticeship for five years, to work with your hands and your wits out there in the field, but now the emphasis is all about going to college and studying for paper qualifications. I've worked with someone who was a lecturer at Aberdeen College, who was then offered a big rise in pay to go out on a job. So there I was, laying out the sleeper joists for our job at Cornhill and there he was, looking blankly at what I was doing: measuring, sizing – he hadn't a clue where to start. But he had all the diplomas under the sun.

David Allan, b.1919. Clark and Donaldson. Interviewed 2014

In the early days of TV for the North-east. Bill checking on connections at the Oldmeldrum transmitter.

The TV repair man:
The Queen Mother wore pink slippers

I was doing well at the school and my mother had ambitions that I could stay on and study to become a doctor but my father wouldn't hear of such a thing. Not enough money. So I left school and became a message boy for a radio firm in John Street.

I'd always had a fancy for such a career ever since that day when my father had taken me to visit a man at Dyce who was an early radio enthusiast. I remember his living room was all strung up with wires, and the man was listening on an earpiece. You could hear London calling, right there in a house in Dyce. To me that was magic.

So I was quite happy to serve my two pre-apprenticeship years at that shop and then be taken on for a full five-year apprenticeship.

Then came the war and several years in the Army. I came home to get married. I went straight back into my old job. But I only stayed there one week; my old boss was trying to get away with paying me only my pre-war amount – 19 shillings a week – despite all my war experience and new skills.

I joined another radio firm. Wireless sets were now in almost all homes. But being valve operated, they still needed regular attention so, as a radio engineer, there was plenty of work to do. But then in the Fifties television came to Aberdeen and that gave me fresh

A young Bill Dalgarno (left) with sister Cath and elder brother Jack.

Home on leave during war service, taken in garden of the family's Holburn Road home. Bill and father standing; Sisters Cath and Margaret with brother Jack sitting.

challenges. Nowadays people never think of repairing their TV set; a set will usually last for years and if ever it does go wrong then it'll be thrown out and a new one bought. But back then the sets were so large and cumbersome yet the screen so tiny – nine inches was the norm – that there were always customers wanting you to go to their homes and put their sets right. I'd travel out into the country in a van with great piles of valves in the back.

I came across a fascinating cross-section of society. One customer was Snuffy Ivy, a well-known lady of the night in Aberdeen. She lived in Mount Street and the shop always followed a policy of sending only one of the older men like myself to her apartment – there was this fear that the younger men might, shall we say, lose their heads. I remember seeing to her set in her house one afternoon and she asked me: 'Will you be long?' 'Oh no, I'll have it fixed in a jiffy.' 'Oh, that's good – I'm expecting one of my clients at 3.15.'

Bill Dalgarno:
A late-life photograph.

A new career:
After the earlier TV and war years, Bill made a career as a member of the Technical Department at Aberdeen College of Education.
A departmental photograph with Bill next to Bob Cooper, Head of Department.

Another lady I had to serve was the Queen Mother herself out at Birkhall on the Balmoral estate. Reception was very tricky out there, maybe three nights in the week for a picture if you were lucky. But you'd get this phone call and it would be a case of right away. She would always see that you got offered a cup of tea and she would sit there on her settee in these rather old fashioned pink slippers. I told my mother-in-law about this and she spread the tale around all her pals, about how her son-in-law had mended the Queen's Murphy set while she sat watching in her ordinary pink slippers, just like the ones she herself wore.

William (Bill) Dalgarno, b.1925. John Street. Interviewed 2014

The Baker: A trade's a trade – but I lost interest

When I was about eight or nine, I had a good job working at a bakery in Crown Street. I delivered morning rolls and then off to school; I also worked on a Saturday delivering rolls. In that bakery, they made apple tarts, a good size, round and thick. The baker had the contract to supply the Harbour Café and they dealt mainly with the fish market porters who got their meals there. The porters started their work very early and they had their breakfast between eight and nine o'clock – bacon, eggs, sausages, mealie puddings, black puddings, beans – and then they had these apple tarts. They had a huge plate of stuff that I delivered to the harbour on a message bike. That was some job, that was, and the pies were some weight as well.

My mate's brother said: 'You start early at your work, and you finish early, then you can go down to the beach.'

I was due to leave school and they asked me 'What are you going to do?' I hadn't a clue really but my mate's older brother had already left and become an apprentice baker. And he said: 'You see, you start early at your work, and you finish early, then you can go down to the beach.' I thought that's a good idea: start early and finish early.

I started an apprenticeship at Mitchell & Muil's bakery at 16 after I'd been working for them for two years. I didn't much like the jobs I got first in my training but then it got better and I started going to classes held at Robert Gordon's. This was on the theory of baking, away back to the Roman and Egyptian times, that sort of stuff – how wheat evolved from grasses, growing the grasses for the best wheat heads, and making flour; from right back then up to the present time. I found that interesting and I won a prize.

Then the war started while I was still in the bakery. I should have gone back to it after the war. I'll admit I was daft because, I mean, an apprenticeship's an apprenticeship, a trade's a trade – but I'd lost interest.

Jim Butler, b.1923. Mitchell & Muil. Interviewed 2015

Union Street, 1947: Ian with mother and twin brother Douglas. Sister Emma is lagging behind.

The Laundry Boy: We handled thousands of items each week

The family home was at 106 Great Western Road, a tenement; we were the first floor up. I grew up surrounded by the sights and sounds and smells of all sorts of small industries and businesses which in those days operated from back-street premises, cheek by jowl with people's homes.

Maybe that's one of the reasons I've always liked to keep busy. When I was eight I went round to the horse and cart business in Ashvale Place and asked: 'Any chance of a job?' 'How old are you? Only eight? – well, come back when you're a bitty older.' But I started more or less straight away. I'd help Bob Beaton out on a Saturday and get 6d for it. Every Saturday, I'd catch the bus at seven in the morning, up to the Woodend terminus, and help get the horse into the shafts. We delivered tatties; I'd pop in and out of the lobbies in Springhill Road, in Ashvale and Nellfield and shout out, 'Tatties!' A stone of tatties came to half a crown and a dozen eggs from his own hens the same price. We had plenty of takers.

In those days there were still plenty of carts going around the streets, making their deliveries. I got to know them all and was always on the lookout for opportunities of earning an extra bob or two. When I got out of school at four o'clock, I'd rush home, change out of my school clothes and hurry off to Holburn Street so as to meet up with Willie Mowat, who I knew would having a cup of tea in Zecca's ice cream parlour. He worked for the Claremont laundry and he'd be collecting and delivering. I'd climb up on to the back of his cart and help him with the deliveries.

Then one Saturday another laundry driver came to the house and asked: 'Any chance of getting some help from you? There's five bob in it.' That was a lot of money on those

days. So we'd go round various hotels and often get a cup of tea and a bit of cake as we went.

I got to know all the drivers and could name them and their horses too. I'd also work in the laundry and could follow the whole process. The clothing would be put into big wicker baskets which could be wheeled into the laundry. When you delivered the clothing to the laundry the girls would open it up, sort out the items and ensure that each of them got its own identification tag. When the laundry was completed they folded it all and put it into brown paper packages, secured by sellotape. They'd tie a book onto the package and each district had its own colour. The customer also had their own book copy with the items written in and the two would be exchanged as the laundry was delivered. When the laundry came in and was sorted out, each item had a label with its identification code and this was machined on, complete with date.

The laundry was very big business, handling thousands of items every week. Many of its customers were local hotels with their towels, sheets and bedding. Another service that they offered was carpet beating; the carpet would put through a machine, which had a series of paddles that carried out the beating.

At 1.25 the siren would sound out its five minute warning with three short peeps followed five minutes later by one long one and you'd see the girls hurrying to clock in on time. The heating for the boilers was provided by huge furnaces fed by coal – like down below in a ship. The rotary tubs were driven by leather belts and then the clothes would be transferred to the driers to spin round in them, When they were taken out they'd be compacted into a big block which the girls had to sort out by hand. Ironing

Maggie the horse and Dod McConnachie delivering vegetables up the Lang Stracht, early 1950s

Another Great Western Road shot of the twins, several years on. Ian is on the left.

ABOVE, LEFT: The imposing Claremont Laundry site with its landmark 120-feet chimney, before demolition in 1977. **ABOVE, RIGHT:** The ironing room at Claremont Laundry in the 1890s.

was done partly by steam machines. The main part of a shirt could be done that way but the sleeves and the cuffs and the collars had to be finished off by hand. In those days a lot of the collars were separate and these would be carefully put into a cardboard frame. Every item had its own identification tag.

Since those early days my life has been one of work, work, work. I've been a van boy, a paper boy, a milk boy, a butcher's boy and a laundry boy; I've worked for the Co-op groceries and was many years a handyman/driver for the BBC in Beechgrove Terrace – I was forced to retire from there when I reached 60 but I quickly returned as their meet-and-greet person. That's where I am yet, at the age of 71. I haven't resented any of this. I

A family of workers: Ian's mother taking a pensive break in the kitchen at 106 Great Western Road.

was brought up in the 1950s in a part of Aberdeen that had workshops and small back street industries all around me and in a home with parents who were always hard at it, filling their days with any task that made life more manageable. I followed on from this example, not just to help get by but because it gave me satisfaction, because it came naturally to me.

Ian Leask, b.1944. Claremont Laundry. Interviewed 2015

I was brought up in the 1950s in a part of Aberdeen that had workshops and small back street industries all around me and in a home with parents who were always hard at work.

The Plumber:
I was brought up to put the customer first

I served my time as a plumber in Huntly. I came into Aberdeen after I'd qualified and done my National Service – originally for six months, but I'm still here. I saw an advert for a 'plumber wanted' in a firm in Chattan Place and decided to apply. It turned out this was a small one-man business run by Jonny Still, who was nearing 80 and looking for some help to take a bit of the load off his old shoulders.

We did all sorts of domestic jobs – kettles, irons, frozen pipes, sink units, anything. It was this sort of personal service that I had been brought up on in Huntly and it suited me down to the ground. Jonny Still and I got on famously together; we had the same customer-first attitude.

Our customers appreciated our efforts. A fly cup was the norm and on more than one occasion the call went out at lunchtime: 'Come through and have a bowl of soup with us.' Our approach was no job was impossible; there would always be a way round any problem.

To my mind, things have changed drastically since my early days – and not really for the better. Take the business of going to the wholesalers to get a part. In the old days when Wilson's had their business in Bridge Street, you'd simply pop in, explain what you were looking for and then discuss it with the man behind the counter. He would know his stock backwards and would take the trouble to work out exactly what you needed.

But now the first and only thing they'll do is scroll up a page on a computer, tell you whether the part is available and that will be that. The old personal service is gone; the attitude now is 'take it or leave it.' Back when I started you were working with metal and a bit of soldering might well fix the problem on the spot. Now it's all plastic and the approach is that if something goes wrong then you just rip it out and put in a new part. Plumbers have tended to become fitters rather than repairmen.

I was brought up to take a personal interest in my customer's problems and to take pride in leaving them satisfied with the care I was giving them. This meant that even if what you were doing was going to be out of sight and behind a wall or beneath a floorboard, then it had to be finished to the same standard as anything above the surface – pipes had to be lined up properly and wires had to be neatly tied up. But now the attitude is, why waste time and money on something nobody's going to see? Now it's all

In my opinion wages have been pushed up so high that often plumbers are getting their money too easily.

about time and money and not the quality of the finished article. I could never leave a job not properly finished off because I hated the thought that at some time in the future another plumber would come along, lift up the floorboard and see that I hadn't left the job in good order.

I was four years working alongside Jonny Still. In the end he came to retirement and asked whether I had ever thought of buying over the business. The attraction of owning my own business was too much and so I took it over. But with the business I bought a whole lot of worries that I hadn't had before. The real problem was my attitude; because of the way I had been brought up of always putting the customer first I just didn't know when to stop. I went at things like a bulldozer, working all around the clock. It became a 24-hour concern. I would arrive home at midnight so tired all I could do was totter into bed and lie there going over the next day's tasks in my mind. I was ignoring the family.

Another big difficulty was finding the right sort of plumber to take on as a help. Back then, in the late 1970s, there was a lot of construction work going on in the city and it was proving almost impossible to compete with the wages plumbers were getting from the big construction firms. I was left to struggle along with what I could get and very often that was simply the dregs of the trade.

I took on one lad in his early 20s who made me all the promises under the sun. One of his first jobs was to fit in a new toilet by the stairs in a tenement. I got home late as usual at 10PM only to find a phone message had been left for me. It was the customer and she was complaining that my man had left a smell of burning behind him. I assured her I would be round first thing in the morning to sort it out but she insisted I go round immediately.

So I went round, took my torch and inspected the job. The smell of burning I could put down to the blow lamp he'd been using but that was only half of it because, when I examined his job, I found myself looking down through a large crack in the floor and there, right below my eyes, was the lady from the downstairs flat sitting on her toilet. He'd left the job with rotten floorboards and a floor likely to give way at any moment.

I went into the shop the next morning and found my man waiting for his orders for the day. But I could only give him the one order and that was to leave my employment at once.

Like many of my old customers I can be frustrated at the way plumbing is done nowadays. In my opinion wages have been pushed up so high that often plumbers are getting their money too easily. A lot of them will charge a call-out fee just for crossing the threshold, so you can find yourself forking out £70 simply to get a new washer fitted. I hear of attitudes and incompetence that horrify me. There's a chap at my bowling club who was telling me he had a plumber in to fix a toilet seat and that he'd been back three times and the job was still not right; five minutes after he'd left the seat was moving about all over the place. Yet he'd been charged three times over and the job still wasn't done.

Perhaps one problem is that a young plumber no longer gets the same sort of training as my generation did, where you had to turn your hand to anything. Now an apprenticeship is very much college based with lots of theory. The old sort of jobbing work tends to be neglected in favour of focusing on central heating systems and fitting in new parts. They are no longer encouraged to improvise, to think their way round a problem and so give the customer the best value for her money possible. Instead it's all about following laid down procedures.

But I can't say I look back on my time with any huge regrets. I have found great satisfaction in the work I've done. Above all, I have enjoyed working with so many different and interesting folk, over the years, here in Aberdeen.

James (Jim) Leslie, b.1935. Great Western Road. Interviewed 2015

Never a dull moment for the TV reporter. Steven Duff interviewing Jeremy Corbyn outside Marks & Spencer's.

THE MEDIA PEOPLE

The TV reporter: You can get 10 stories a day to deal with

Journalism was just something I seemed to wander into but once there I've pushed myself as hard as I could to advance in it. One thing I brought to it was an abiding fascination for politics. For me it was an individual pursuit, almost a boyhood hobby that just grew and grew. I watched the TV and I read the papers and fed on them. By the time I was 14 I could have named each single member of the cabinet. At home on a Sunday we took in the 'Sunday Post' but as I got older I would sneak out and get hold of a 'Sunday Times.' But the highlight of the day was to watch the lunchtime politics programme that Ian McWhirter and Brian Taylor ran on TV. I would sit and watch it all by myself. And there I was just yesterday, at the broadcasting of a memorial service, actually working alongside Brian Taylor.

When I left Mackie Academy I enrolled in a 'Legal Administration' course at RGU. Big mistake; I found the whole thing so depressing that some mornings I was physically sick just at the thought that I would have to be spending another day listening to lectures on some legal nicety or other. I dropped out after a year and joined the Journalism course at Aberdeen College. This was the very first year of it and although the course itself wasn't all that exciting I knew that this was where I wanted to be.

It got me through the door at NorthSound. I did a day a week placement there and they liked me. In the summer holidays I had a job at Dunnottar Castle. I remember there was this day when the summer was wearing through and I still had nothing fixed for my future. I went home preoccupied by this and was just sitting there at my tea. Then the phone rang. It was the newsroom secretary at NorthSound: 'Everyone's away on holiday – could you come in and help out?'

I was to be there for a few days only – and stayed on for two years. It was the classic lucky break. I found I was involved in something I was suited to, one which I loved. I quickly realised that one of the secrets of being a good reporter is to chase stories, to follow them up, whatever the effort needed. I'd go in at seven in the morning; I'd chase anything that came my way; I'd give as much attention to the small story as to the dramatic big ones.

Always on the lookout for a story: Steven, on the street, poised with his equipment.

Yesterday I was covering the memorial service in the city's 'Mither Kirk' for the victims of the helicopter disaster. It has been a huge story, one that was covered by all the media and which went right round the world. It's easy to put something into a consignment like that; the next day can seem very flat indeed, but what I've learned is that you have to pick yourself up and be ready to go for it, even if it's only the local concern over the closure of Bucksburn Post office or the traffic problems at the bottom of Market Street. I'm a professional and I need to ensure that I'm pitch perfect, however big or small the next story might be. You might find yourself having to get through five bulletins in a day, 25 for the week, and each one of them will require its own professional attention.

I was lucky when I started out in that there were a number of interesting stories around. There was the whole Ian Oliver saga and whether he should resign or not. There was the Scott Simpson murder at the hands of a paedophile. I had to cover the funeral. It was a steep learning curve. You could get 10 stories a day to deal with and you'd have to try to make each one as fresh as possible. I always took the trouble to avoid clichés, to approach each script as a blank page which deserved its own treatment. I believe that the viewer or listener deserves something fresh when they switch on to catch up with the latest news.

That doesn't alter the fact that yesterday was a very big day indeed, the kind that as a reporter of news you just live for. I fully understand the tragedy of the loss of life and the feelings involved but any reporter will tell you the same: the knowledge that it's a highly important event and that the eyes of the nation will be upon it gives you a real challenge.

I had just finished an interview with Joe Harper, an interesting but a routine enough event, and then suddenly the world falls in on you.

There's tragedy, there's loss of life – but you wouldn't want to miss it, you wouldn't want to sit there and see someone else doing your job.

On the day of the accident I got a phone call at 2.30; by 2.50 I was here for 'News 24'. I had just finished an interview with Joe Harper, an interesting but a routine enough event, and then suddenly the world falls in you. The victims were being flown to ARI so the satellite truck was sent there; I had to go there for the News Channel. Then at 5, just before we were due on the air, came the phone call: 'Eight missing; eight dead.' Of course, I felt for those involved but I knew I had to be professional about it all and get on with the job. I knew to that I had to offer more than just the bare news and more than a bit of fluff to go with it, that I must try to draw on my experience to come up with some insight and something that would catch the atmosphere of the occasion.

My experience has shown me that North-east folk are a bit different. Compared to those in the South, we are more reticent about expressing our feelings. I did a three-month placement in Glasgow and immediately found myself in a different world. I remember one story where I'd been trying to follow up a report that crop tops were now reckoned to be a hazard for pregnant mothers because they let in cold air around the mid body. I interviewed Andrew Kerr, the Health Minister, and then I went out onto the streets to canvass public opinion. Try a vox pop in Union Street and people will cross the road to avoid you; in Byres Road they came flocking around the mike. I'd ask an obviously pregnant woman and within a second she'd be lifting up her top to show you her bump and let you know what her baby was going to be called, how many other children she had, how she met the father and so on. In Aberdeen you'd be lucky to get an embarrassed mumble.

We have our own way of dealing with things here. I remember having to go to the Moray Firth to report on a terrible road accident. Two sisters and a boyfriend had been killed, a tragic loss of young lives. I spoke, with the village in shot behind me. Now, the expected intro would have run along the lines of: 'Portsoy is in shock today. There is a stillness about the place – etc. etc.' But I knew that wasn't really appropriate; in any other region that might have been accurate but here people were dealing with matters privately, behind their own doors. The normal 'Community in Shock' drama just didn't fit; it was more a case of 'while behind these doors there is untold grief, on the streets themselves life goes on'.

People in the North-east are stoical, they understand that life will bring along its share of suffering, that there is no need to take to the streets wailing, that display of that kind can't bring back the dead. Maybe it's the sea and the long history of fishing disasters, maybe it's the struggle to wrest a hard living from the land, but we seem to have a grasp of the basic truths of life and that it must include pain and death.

So, yes, for the reporter and the journalist, the North-east can be a difficult patch but its people demand respect. Totally.

Steven Duff, b.1975. BBC Beechgrove. Interviewed 2009

The Journalist:
Starting from scratch

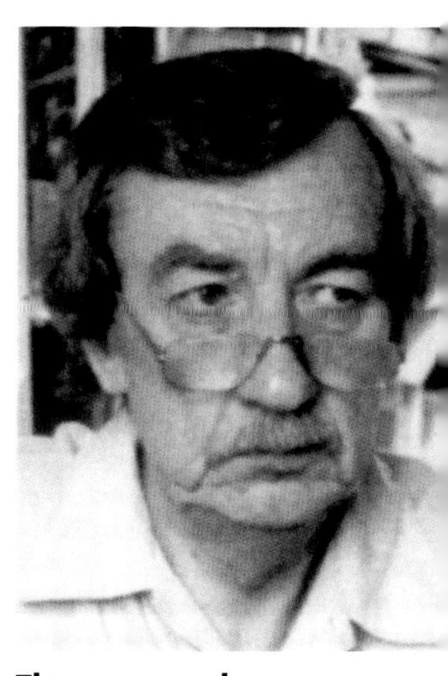

The seasoned journalist: a 1990s shot of Bob Gibb.

Then, at Hilton Junior Secondary School, with three months to go, in walked this man in military uniform. His name was Ross, Edward Ross. 'Good morning, boys and girls, I'm to be your new English teacher.' He was my saviour; a wonderful teacher and man. He made English so easy for us. He could turn learning into a game. We would discuss all sorts of things with him.

He told me: 'Robert, you are a natural writer.' He asked me one day: 'Robert what do you intend to be once you've left this school?' 'A veterinary surgeon, sir.' 'I'm afraid that's impossible – you need to go to university for that. I'll tell you exactly what you are going to be: you are going to be a journalist.' A wonderful man; I owe so much to him.

I stayed on for the full three years and came away with the Junior Leaving Certificate. That was my only academic qualification. I owe the rest to my teachers. We obviously got a good grounding at their hands. They were always with us. Any spare time they had seemed to be devoted to us. Each school had its 'junior recreation club', which would meet two or three times a week and they would always be there. There was a drama club – we won the Aberdeen Festival three years running. There was a Scottish country dancing club – and we became North of Scotland champions. These teachers were heroes, and heroines.

The actual teaching was pretty book-based. Right from the start I was thrown into learning how to count. I consider myself one of the world's best spellers. We would get lists of words to learn up each night and then be tested on them at the end of the week. There was a lot of repetitive work and some of it could be boring. The way History was taught bored me stiff – dates and kings and queens. But English was different. Mr Ross would give me a reading list of novels. I'd go to the library and be told: 'You can't have that one – that's in the Adult section.' I returned next day with a note from Mr Ross and from then on I was given the run of the whole library. The Sir John Anderson library was the place I would go to practically each day; I just read and read.

I remember that when I left school, the Headmaster wrote to me to inform me that there was a job going as clerk at ICI and that he was recommending me as 'a good prospect.' I wrote back to tell him I was going to be a journalist. I spent six months in the Rector's office at Robert Gordon's while I was pestering every newspaper in the land for an opening. I finally got taken on by the 'Press and Journal'.

I joined the 'Press & Journal' at 15. I rose to become a senior member of the staff. Thomson's took over from Kemsley Newspapers and that brought in a policy of appointing graduate journalists. In they came – and they couldn't spell, they couldn't produce correct copy, they had no street cred, they knew nothing of life. I remember saying to this guy – I was Features Editor at the time – 'Look, there's an Easter Egg painting competition at Walker Road School tonight. I want you to go along and come back with a nice light piece on it.' 'But, I'm an MA. I can't do that kind of thing.' 'Yes, and another thing you can't do is spell properly. Now go and do it.'

You were thrown in at the deep-end and you just had to use your wits.

There were exceptions but a lot of these brand new graduate types used to annoy the life out of me. We had to teach them everything. They hadn't served an apprenticeship. I'll tell you just how scratch we had to learn from: I was put on the sports side because I used to write sports reports for the 'Green Final 'off my own bat when I was still at school. I'd go along to St Clement's matches and send in 50 words at half-time, 100 at full time.

I'd only been a week or two into the job when I was told: 'You're to go down to King's and report on the University match there.' 'But I didn't even know they had a football team at that place.' 'That's right – it's a rugby match.' Well, the only thing I knew then about rugby was that the shape of the ball was different. But I went and immediately sussed out the most important people grouped together on the touch-line. I approached them and explained that I was to produce the day's newspaper report. 'Right, son – just stand with us and we'll tell you what to write.' They were the committee members. That's the kind of thing you had to do; you were thrown in at the deep-end and you just had to use your wits.

My schooling had given me a full preparation for that kind of thing. All I had left with was a Junior Leaving Certificate – and now I'm a registered lecturer in journalism. I hold two diplomas in Law through the NCTJ, one for England, the other for Scotland. I ended up lecturing in the subject at Aberdeen College. This has been a wonderful experience: I can now go to a press conference and find that I'm competing for the stories against my ex-students. That thrills me.

Robert (Bob) Gibb, b.1932. Aberdeen Journals. Interviewed 2004

The Television Announcer: a curious existence

A new TV station – and a young announcer to go with it. At Grampian TV in the early days.

Drama, then, was a significant part of Aberdeen Grammar School life with an annual production involving a large cast. For the first two years I was a rapt spectator, knowing this was what I wanted to get into; and from Year 3 onwards I was a regular performer. Drama came to be absolutely crucial to my psychological well-being. It was an alternative world that I could enter into as a relief from everything else – including my normal inhibited self. Otherwise, in class, I kept as low a profile as possible. I was really a rather timid boy, anxious to keep out of trouble.

This is where I made my mark at school. I was no use at sport and not outstanding as a scholar, but put me on a stage and I was in my element and quite without nerves. Drama was my escape from myself. I would lose my identity in someone else's. It reassured me that I was good at something, that I was making my contribution to school life.

So at university, I naturally turned to drama. I went into the student shows and any other theatre activity I could, from revue to the classics. Bliss. I mingled with some

talented writers and performers, people like Buff Hardie, Steve Robertson, Derek Brechin, David Buchan and Angus Robbie.

After college, I couldn't find a post in Aberdeen so I took a year out to take on a teaching job in Germany. I enjoyed the experience and made some life-long friends; but, at the end of the year, I returned to Aberdeen, where Grampian TV was about to set up. I did a bit of supply teaching first, then did an audition for Grampian TV, who were looking for local people for their new North-east television service. Like my university friend, June Imray, I landed a job as continuity announcer and newsreader and began my career in broadcasting. My years of stage work had stood me in good stead, as I was used to reading scripts. That was my gift: being able to read the written word and turn it into the spoken word with all the appropriate intonation and stresses. Even today when listening to a news bulletin I can find myself roaring at the radio whenever announcers don't get the stresses right.

I was brought up on the spoken word. I was a member of the radio generation, one where you sat quietly and lost yourself in the world of a radio serial or simply listened to somebody reading out a story. I loved the comedy programmes like 'Much-Binding-in-the-Marsh' with their various voices and word play. I'm told that when asked as a child what I wanted to be, my answer would be: 'A BBC announcer.'

So drama and radio were my preparation for the professional life I was able to follow years later. There were other formative experiences too. My mother bought me a book of Scots verse which I would commit to memory and recite at weddings. To be honest, I

The BBC years: Celebrating the 100th edition of 'Good morning Scotland' with, from left, Magnus Magnusson, David Findlay, Mary Marquis, John Milne, Bob Cox, DK, Chris Niven.

Behind the camera: Chatting with Jackie Bird in the BBC studios

didn't always know what I was saying – sometimes the country dialect was quite foreign to me – but somehow I could capture the humour and the spirit of the piece and the adults were always very indulgent. By the time I got to university, I was able to write and speak Doric for the student shows.

Working at Grampian was quite exciting in the early days. With the station just starting up, the announcers quickly became recognised faces and you'd be invited to open things like fêtes and Highland Games. We read the local news; and in time, we all presented programmes; but the basic work was continuity announcing. In those days, the announcers appeared in vision; nowadays it's done by voice-over and I think that would have suited me better. But back then, with the station still struggling to sell its advertising slots, there were plenty of gaps between programmes which had to be filled somehow. Sometimes they would use short films from the Central Office of Information – 'Don't be a boot bumper ' or 'Tufty's rules for crossing the road', that sort of thing – but often enough it would be left to you to fill the gap. That could be tricky, because you'd memorise a script and time it to the second, only to find that the programme before had overrun, leaving you to edit as you spoke.

It was a curious existence altogether. You had to sit there in a darkened cubicle, waiting your turn, and then suddenly the lights would come on and you had to face the camera, trying not to blink. It was like a puppet having to jump out of its box and put on a performance, every half hour or so.

In retirement, but still producing: Douglas with one of his several books in Doric.

Douglas Kynoch, b.1938. Grampian TV. Interviewed 2014

Since his TV days, Douglas Kynoch has contributed to magazines and written a number of books, including 'Here's tae us. A Personal View of Scottish History' and 'A Doric Dictionary'.

The Hotelier Supreme:
Stewart Spence and his New Marcliffe

The reason I got into the hotel business can be traced back to my boyhood years in the 1950s. In those days the family rented a holiday home in Ballater for a month, each August. But I began to get a bit fed up, being stuck there for all that length of time, so to get me out from under her feet my mother approached her cousin. This relative lived all the year round in the village and owned a hotel there. 'Can you possibly find something for Stewart to occupy himself with?'

So I started doing jobs in the hotel at the age of 12. I took to it straight away; I just loved the bustle and the comings and goings of a hotel; from that point on all I ever wanted to do was to work in a hotel. I always tell any youngster who is thinking of following my path: 'Go into a hotel, do any jobs you are given, however menial. The vital thing is to breathe in the smell of hotel life – do that and as like or not you will be smitten just as I was and want to stick at it for the rest of your working life'.

I did all the odd jobs at that hotel under the sun: I would polish the guests' shoes before breakfast; I would wash the dishes; I would help with the luggage as they came and as they went. I was fortunate in that the hotel my mother's cousin owned was the famous Invercauld Hotel, and was reckoned to be just about the finest on Deeside. And in those days rich families from the south would come up to Ballater, first for the fishing and then for the grouse shooting.

So the Invercauld was right at the centre of a high quality leisure business. I found the excitement of all these comings and goings quite captivating. I've always been lucky that the hotels I got my training in all had an aura about them; they prided themselves on high standards and that has set the mark for all that I have tried to achieve.

The main lesson I imbibed in those places is that the hotel business is really a people business. It's not about the artwork on the walls or the carpets beneath the feet – it's about the quality of the staff and the manner in which they interact with the guests. That's what counts – people.

Nowadays we are in danger of losing that vision. A lot of the more modern hotels have sacrificed real communication for a machine-like approach where you go in, stick your credit card in a slot and print out your own room key and number. For me that is losing that vital personal touch, the welcoming moment when a friendly face at the reception can invite the guest into the hotel, ask whether they have had a good journey and give out information about the weather forecast and, generally, make the guests feel they matter and are truly welcome. We run a 'guest history' on our computers

Owner of Aberdeen's premier hotel: Stewart Spence.

'No ordinary hotel': The Marcliffe in its Pitfodels setting.

Advertisement for the Marcliffe.

so that we know exactly who has stayed with us before and who is new. That means we can greet them with a 'Welcome back to our hotel, Mr Smith. It's good to see you again'.

I draw a distinction between the sort of individualised hotel we offer here and what I would term a mere bed factory. Whenever I go away to sample another hotel, my staff will ask me on my return: 'What was the hotel like?' and if I can answer: 'The people were fantastic,' then they know that my stay has been at a first-class place. That's the first thing to report, not the cuisine, not the furnishings or the bedrooms, but the people.

My father had shone at school but he understood that all I wanted to do was to leave Robert Gordon's College as soon as I legally could and enter the hotel business. In those days the best hotel in Aberdeen was recognised to be the Station Hotel and as it happened he knew the head waiter there from days at dancing classes. I got fixed up with an interview with the manager and was in.

So at the age of 15 I started my training in the best line of hotels in the country, the British Transport Hotels, which were situated next to the great railway stations of the land. The later generations can't appreciate what those hotels meant in those days. The other day a young chef asked me where I did my training as a chef and when I answered: 'with British Rail' he looked puzzled and then came up with: 'Oh, do you mean making sandwiches?'

Making sandwiches! Why, when I was starting out BR had some 34 prestigious hotels dotted around the country, from Aberdeen right down to Cornwall. Gleneagles, St Pancras, the Great Eastern and the Great Northern in London, the North British in Edinburgh, the Grand Central in Glasgow – the very best hotels in the land, ones which were a hallmark for fine cuisine and luxurious accommodation.

I started, as all young would-be hotel managers did, working in the kitchens, as a commis chef. Kitchen life in a prestigious hotel at the age of 15 is a high pressure situation; the curtain goes up, the food has to be put on the stage and the show must go on without any false step. One of the reasons hotels insist on an early training in the kitchen is to test you out, to see whether you can handle the pressure; the attitude is very much: 'If you can't stand the heat, get out of the kitchen.' You are expected to watch, to learn and to obey so that if the moment arrives when the chef calls off you can step in and take his place.

My aim was to train as a manager but places as a trainee manager were usually reserved for those who were a year or two older than my 15 years. So I had to do my two years in the kitchen and then six months as a waiter. Then, when I reached 18, I went to Paris for a couple of years. British Transport operated an exchange scheme so that their young staff could experience the methods and the language of a different culture. I rented a small room right in the heart of Paris – if my father hadn't put his foot down I might still be living that Parisian life. I thrived in the whole Parisian scene.

I was posted to Fouquet's in the Champs Elysée. This was a really prestigious restaurant. It was the spot that the film stars used to frequent. The day came when I got summoned to serve in the Salon Privé which was where the VIPs dined if they desired some privacy.

The waiter told me that I had to offer the couple soup to be served from a silver tureen. He opened the door, I entered and discovered who this couple was – Richard Burton and Elizabeth Taylor.

With his famous piano-top photos of some of the many celebrated Marclife guests.

I was asked to go because the waiter there couldn't speak English and the couple he was serving couldn't speak French. When I arrived, the waiter told me that I had to offer the couple soup to be served from a silver tureen. He opened the door, I entered and discovered who this couple was – it was Richard Burton and Elizabeth Taylor. I set the tureen onto a side table and enquired: 'Madame, would you care for soup? Sir, would you care for soup?' Hearing my accent, Richard Burton immediately said: 'And where might you come from?' 'Scotland ', I replied. 'Yes, I can hear that – but which part of Scotland?' 'Aberdeen, sir.' 'Quick as a flash he came back with, 'Aberdeen. Don't you mean Aiberdeeen? I remember appearing at His Majesty's Theatre up there and I know that's how the locals speak.'

After that, they returned several times for lunch and I was asked to serve them again. Elizabeth Taylor was a very beautiful woman, of course, but the feature that really struck me was her eyes – such a dark blue, so large; eyes that would stare right into you.

Then there came the Saturday when a pair of guests entered and I was ordered to stand to respectful attention as they swept in, accompanied by their dogs. I recognised them at once; it was the Duke and the Duchess of Windsor and they dined with us every second Saturday. The French treated them as royalty – having murdered their own royal family they were quite fascinated by ours.

So my sojourn in Paris gave me some memorable experiences, ones that have stood me in good stead here at the Marcliffe. I learnt that when a big VIP comes to eat or to stay what they are really demanding more than anything else is to be able to relax in a warm and secure environment. Denis Law, Sir Alec Ferguson, politicians, sportsmen and sportswomen, entertainment stars have stayed here and they have all appreciated the

With another notable Aberdeen son: Denis Law, a frequent guest on his return visits to his native city.

welcoming yet unobtrusive ambiance we can give them.

So I was quickly learning how to adapt myself to all sorts of situations and to handle myself with any kind of guest, however celebrated he or she might be. I also found that once I got the message over that: '*Non, je ne suis pas anglais – je suis écossais,*' I got a ready welcome everywhere I went.

But eventually I had to return to the UK. I was now posted to London and in the great Northern Hotel for one year, working in the cocktail bar. By now I had completed six years of training and was ready for a permanent posting. So in July 1968, at the age of just 21, I became the assistant manager at the Treetops in Aberdeen, which at that time was the busiest hotel in the city.

Why had I got on so well and so fast? Well, a feel for people and the ability to adapt and to learn on the spot had proved to be the obvious requirements. But beneath all of that, there is one basic quality and that is quite simply the willingness to work and to work, to never pass up the opportunity of taking on that bit extra, both for what the experience will give you but, just as important, because that is the way you can demonstrate your absolute commitment to making progress.

You have to accept that running a hotel is a 24/7 business. Attention to detail is the key; guests have the right to expect the best and we have to make sure they get it. That's why just about the first thing I will do in the morning is to go to the reception desk and enquire what the check outs have been saying about their stay. I'm not interested in the complimentary ones; it's the negative comments which count because they are the ones which tell us how we can improve. You can never stay still in this business.

But now came a big break. Peter Cameron, the building firm magnate, was erecting a brand new hotel in Stonehaven, the Commodore. He was a friend of my father's and a golfing buddie at Murcar. The hotel opened in May 1970 and I was offered the position of becoming its first manager; all this at the age of 22.

This was huge opportunity, the chance to furnish and to staff a brand new hotel right from the very start. The Commodore could act as an example of what a modern hotel in the North-east should be like. For example, it was built to be completely *en-suite* and this at a time when a good class establishment like the Atholl in the city still had only five bathrooms for its 22 bedrooms.

I was then offered the chance of running a hotel in Bermuda. My wife and I were keen to grab at the opportunity. We gave the news to my in-laws; my father-in-law was Dick Donald of the Aberdeen FC and cinema people in Aberdeen. On our next visit to their home we burst in with 'We've got something to tell you.' But when we told them what it was the faces dropped – they had assumed that we were about to announce the imminent arrival of a grandchild.

They clearly were unhappy at the prospect of losing the next generation to a far off posting. 'Is there anything we can do to change your mind?' 'Well, the only thing that would make me think twice would be the chance of owning my own hotel here.'

My father-in-law asked whether there were any suitable hotels for sale in the city and when he was told: 'Yes, I believe the Atholl is up for sale', followed up with a 'How much?' The asking price was £150,000; he agreed to act as our guarantor and that, along with the £20,000 we had saved up during my time at the Commodore, meant we were able to bid £140,000. It was accepted.

Deal done. So there I was at the age of 25 back in 1972, the owner of a prestigious west-end Aberdeen establishment. This was the start of my hotel empire building. A year later the Queen's Hotel was on the market. This was then the hotel with the biggest function room in Aberdeen and that was something the Atholl lacked. Putting on functions was very much my thing so I was keen to buy. The owner agreed to sell so that was a pair of excellent hotels in the west-end of the city acquired within the one year. It was now 1973; I was 26 years old.

Back then, in the early 1970s, just before the oil struck, the Aberdeen hotel scene was very conservative. In fact, there were only four real restaurants in the city – now it has 500; people would go to a hotel if they wanted to dine out in something more than a café. But the city has always had money; you only have to drive round the west-end to realise that there had always been a lot of wealth here – and a market right for exploitation. So although I was now acquiring hotel property at a fast rate, I felt I was on safe ground.

In 1979 I acquired the Marcliffe in Queen's Terrace. By now the oil industry was bringing in new sets of customers; the Marcliffe attracted American clients. Then I ran the Capitol restaurant for several years in the late Seventies.

The young hotelier: Stewart Spence and family taken at his Atholl hotel 1983.

In 1982 I bought the Belvedere in Queen's Road – now the Chester Hotel – and the following year moved the Marcliffe from Queen's Terrace to the Queen's Hotel in Queen's Road, re-naming it The New Marcliffe.

The next break, and the one that led me to this site in Pitfodels, involved the Rio Stakis group. After the disastrous gas explosion which demolished their Royal Darroch Hotel in Cults, they had acquired a replacement site at Pitfodels where a lovely old house, Beechwood, was up for sale.

But for a number of reasons their plan to erect a brand new hotel on the site never materialised. The property lay untouched for several years until it was sold on, eventually falling into my hands in 1991. It came with full planning permission but my plan was to

The North-east might never be able to sell itself as a sunshine resort but what it does have in abundance are its landscapes, its history and a wonderful array of golf courses.

keep it as a fine old house and to build up the hotel around that. The property was set in a secluded, picturesque site in eight acres on the north side of the Dee.

I knew exactly what I wanted to do with this wonderful opportunity. For several years beforehand I had been the owner of a very fine hotel out at Banchory, the Invery, an old mansion house which stood on the banks of the Feugh. I had developed it as a real upmarket establishment, the sort of place where important visitors to the North-east would want to stay – such as Maggie Thatcher and Rod Stewart. I ran it for seven years and this was the hotel which took me up to another high level.

When the Beechwood opportunity came up I knew I had to go for it. I sold Invery House, not as a hotel but as a private home – the last thing I wanted was competition for what I had decided to build up here at Pitfodels. This also meant that I could retain my staff and transfer them over to my new venture.

When I took over the Beechwood site I decided I wouldn't put all the eggs in the one oil basket. Instead I would attempt to re-establish the North-east tourism market. I realised that the nature of that market had changed from the time when almost all holidays had been booked through travel agents who had been able to screw the hotels down with their demands for costly commissions. But by now more and more people were making their own holiday arrangements on-line and it was to this more individualist market that we now had to turn.

In 1986 I had joined a small elite organisation called the 'Small Luxury Hotels of the World.' At that point it had 30 members only; now it has grown to 540. But I saw this as an important act of branding, a declaration that we would be going for the discerning individual traveller. I began to attract the attention of the Americans and especially the niche golf business. The North-east might never be able to sell itself as a sunshine resort but what it does have in abundance are its landscapes, its history and a wonderful array of golf courses.

Another important statement of intent was made at the very start of the business. Originally I had wanted Princess Margaret to perform the opening ceremony but then Mikhail Gorbachev was invited to Aberdeen to accept the Freedom of the City. I seized the opportunity to invite the great man to perform the opening ceremony. Gorbachev proved to be a charming and affable guest.

After that successful visit the publicity was enormous and the floodgates opened. Soon we were taking in guests from all over the world. We've been able to attract most of the world's leading golf people – Nicklaus, Palmer, Player, Donald Trump, Tom Watson – they've all stayed here and then gone home to spread the word. On my grand piano in the drawing room the lid is covered by photo after photo of the well-known people who've enjoyed our hospitality – from Margaret Thatcher to Tony Blair to Alec Salmond and from Sean Connery to Paul McCartney, from the Sultan of Brunei to Prince Charles.

Stewart Spence, b.1947. The Marcliffe at Pitfodels. Interviewed 2015

The Marcliffe at Pitfodels, owned and run by Stewart Spence, is the city's only five-star hotel.

SHOPS AND BANKS

George Fraser with his ever present smile.

The staff at the Bank Street shop: from left – Andrew Thom, cashier, the long-serving Annie Davidson, brothers Atholl and George Fraser.

The grocer:
There aren't any shops like ours left

The shop in Bank Street was established in 1856 by George Angus from Ballater. My father took it over in 1914. I started at the shop as soon as I left school in 1934. But I had to begin at the bottom, as a message boy on a bike. I had to go out in all weathers. We had customers all over then. There were west-end houses in

The war hero: George served in Burma in the war and was a long standing member of the Aberdeen branch of Burma Star.

Queen's Road, there was the Palace Hotel, the Station, the Imperial; we supplied coffee to Esslemont & McIntosh and provisions to Aberdeen Royal Infirmary. We had customers all up Deeside, right up to Ballater. We supplied the hospital at Woodend.

I spent my first year on the bike, as a message boy. Then I went into the shop: white apron, grey jacket and, always, a tie. Aprons had to be kept absolutely spotless. Every second day, home with them for soaking, boiling, starching. We had standards to keep up. We had dark mahogany counters, wooden floors, with scattered sawdust on them. Then we got Robertson of Union Street to come in one Saturday night and lay down these thick quality linoleum squares. They worked all through the night, the whole of Sunday and overnight into Monday morning. The job was finished at 8AM, ready for us it open at 9AM.

Our success was due to hard work and complete dedication. Before we retired a lot of our customers came in to take photos. This was in 1991. I worked on till I was 71 and would have carried on but as soon as Atholl [brother and partner] got to 65 he told me he didn't want to work any longer. So that was that: the old business came to an end.

I'd never had the time till then to go into a supermarket and when I did my first thought was: 'Oh my goodness, so this is what we've been up against. How on earth did we ever survive for so long?' But we did it by personal contact and by concentrating on good quality and personal service to our customers. We would search all over Britain for that and people would come from far and near to get it. We would sell these extra-large prunes – you'd call them 'jumbo prunes' today. One well-known customer – Professor R.V. Jones from Queen Street – would always call in each Saturday to get his bacon, his boiled ham and his extra-large prunes.

With brother Atholl outside their shop.

Our shop worked by building up a network of contacts and suppliers. For example, we got eggs and chickens from a farm out at Dunecht. But we would also go all over to get high-quality produce. Our bacon came from C.&D. Harrison, Wiltshire – lovely back bacon. Our ham was top quality gammon, rolled and cooked in tanks. We'd get raw coffee beans from 'Appleton, Macklin & Smiles' of London.

Everything was done by post and by telegram. If they had a special offer on, Harrison's would telegraph us from Wiltshire; the order would go down by return, they would pack it and send it up by passenger train and we would receive it within 24 hours. We'd get Stilton cheese from Stilton itself, in Leicestershire. For our pork pies we would go to Hadfields of Chesterfield – beautiful pies. Every day, sausages would come up to us from Palethorp from Tipton, Staffordshire. The finest in Britain.

Now it's all telesales but then there were reps galore. My father would always tell me: 'Always treat a representative as you would wish to be treated if you were in his place.' That's what we did and did it pay off! When the war came and goods were scarce they would make sure we got the best allocations.

We had our own regular customers; we looked after them. We knew all their names, all their telephone numbers. Each week they would phone in their order, we would send it out to them and then get their cheque at the end of the month. We were quite formal, never used first names. It was never: 'Hi there, Jessie!' but 'Good morning, Mrs Davidson!' We never had to advertise, never had to spend a penny on that. It was all done by word of mouth.

We had to develop special skills in those days. When I started there was no pre-packed sugar. It would come to us in large sacks and it was our job to weigh and wrap it up into one pound, two-pound bags. Tea came in chests. Tea bags didn't come into this country till the 1950s. Selecting the tea was an art. We had these special cups and scales; Father would do all the tea tasting. Samples would come by post from Glasgow and from London. At our centenary in 1956 we ordered 500 caddies and printed on them 'George Angus & Company, 1856–1956'. Each of our regular customers was presented with one.

Biscuits also came in loose. We had a metal display stand in the shop for customers to make their choice from. Syrup all came up in barrels and we had to fill it into jars. Tate & Lyle. We would bottle our own vinegar: 'Champion & Sleighs Vinegar' from London. We bottled our own whisky: 'Royal Strathangus.' Father would take in malt from Glen Grant of Speyside. He would tell us: 'The secret of a good whisky is plenty of the very finest malt.' He would blend it, not by taste, but by the smell. We also bottled our own port and our own sherry. We would get big cheeses in and keep them till they were properly mature, turning them regularly.

We got a good hard training in that shop. As my father would always say: 'If you're going to do something, do it right.' If you were cutting cheese and if you did it squint you'd get a bash round the ear.

Our Miss Davidson was very efficient. She was with us all her working life: she came to us from the Central when she was 17 and stayed on till she was in her 80s. She kept us all in order. Her job was to look after the books. She had this little office at the back and sat at a desk on a high stool. She never used a calculator. Like me, she could add up any set of figures just like that.

There aren't any shops like ours left now, not one. I use the supermarket nowadays: you have to, there's no other choice. But I'll tell you this – I won't live to see it but it will come – the number of supermarkets will dwindle down to two, Asda and Tesco, and then the supermarket will have the ball at its feet – and then we'll see how much we miss the small corner shop.

George Fraser, b. 1919. George Angus & Co. Interviewed 2006

George Fraser with his wife Alma, married in 1948 and only parted by death in 2016.

Moira's parents on the brink of retirement.

The Butcher:
Best was too good to waste on his family!

It was an old fashioned butcher's such as you never see nowadays, with carcasses hanging up and blood dripping down onto the floor. It was the family trade and when Granda died in 1948, Dad continued the shop in Holburn Street. He took great pride in his calling. He hadn't an academic head on him but he was very good with his hands and had something of an artistic bent which came out in the way he set about his business. To watch him boning a leg of beef was quite something. He loved to hoist a good side of beef up on his shoulder and to stride along with it. For him being a proper butcher was a matter of pride.

He loved the butchering side of the business and also the interaction with the customers. But he simply hated having to keep the books in order. He was a practical man, someone who had to be on the go, not sitting still at a table, poring over accounts.

The best cuts were reserved for his customers. In fact, quite often he'd demand that Mum return a cut to him because a customer needed it – the best meat was too good to waste on his own family.

I was in the shop quite a lot. Christmas was a busy time; we got our turkeys from farms out at Banchory-Devenick and I would go out to assist with the plucking. It was fascinating to watch Dad and the farmer negotiating a fair price and then settling the matter over a dram. When the deep freezes came in he would go out to fetch a dead sheep or pig, take it back to the shop to break it up into sausages and chops. I remember once we had this bright idea of using a Hoover to suck the air out of the vacuum packs, and ending up by hoovering up the livers into it.

The shop was kept cold with a stone floor and sawdust; there was the chill in the corner and a chill cabinet to store the beef in. There was a small office which had that rarity in those days, a phone. Downstairs was the lair of Nelson, the cat, and also the delivery boy's bike. We had a number of message boys and they would be carefully inspected as they arrived for duty to check on their cleanliness. They'd get their necks scrubbed if they didn't pass muster. My dad wore a stripy apron; our daughter, Carol, would give him a cuddle and come out of it smothered in blood and mince.

In the shop, the attitude was, the customer is always king. That meant good service and it also meant taking a personal interest in people: my father was always ready to take time to enquire after a customer's welfare or to pass on a joke or a bit of news. And Mum would always read the announcements in the paper so that Dad was up to speed and didn't put his foot in it with any of his customers if they'd had a bereavement.

After he died a lot of folk would tell me how much they 'missed Jock and all his stories.' He looked after his poorer customers. He wasn't above bending the results of the Christmas raffle to make sure it was a deserving case which won the turkey.

But towards the end, the standing of the local neighbourhood butcher changed. This was partly because the supermarkets began to encroach on his trade, partly because the arrival of domestic fridges and the deep freeze meant that folk no longer had to pop along

A shot taken of 'Jock the Butcher' just before retirement.

to the shop just down the road to buy in that day's sausages or a nice chop for the family dinner. Then the regulations became more and more heavy. The sanitary people were the bane of my father's life; there seemed to be always something new to comply with, whether it was providing separate cutters for cooked and for raw meat, fitting in stainless steel worktops or fixing banisters to the stairs. They banned sawdust because it was deemed that that held blood, even though my father would diligently sweep and scrape all the old sawdust off and lay fresh stuff regularly.

The shop is now occupied by a bathroom place – 'Affordable Bathrooms' – and when they were fitting it up I asked them whether they had come across the bottle of whisky my father kept hidden on the top of the office. 'No,' they said, 'but we did come across a pun o' mince.'

Moira Mapley, b.1950. Holburn Street. Interviewed 2014

The shop Cashier:
A super shop to work for

After I left school, I went to Shirras Laing in Schoolhill to work. I was on the cash desk where my role was to handle sales and accounts and to tot up the totals at the end of the day. No calculators or even adding machines so I quickly

'A super store': Shirras Laing in its Schoolhill pomp.

had to master adding up rows of figures. Now when you go to the bank and if the teller has to handle more than three sums there seems to be a problem; I've often found myself standing there staring at the tiny figurers and find I can beat the teller to the answer even though I'm looking at them all upside down.

Shirras Laing was a super shop, just about the best of its kind in the North-east: it handled the full range of household goods from washing machines to silverware. We had a big clientele from the country who would pop in on their day in the city. One of them was Lord Aberdeen and he would appear every other month to buy stuff for Haddo House and to settle accounts. He was such a gentleman. If he happened to pass you by on the street afterwards he would raise his hat and wish you 'Good day.' I usually found that the gentry folk were more inclined to be nice and polite to a young shop girl like myself than a number of the city's businessmen, who would simply throw their cheques at you with never a word of 'please' or 'thank you'.

I liked being down at the front of the shop, able to see people coming and going and to interact with the customers. The director was Mr Stevenson, a man I found to be very fair and good to work for. He looked like Winston Churchill with a red face all crisscrossed by broken purple veins.

He would award you a bonus at New Year and mine usually came to a handsome £25. It was interesting to witness how he acted with some of the country customers. One of them was from the Old Meldrum Games committee and he came to us to hire marquees each year. Once, I overheard his reply to Mr Stevenson's query: 'Was everything to your satisfaction for the Games? I trust our Mr Donald looked after everything for you?' 'Yes, everything was just right.' 'Ah, yes, a good man, our Mr Donald.' To which the farmer replied: 'A geed man, no; he's a bliddy geed man!'

You'd also overhear him responding to the regular country customer's requests for 'a luck penny' on any sale – and sometimes they would be successful and get a discount. He knew how to play his clientele, did Mr Stevenson, and he ran a very successful business.

We all had to dress quite formally in dark clothes and white blouses. When one of the girls reported for work in a red dress she was promptly told: 'Elizabeth, you are here to work; this is not some cocktail party.' At the end of the day – we worked from nine to six – he would stand at the bottom of the stairs to see the staff trooping down to clock off. If they were even one minute on the early side they would hear him tell them: 'Well, ladies, I see it's not actually six o'clock yet. But quite right – after all I noticed what time you all reported for duty this morning and I quite agree – there's no point in being late twice in the same day.'

Margaret Dundas, b.1938. Shirras Laing. Interviewed 2016

'I trust our Mr Donald looked after everything for you?'

'Yes, everything was just right.'

'A good man, our Mr Donald.'

'A geed man, no; he's a bliddy geed man!'

The Banker: Still an honourable profession

It so happened that my parents had a friend of a friend who worked for the North of Scotland Bank and he was prepared to write a letter of introduction to the Staff Manager. And that's how I became a career-long banker.

I felt proud to be joining such an important and respected profession. Banking was seen as a substantial position, one that parents were happy to see their sons enter. Not so long ago I was swapping experiences with a retired bank manager, someone who rose to the heights of the profession, and who had joined at about the same period as myself. He said that, like me, he had been determined to leave school early rather than slog on to get into university. He was fishing around for a promising opening when his mother remarked: 'Do you know, there's a pair of young lads who pass the house every morning on their way to work in the bank and they are always so nicely dressed.' So he said: 'That's how I came to be a banker – all because of those two nicely dressed boys.'

After a number of various postings all over the north of Scotland, in 1973 it was back to the city as manager at the Kittybrewster branch. After one more shift – to become manager at the George Street branch – I retired in 1990 after some 45 years as a banker. Of course, that period brought in many changes. When I started out in 1945, everything

Formal wear was de rigeur. For us that meant a dark suit, collar and tie, a white shirt and polished shoes. Hair had to be properly combed and not too long.

was still done by hand and by brain power. Accounts and transactions had to be entered in big ledgers, by hand, in impeccable script. For my entry into the world of banking I had armed myself with a brand new fountain pen only to be sternly informed that I must put it away and use the standard dip pens in which all bank business was then recorded. You were given a box of nibs, ranging from very fine to broad, and allowed to select the one which suited you best. Any untidiness would result in a prompt ticking off; really it was all a bit like being back at school.

And naturally, formal wear was *de rigeur*. For us that meant a dark suit, collar and tie, a white shirt and polished shoes. Hair had to be properly combed and not too long. We were always made aware that we were on show to the public and must meet their expectations as to what a respectable bank branch official should look like.

In fact, it was a long time before we were even allowed to take our jackets off. It wasn't till the 1970s that an edict came out from Head Office which permitted such casualness – but with the proviso that a tie must be in place at all times. I remember having a member of my staff turn up in waistcoat and suit. That was fine but only as long as he kept his jacket on. When he attempted to take it off I had to remind him that he wasn't a snooker player and that he had to remove it along with his jacket.

Handling cash is only a small part of the bank's business though that is what the public will always think of as being its essential role. The most important job that the manager has to do is to make decisions regarding advice and loans.

Here the responsibility is very great; after all you could be dealing with a million pounds and more. You had to learn as a manager to get to know your community, your customers and to draw on both experience and plain common sense. The key is sound judgement. Each case had to be treated on how you saw its merits.

I always saw it as my duty to advise and not simply to pronounce. I would try to take the client who came to me with a proposal through the details and to help him or her to anticipate any likely issues. Even if the decision had to be a negative one I would attempt to explain the reasons and never simply send a customer away with a blunt: 'You're not on.' Not only might you want to see them back some time in the future but you also had a responsibility to save people from themselves.

This was an attitude of polite helpfulness which I tried to spread throughout all the staff. I would advise my tellers always to be respectfully friendly, to watch out for the customer's name on the cheques they were handling so as to be able to greet them by name. The last thing I wanted was the practice of calling out to the queue: 'Next.'

It's certainly true that the old traditional North-east thrift has largely gone and that credit has become a way of life here as it is elsewhere in the UK. My own father would never pay out for anything which he hadn't actually got the ready cash for. When he at last bought a car in the 1950s, he paid for it straight out.

But you know, the other traditional values of the North-east in the sense of honesty, reliability, your word is your bond, are still pretty well intact. And that is still the case among the banking fraternity, I can assure you. That is why what has happened to the good name of my profession over the last decade makes me so sad. It is really only the antics of the people at the very top – the Fred Goodwins – that have brought us into disrepute and for that I accuse the negligence of the directors for the freedom which they gave to them to gamble with other people's money, that and the bonus culture which encourages the top bankers to go flat out for quick profits.

That wasn't real banking; it was casino gambling and as such a million miles away from the values I was brought up on. I was speaking to an old colleague recently and he was shaking his head and saying that once he had been proud to tell people what he used to do for a living but now he shudders at that question and tries to keep it quiet.

But I know that I and hundreds of other bank people scattered right through the land have given their lives to help bring financial stability and support to the community. I would go into work each day knowing that, through the advice I would be called on to proffer, I would be able to involve myself in the financial welfare of my fellow citizens and the commercial development of the small towns and the city in which I held such a trusted position. Banking? Despite it all, I have no regrets about devoting my working life to such an honourable profession.

Gordon Smith, b.1930. The Clydesdale Bank. Interviewed 2016

The Milkman: You can't strike up a bond with a van

I landed a job with the Co-op. I worked as a dairy roundsman, mostly delivering milk in the Ferryhill area. Up till 1956 when the vans came in, this was done by horse and cart. The routine was to report to the depot at 6AM at Berryden Road. My first round was in Belmont Road, up the Great Northern Road and into the Hilton area. There was this little sweetie shop at the back of the Northern Hotel and I used to pop in and feed the horse with a sweetie or two. 'You're spoiling that horse,' I'd be told but I still did it.

17-year-old milkman Kenny Courage, with the faithful Dobbie.

We had this huge Belgian horse, very big, very strong, called Sandy. In 1947 an epidemic of horse flu struck and we had to prepare for the worst. Sandy caught it and had to be placed in his stall with straps around his tummy so he could be lifted out more easily if his body had to be collected by the knackers. But Sandy did survive, although he lost a lot of weight.

I had a real bond with my horses and was good to them. But more than once I got into some bother over my care of them. I was delivering milk at 22 Prospect Terrace – the number is engraved on my mind – and the lady there would always give the horse some bread or buns. Now, the horse was well aware of this treat so as we approached the house it would get excited. On one occasion he was pulling and tugging so fiercely that I simply had to give him a sharp tug on the reins. She saw this and phoned up the SSPCA. They sent officials up to the stables and interviewed me. Fortunately, the stableman put in a good word for me, besides which they didn't find any signs of distress on the horse. I really felt hurt because I would never dream of being anything but kind towards my horses.

Charlie Archibald, Kenny Courage's deliveryman boss.

Icy weather could cause more difficulties, especially in getting purchase on hills. Then you would have to fix cogs to the hooves and stop now and then to make sure the cogs were still holding. You had to get to know your particular horse, whether, for example, he was the sort who lifted up his front feet as he trotted along or the sort that didn't. They each required sensitive handling.

Over the years I saw a spread of rounds. Ferryhill was a good one, with pleasant people and regular payers. When I was allocated to Tillydrone I was warned: 'That's a bad round for payers.' But I never had much difficulty. I found it was important to get to know the problems of your customers and to adapt accordingly. If they came up to you and said: 'Look, Kenny, I'm a wee bittie short this week – can you wait till the next ane?' I would accept their word. After all, these were working-class folk up against it whenever rent day approached. I was never let down.

You had to be careful with your horses. I would sometimes be invited in for a cup of tea and whether I accepted or not depended on my knowledge of the horse and whether he was the sort who could be safely left standing outside a house by himself. There was this Italian customer in Causewayend who came out with a basin of water for the horse. But the horse refused it and so the Italian simply threw the water into the ground, making a big splash as he did so. That was enough to spook the horse and set it off. It took to its hooves and galloped away, not stopping till it got back home to Berryden.

But I missed the horses when they were sold off and replaced by vans in 1956. It's difficult to strike up a bond with a van.

Kenny Courage, b.1932. Berryden milk depot

While at University, Norman enjoyed a notable swimming career. A wide-eyed Norman, with the University water polo team, 1961.

The Retail Manager:
Look after the customers and the shop will look after itself

My father, Harold Esslemont, was a director and then Chairman of Esslemont & Macintosh, the large department store on Aberdeen. He proved to be a shrewd businessman when he became Chairman in 1972. His main qualities were a strong work ethic and a sense of integrity. Everything was done straight down the middle, and that included paying your taxes on time and strictly no fiddling the books.

His philosophy was: 'Look after your staff and they will look after the customers.' You could call this a paternalistic approach but it was one that succeeded in gaining loyalty. If any member of staff fell ill he would take care to enquire after them; and if they had a few years service he would ensure they would be helped financially until better times came round (there was no statutory sickness pay in those days). He made a point of being able to address each one personally and of knowing about their family circumstances. So when we celebrated 100 years of operation it wasn't surprising to be able to look around and note the significant number of staff who had been with the firm for 40, even 50 years – their whole working lives in fact.

I was always destined to join the family firm after university. But my father insisted that I first have spells at Bradford and London, in department stores – so as to make my

Always a fashionable store. A 1913 advertisement.

mistakes down there. It proved to be a happy choice; I took to the life and showed some aptitude for it. I enjoyed meeting the public and other members of staff and proved to be something of a people person. I didn't receive much in the way of formal training; it was more a matter of learning by observation.

Back in Aberdeen I started off as a salesman on the shop floor, in the Men's department. Then when my second cousin, who was a buyer for the department, gave it up, I replaced him in that position. This was accelerated promotion but I did show I could do it.

There are some basic rules of customer psychology that you master through experience and observation. The key one is to listen to the customer and try to develop a dialogue with them. You talk, you listen and all the while you are trying to feel out the little signs and inflexions which will guide you towards being able to assist them to arrive at the purchase which they might well have not been certain of when they entered the store.

An early lesson is that customers don't necessarily know precisely what they want and it's your job to help them to discover it. Communication is the key. You must strike up a rapport and gain trust by showing a sensitive interest in their needs. The worst thing you can do, as a customer is peacefully browsing the goods, is to advance upon them with a 'Can I help you?' That's a question that can only invite a definite reply and most customers will fend you off with a 'No thank you – I'm just looking.' The best way is to let them settle into the store and then gently open up a conversation – about the weather or the item they happen to be looking at. That gives you the chance to win the

The Board of directors, 1991. Left to right: G. Birnie Esslemont, Pauline Esslemont, Norman Esslemont, Colin Murray.

customer's trust and then gradually to help them feel their way towards a decision.

Esslemont & Macintosh was one of several department stores in Aberdeen at that time. Our particular niche was that of a higher class store, one that was frequented by customers from the west-end, by well set up farmers and by the business community. Our big rival was Watt & Grant's in that respect rather than, say, Isaac Benzie's. This meant, too, that we could attract and maintain good class staff, often capturing them from rival stores.

Now as we move deeper into the 21st century, it is clear that the heyday of the large department store has passed. They can still survive, I think, but only by becoming more specialist and ceasing to attempt to handle every single item of goods under the one roof. In these days of the internet it's too easy for customers to browse through pages and pages of offers and order their choices that way. In the old days, once you acquired a satisfied customer, you could be fairly sure he or she would always turn to you first when seeking a purchase; but now that sort of loyalty has gone. People like to shop around nowadays.

But I only realised that the writing was on the wall for me at E&M's when I was actually served with my jotters in 1997. The end came completely without warning when I was called to a meeting of the directors on Monday, 27 March 1997 – that date is engraved on my heart. I had assumed this was to be a fairly routine administrative meeting but when I took my chair it was to be informed that I was no longer considered to be the 'future' and that it was now time to pass on the baton to younger people, those who – it was claimed – had the sort of fresh thinking that the store needed.

The Board consisted of my second cousin, who was the Chairman, and his daughter, Pauline, plus the firm's accountant. I'm not sure who exactly initiated the coup but their

A loyal and long serving staff: Mrs Harold Esslemont presents awards to staff with 25 years service at the firm's Centenary Dinner. Standing, left to right: Norman Stewart, Arthur Walker, Bill Robb, Bill Chalmers, Harold Smith, David Graham, James McKay, David Kemp, Mrs Esslemont, William Smith. Seated: Sheila Currie, Frances Allan, Eva Westland, Rita Smith.

The publication of *'A Store of Memories,* 1991. From left: G. Birnie Esslemont, Sheila Currie, Charlie Gordon, author Shirley Cunningham, Norman Esslemont.

decision came as a huge shock to me. And what added to my pain was that I was peremptorily told that there was to be no further discussion; instead I was given the advice that 'I should ask my lawyer to speak to their lawyer.' After 33 years working for the store and the last 10 years as its Managing Director I was shell shocked.

In hindsight the months after I left proved to be most rewarding ones. I was inundated with letters and expressions of warm support, ones which assured me that the loss was E&M's not mine. Most people have to wait till their obituaries to receive that sort of appreciation.

And now E&M's is no more and that grand building at the corner of Union Street and Broad Street is the site of a Jamie Oliver restaurant [now closed] while the rest is boarded up to await possible conversion into yet another city hotel – while here I am running two west-end shops in Thistle Street with my wife and my son. Whilst I have a resilient temper, the support I have received from friends, family and staff has been a major factor in helping me to adjust to the new scenario and to maintain a positive attitude.

I suppose you could say I am entitled to feel a little smug about this turn of events but that is not my nature. There is no satisfaction for me in the demise of E&Ms but I am pleased that I have managed to keep the Esslemont name on the Aberdeen retail scene.

Norman Esslemont, b.1943. Esslemont and Macintosh. Interviewed 2015

Following the departure from the old family firm, Norman Esslemont, with his son Mark and wife, Ros, have set up and run his own male and female clothing stores in Thistle Street.

The Window Dresser: There's a lot of psychology involved

I'd always been drawn to Art so at the age of 15, I was happy to land a job at Isaac Benzie's as a window dresser. I began to attend classes twice a week at the college in Commerce Street, in the evenings. The classes were in 'Display': one evening for theory, the next for the practical. I did well, gaining 100% for those two elements and 99% for Art.

I decided to sit the British Display Society's qualification. This was quite a rarefied qualification and only 26 in the whole of the UK possessed it, none of them being under 40. Fortunately, my boss at Isaac Benzie's was one of them and he proved an excellently hard taskmaster. You had to master a whole range of skills: electric lighting; joinery – to make the props; store work; how to design the whole construction of a window.

Those are the practical skills but there's a lot of psychology involved too. After all, a window only has a second or two to do its work in attracting attention from the average passer-by on the street.

You have to come up with a window design that will be sufficiently arresting to draw them into its contents. For example, straight lines might seem all very neat and tidy but by themselves will simply be glanced at because that is what the passer-by expects to see.

The psychology of window dressing. The author's eye is caught by this Stockholm store display, 1996.

So you need to create some variety; if you have a line of cans then there is no use in simply laying them out in a straight row; you should also create perpendicular lines so as to arrest the vision.

Pots and pans, wallpaper, fabrics, gents' clothes, ladies wear – I did the lot at Isaac Benzie's. My boss, Sandy Shepherd, was meticulous in his work and demanded the same high standards from me. He would come in and examine your work, stand there for a minute and then say:'No, there's something not quite right with this window.' Then he would go off, leaving you to spot the fault. It might be no more than a squint ticket or a stray pin lying in the corner but it had to be corrected. Everything had got its place in relation to everything else – that is what he taught me and I took it all to heart.

I was now offered a post as Display Manager at Falconer's, a shop with a long arcade and seven of a display staff. I went there for a couple of years, then onto Watt & Grant's. It was at this time that Reid & Pearson's was converting its Junior department into 'Young World' and I was asked to take it over as well. All this time I had been teaching evening classes at the college and after two further years I was invited to become a full time lecturer there.

You would put a dress, a hat and accessories on a ladieswear window model. You would also place a shoe – but only one shoe. The signal will go out that there's another shoe waiting to be tried on.

I stopped full-time work in 1970 when my daughter was born. That was the start of my freelance career. In the November, just when they were gearing up for the Christmas rush, the manager at Esslemont & McIntosh broke his leg and I was called in to replace him. When he returned I was invited to stay on for two mornings a week to take care of the menswear windows.

That was the start of building up a folio of work in various parts of the city. One day I was walking past Lizar's in Union Street and noticed that its window was standing empty. Now, that is a crime for any shop since its window displays are its main point of contact with any potential customers. I went into the shop and told them what I thought of this situation. The upshot was that I offered to do their windows for three weeks for nothing and then if they were pleased I would negotiate a more permanent arrangement. After the first two weeks and a noticeable rise in their custom, I was invited to take on their windows on a two mornings a week basis. I came to a similar arrangement with Pitlochry Knitwear. I also did a motorbike shop in Crown Street.

So I was now covering a wide range of shops. But the skills involved are generic ones; the same principles of display and psychology go right across the board. Take a clothing store. If it's a ladieswear window then you would put a dress on the model, a hat and accessories such as handbag, scarf and necklace. You would also place a shoe – but only the one shoe. That's because the signal will go out to the female onlooker that there's another shoe waiting for her to try it on. With menswear, you must show a pair since men don't respond in the same way.

So there I was, working in Aberdeen at the heyday of the department store. But they were places where a hierarchy among the staff operated. At Watt & Grant's the buyers felt themselves to be a superior elite and acted in a snooty way. They had use of the public restaurant while the rest of the staff had a canteen. A strict dress code was expected. Now, as a hands-on window dresser who often did her work in trousers and was sometimes smeared with paint, I resented being expected to change my clothes simply to have a cup of coffee. But the buyers would come swanning in in their fur coats and heavy make-up. First names were not to be used: it was all a matter of 'Mr': 'Mrs' and 'Mistress'.

But now all has changed and the role of the window dresser has greatly diminished. Some stores have done away with the shop front window entirely: at Marks & Spencer the idea is that you simply look right through the windows into the store within. And even when that isn't the case the system now is for there to be one centralised window dressing unit in London and for that to make up a display which is then copied throughout the rest of the country. With computerisation it's easy for headquarters to have photo shots of each separate store, to have its measurements and angles, and thus to prescribe how and what it should be displaying. In my day to dress a window in an Aberdeen store was to use your creativity and to apply the fruits of your training; now it's just like painting by numbers. You have to follow a plan set by someone else.

Linda Muller, b.1945. Isaac Benzie's and others. Interviewed 2015

The Waitress:
I'm not staying here!

The first job I had when I left the school was at the Gentleman's Club next to the Music Hall. I was a waitress there, and I lived in.

What I didn't like was the head ones, because they were old and crabbit (like I am now). I wore a black dress and a head-dress with little pleats, and a white apron. In the morning, when you weren't serving, you cleaned the cutlery. They gave the worst jobs to the young one – me.

Not only that, the dress that I had was one my mother had sewn little flowers on at the top of the sleeve; they made me get my mother to cut them all off. I just hated it and one day, when I still had on this dress and this hat and this pinafore apron, I said: 'I'm not staying here.'

So I took off the hat and I ran all the way home to my mother.

Kathleen Porter, b.1932. The Gentleman's Club. Interviewed 2016

Just left school and ready to have a go at waitressing. A 1940s shot of Kathleen Porter.

The Florist:
It's not always a gentlelady's occupation!

I'd always been drawn to the world of flowers. As a girl we would spend hours in the garden, gathering the moss together to turn it into little houses and using the daisies as our own garden for it. My father kept a good garden, one that not only included vegetables but flowers too. He was especially fond of roses; once he planted a special variety called Blue Moon in honour of my mother. That was when disaster struck. Both our parents were out and we girls were playing in the garden with a ball. Unfortunately I sent the ball crashing into Blue Moon, knocking the head off just as it was about to come into bloom. Panic. I tried to cover up the misdeed by sticking the head back on with sellotape and then had to listen to my mother puzzling over the fact that her precious flower never seemed to be coming into bloom.

People imagine that being a florist is a nice gentlelady's occupation, a matter of leisurely arranging lovely flowers in long vases and then standing around waiting for our nice customers to come along to admire our arrangements. But that is only a small part of what we have to do. If, for example, you want to make up an oasis then you have to wire every single flower and that is intricate work, believe me.

When the orders arrive they come in heavy crates and require to be conditioned. That

I loved my work. Flowers are lovely natural things to work with and there were always new ideas and varieties coming along.

means being tidied up with any thorns or stray bits removed, cut to size and then put in water so as to make them shop ready. The hours can be very long and often in winter it's freezing cold since any heating would mean that the flowers would lose their freshness. And then, when you receive an order for a special event such as a funeral, you can be up all night, working against the clock to get everything absolutely right.

I had to serve a full apprenticeship and that meant five years, starting out on a five-and-a-half day week, with all day on a Saturday and a half day on the Wednesday. My first wage was £4.50 a week; after training, at the age of 19, it went up to £19.

Of course, you have to have a feeling for flowers and the imagination to see what the various arrangements would look like. But one of the main requirements is stamina. When you are hard at it to get an order out then you can be working till three in the morning and have to start again at six. You are on your feet all day long

Next to sheer stamina I would put sensitiveness as the next most important attribute. You have to be a trusted guide for your customers, and you have to tune into exactly what will suit them at a particularly important moment in their lives such as a wedding or a funeral. This can be an especially demanding role when you are dealing with a bereavement. That is when the personal touch is so vital.

Another skill, one that can only come through years of training and experience, is a knowledge of how to blend colours together, a sense of harmony and the interplay of fungi, blooms, stems, foliage – how they all set each other off, how the whole texture of the arrangement works in a way that satisfies the eye.

These are qualities which no garage or supermarket can reproduce. Their recent growth does pose a threat to the specialist shop but I accept that they have their place. If you are only after a quick, cheap flower fix and are not too bothered about getting anything that will last more than a day or two then the local garage or supermarket might well be the easy solution. But the flowers you get there will never compete in size, weight, head size, stem strength or durability to what you can acquire in a florist's. And then so many supermarket blooms are pepped up to unnaturally vivid colours by the use of artificial colourings.

I loved my work. Flowers are lovely natural things to work with and there were always new ideas and varieties coming along. The key is workmanship. That is how to put everything together in terms of design and strength. If you are making up a buttonhole, for instance, you need to cut the flower to the correct size, then you have to gauge the wire, tape it and make sure it falls in a straight line with a proper weighting. If it is a bouquet for a bride, then it must be so she can carry it with comfort and that can only happen if the balance is right. I was brought up in a period when you were constantly being entered into competitions. Interflora would give a prize for the best wreath, one that you could raise to your shoulder, then let it drop to the floor to see whether anything becomes loose or whether it is so well made that it all holds together.

Barbara Irvine, b.1957. Flower Design. 2016

TRANSPORTING GOODS AND PEOPLE

The Coalman:
He worked so hard that it killed him

It's a different world nowadays, especially as regards earning your living. I can think of a few people and the things they did back then. This lad was a chum of mine at school and his father, boy, did he work! And it killed him. He worked in the harbour loading trawlers with coal. It was piece work but with good pay. You had an apron on your back with metal studs to stop the chunks of coal damaging your back – and each bag you carried was a hundredweight.

Loading trawlers on piecework meant they'd to load the trawler as quick as they could so it got away to sea. That was his full-time job, and then he also had a spare-time job. Imagine, a spare time job! He had a horse and a cart in the lane off Crown Terrace. He got his coal from a place in Frederick Street that was a coal store – a mountain of coal – and in the evenings he sold coal round the houses. He bought maybe 10 hundredweight bags of coal for his customers that he delivered on his cart and sold to them in the evenings, and on Saturdays.

He did that for years and it was a helluva hard life. He lived in Marywell Street and wanted the money to better himself. But he was dead by 50.

Jim Butler, b.1923 Marywell Street. Interviewed 2015

You had an apron on your back with metal studs to stop the chunks of coal damaging your back – and each bag you carried was a hundred-weight.

The Corporation Cashier:
You had to do it all in your head

When I went into the cash office at the Corporation Transport the conductors were only allowed 15 minutes cashing up time. Now, they'd come in all at the same time. You all had your own set of conductors in your own queue and

The young Transport Corporation cashier. A 1940 shot of Gladys Morrice, complete with Number 111 bus.

you'd be as quick as you could. You had to count up all their different ticket numbers and then you counted the money they'd collected to see if it matched. You'd to do everything in your head and you'd to be quick because these lads were only getting 15 minutes to cash up. They used to shout: 'C'mon then. C'mon. ' And I always remember if they were 'over' with their money, the company kept it. But if they were under, they had to pay the difference. It was hard for them because they were passed foreign coins and everything in the dark and they'd to make it up; it wasn't fair.

Now we'd one lad – he was a nice lad but, you know, he was one of 'those' and he was half a crown short. I said to him: 'Two-and-six short. ' 'I canna be, Gladys. I canna be.'

I said: 'You are. You're 2/6 short. Look, I've done it twice and you are 2/6 short.'

And I can always remember, Alec something, he was the boss saying: 'C'mon pey up. Own up, ye bought a flamin' pooder puff. ' That sticks in my mind because a ripple of laughter went through the office. He paid up, but I can see that yet.

Not long after I started, I can remember going into the Majestic Picture House on Union Street with my boyfriend and the film was something to do with a hotel; this man was looking for this number, and the number was 400. And I'm sitting in that picture house thinking something like "eight into 400…"; I was dividing it by eight, the number of penny-halfpennies to the shilling.

Gladys Morrice, b.1920. Aberdeen Transport. Interviewed 2016

The Bus Driver: Not a moment's relaxation!

You constantly have to bite your tongue. Most of the public are perfectly pleasant to deal with and will act polite but there will always be some who seem to take a delight in nipping at you as soon as they get on. A common problem is claiming not to have enough money for the fare and so they will ask to be let off that final two pence; then I'll have to ask them whether, when they go to the pub, they expect to get their pint for a couple of pence cheaper than the rest are paying simply because they haven't brought enough money with them. Most get the point – but not all of them.

We are never on the same route two days running nor do we work the same hours. For example, this week I had a Sunday 5PM to midnight shift, then on the Monday it was start at 12.30, Tuesday 1.30, Wednesday and Thursday days off, Friday start at 12.30, Saturday at 4PM. My shifts last for 7 hours 36 minutes, with one break of 30 minutes after three hours.

You are the sole person in charge of maybe 50 passengers and are responsible for their safety and comfort. Any trouble, we are supposed to stop the bus and phone the police; but for small incidents I prefer to try and defuse the situation there and then. A lot of the trouble is drink related or is low level nuisances. A couple might get on, rowing with each other and continue to shout and act aggressively as the bus sets off, or a wheelchair

user comes on and nobody clears a space for her to get into the proper position. But sometimes the trouble can be more severe, even dangerous. Stone-throwing by kids can occur at any point – Cults just as well as Tillydrone. I've had windows smashed, I've been shot at by air rifles or catapults and had lasers shone at my face.

Every bus window has two panes of glass: an outer and an inner skin. Usually a pellet will just break the outer layer but I have had a brick come straight through my windscreen. You need a calm temperament for this job and some drivers can get too tensed up. You can't allow your mind to wander; anything can happen at any moment. Just the other day I was up by Murdo's Bar at the junction there when a car decided it couldn't wait and went to overtake me just as another car was entering from Anderson Drive, and so the overtaking car tried to pull in and clipped its own mirror. A small thing maybe, but it all has to be precisely reported when you get back to the depot and a whole procedure gone through, and this at the end of your shift and you dying to get home.

In my opinion, Aberdeen drivers are among the worst in the country. When I visit Glasgow I notice that there it is customary to let other cars in off the slip roads whereas in Aberdeen you'll often see drivers racing alongside deliberately so as to squeeze the other driver out. Then there are the central island overtakers. A lot of bus stops are

The old and the new. Stanley Irvine (above) with an old 'Albion' Corporation petrol driven bus… And (below) with a state of the art hydrogen powered First Group bus.

One of the best things about driving a bus for a living in Aberdeen – the camaraderie and humour.

positioned just behind a central island placed in the road, the idea being that passengers will be able to cross in front of the bus where you can see them, get to the middle of the road and then see if anything is coming in the opposite direction. The island is also meant to prevent any car from overtaking the stationary bus while all this is going on. But there will always be the odd driver who doesn't feel he has to wait while all this happens and attempts to draw out, go to the wrong side of the road and overtake you that way.

But the biggest bugbear is the number of drivers you see using mobile phones, sometimes not even talking into them but texting. It can be as many as one in three at this game. Sitting up in your cab you can see it all.

We are under constant surveillance, too. Each Aberdeen bus is fitted out with six cameras: two in the middle, one at the back, another at the rear and one at the entrance and one in the cab. The cab is also fitted out with three traffic lights, so to speak. These will show red whenever you are doing something wrong, like taking a corner too fast. The results are recorded and gone over later. Prizes will be awarded to the best driver of the week and disciplinary action taken against those with too many red light counts. Never a moment's relaxation for the Aberdeen bus driver.

A couple of months ago I was approaching Mannofield and the No. 19 to Culter was on the other side of the road. Three lassies jumped off my bus and one of them ran straight across the road, without looking. She got struck by a taxi. I couldn't do anything but sit and watch; my bus was stationary. She wasn't too badly injured as it turned out but an incident like that does give you a turn.

However, the next day at the depot all my colleagues were completely supportive and even made a joke out of the matter. That's one of the best things about driving a bus for a living in Aberdeen – the camaraderie and humour. However much abuse you might be having to put up with from the public, however many times you are attacked by stones and laser beams, you know that back at the depot your mates will be waiting to exchange banter and to cheer you up.

Stanley (Stan) Irvine, b.1955. Firstgroup Buses. Interviewed 2016

The Bus Conductress: I loved working on the buses

A break at the Turriff Show 1956. Kathleen is centre with the ubiquitous 'Hazlehead' tiger.

I was a conductress with Alexanders for 14 years. I liked the buses. The bus routes were in different sections, like 'Inverurie section': 'Dunecht section': 'Peterhead.' Everybody had to take turns of 'Dee and Don', on buses running from Dyce to Culter and back again; that was the busiest route. You had different shifts to do: 'Early Dee and Don': 'Late Dee and Don': 'Early Country': 'Late Country.' So you'd rotate round this every five weeks.

I loved working on the buses. We had parcels to take as well. Some of the drivers

were lazy sods, who'd sit on their backsides and leave us to deliver the big parcels of papers and things while they would sit there and smoke or gawp about them. They fairly thought they were 'it.' When you were younger you'd think 'Ooh, a driver.' But in time you'd realise they're not a bloody pilot.

Kathleen Porter, b.1932. Alexander's Buses. Interviewed 2016

The young clippie at the bus terminus at Culter, waiting at Pie Jean's

Father peeping out of the cab of No.60525, named AH Peppercorn – one of his beloved steam locomotives. He is talking to Ferryhill depot 'Fat Controller'.

The Train Driver: He lived for his job

All my father ever wanted to do was to be a train driver. He was forced to go to sea: in a fishing family that was the expected thing. So when he was 14 and just left school, they took him off to the Faroes with them. He was sick as soon as the boat left the harbour bar and continued to throw up all the way to the Faroes and back again. So my grandfather told him: 'You'll never make a fisherman – it's the railways for you, right enough. '

He went to the Ferryhill depot at 18 and began to work his way up. That was always a long business in those days: you had to start as an engine cleaner, then go onto the footplate as a fireman before you could finally become a driver. When he finally made it he was 44 – but that was one of the youngest drivers around then.

His usual runs were out of Aberdeen down to Edinburgh or Dundee, or up to Inverness or over to Ballater. One of the highlights of my childhood was when the annual Sunday school picnic outing took place. This would be by train to somewhere like Torphins and he would try to arrange to be the driver. He would tell me in the morning that he would be driving us all out on the Deeside line. When we got to the Joint

Station and along the platform, he would come out from the cab to greet us. They would all shout: 'It's Norma's dad; it's Norma's dad!' and I would just about burst with pride.

He lived for his job. The only time he got fed up was when the diesels came in, during the late 1960s. They were just a big machine, whereas the old steam engines were like a living thing that you had to get to know and look after. He would love to go round seeing that everything was in order.

He would tell us how when the engine was at rest in the depot you didn't just switch off and go home; no, you had to go round with this huge oilcan that had a long spout, and make sure that every single wheel was properly lubricated. It was a point of honour that when at the end of your shift you handed it over to the next team, you could tell them: 'She's running well today.' The engine was always a 'she', a person to be coaxed and cared for.

Another thrill for Dad was to drive the Royal Family on their trips up Deeside, towards Balmoral. He would laugh at the way the Queen Mother would have to get her children, the two princesses, in proper order so as to face the public. The station master would be out in his bowler hat to salute her on the platform, and as she approached he would offer an aside: 'Oh no, it's the greetin' geets today.' Often there would be some sulking and protests from either Elizabeth or Margaret, and the Queen would have to calm them down before they got on the train.

Then there were all the royal corgies to cope with. They were yappy little dogs that were always threatening to snap and bite. But, of course, no-one dared to look anything but delighted to see them.

At the end of the journey, the Queen Mother would make a point of going up to my dad and handing him a sweetie: 'Here, this is for you, driver.' My dad had to doff his cap and show proper gratitude.

Norma Reid, b.1943. Ferryhill Railway Depot. Interviewed 2007

The only time he got fed up was when the diesels came in, during the late 1960s. They were just a big machine, whereas the old steam engines were like a living thing that you had to look after.

EVERYDAY PLEASURES

Parks, Pictures, Holidays and Dance Halls

Ayr Butlin's Holiday camp with an excited crew of children, among which is a young Arthur Wyllie (*see* *SPORTS and WORK*). This venue was a popular holiday destination for Aberdeen families in the 1950s when this shot was taken.

~THE JOLLY ROGER~

GOING TO THE DANCING

That fateful Marquee card – still kept as a souvenir, after 65 years of marriage.

It was near enough for us

I met my husband, Kenneth, at Newtonhill. It was at the Marquee Dance there; we'd heard such big things about this Marquee Dance that some of us girls from the Comb Works decided to make the trip out. When you entered the marquee you were given this card with a number on it. It was just a cardboard disc with a bit of silver and a string through it so you could wear it round your neck. Mine was '183'; Kenneth's was '381.' The idea was that you were supposed to look out the male that was wearing the same number as yourself and maybe pair off with him. Kenneth's wasn't exactly the same but it was near enough for us. We became engaged two years later. That was in 1951; we've been together since that time. And I've aye got the card: '381'!

Elizabeth (Betty) McHardy, b.1930. A Marquee dance. Interviewed 2004

Isabel Murray in her younger days at the turn of the century when she was a specialist in physical education and had a spell as Principal of the Aberdeen Physical Training College.

I remember you from Madame Murray's!

One of my great memories from those days is Madame Murray's dancing classes. She ran her classes with the utmost strictness. You usually started to attend when you were 15 or 16, just the age when the opposite sex became of interest, but she made sure that there was absolutely no impropriety. If she considered you were dancing a little bit too close then she would advance upon you and slide her hand down between you so as to push you a safe distance apart.

Dress standards were firmly adhered to. For a few years, circular skirts were popular, skirts that were so full that if you laid them out on the floor then their material would form a complete circle. Beneath them you were expected to wear full petticoats which you had soaked in sugar and water in the bath; this made the whole ensemble stiff and able to stick out.

There were two dancing events in the week: on Saturdays there would be the Saturday Club, which was held in the Cowdray Hall, and during the week there would be classes held after school, on a Wednesday. For her classes, she hired out a variety of rooms in the centre of the city and if you wanted to go to the Saturday nights then you had to be in attendance at those classes.

Madame Murray when I encountered her was by now quite an elderly lady but managed to maintain an erect and dignified appearance. The 'Madame' was, I think, a piece of affectation; I'm sure she was a local through and through. Generations of young Aberdonians passed through her hands; in later life you could always recognise each other by the way we all moved across the dance floor. I say 'generations' but she confined herself to pupils from Robert Gordon's College or Aberdeen Grammar School, the High, the Central plus the private schools.

I still meet people who are now old but are recognisable as fellow Madame Murray graduates; it's quite common in Aberdeen for folk of my age group to greet each other with: 'Oh, I remember you from Madame Murray's.' All this common experience made you aware how small a world we shared with one another – Madame Murray is one of the bonding experiences of people from my age group and my background.

Marjory Rose, b.1937. Madame Murray's. Interviewed 2015.

Sixty years later Madame Murray was running the dancing classes which generations of young Aberdonians attended – if they were from the right schools.

'We had some really good bands': A crowded floor at the Beach Ballroom, dancing to the music of Syd Lawrence's band, 1977. [PHOTO: ABERDEEN JOURNALS]

I would go dancing every night of the week

When I got older my great pleasure became the dancing. I started when I was just nearly 16. In those days there were plenty of dance halls in Aberdeen. There was one in Spring Garden, another in Gray Street, another in George Street, then there was the Abergeldie and a hall out at Bucksburn. Then there was the

Palais, which had its own dance teacher, Colin Smith, in a room up the stairs. On a Saturday afternoon I'd go to the Beach Ballroom or to the Swing Club at the top of Market Street.

I would go off to the dancing every night of the week, except Tuesday, when I stayed in to wash my hair. I had two skirts and two blouses and would alternate them but I also had a special pair of dancing shoes which I'd acquired from Findlater's. They were of satin and pure white, with high heels. One day I decided I would dye them black but I discovered that when I got them under the lights they shone out a sort of electric blue. All the others came round: 'Oh, I like your shoes – real bonny. Far did you get such a pair?' 'Oh, that's a secret,' I would reply.

So that became my life: work for the Co-op in Loch Street by day, dancing at night. Even after I'd started going out with the man who became my husband, and he was away working for Ford Motors down in Dagenham, I would still go out. For a spell we could only see each other during our fortnight's holidays, either up here or down there, but that didn't stop me. He knew it was the dancing I was interested in and that the opposite sex was no more than dancing partners.

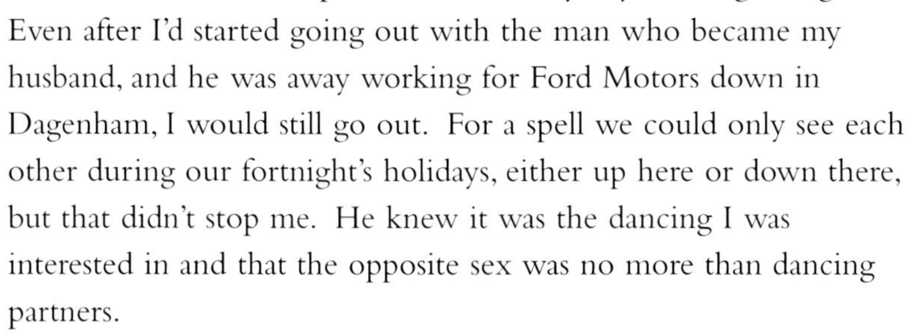

'There was dancing every night of the week'. A 1940s advertisement for one of the city's most popular halls.

I would love the whole thing: the dressing up, the music, the crowd, the atmosphere. The Locarno was good because the crowd there were so open and friendly whereas the Palais could be a bit stiff, with an office set, then a police set and so on, never really mixing with each other.

You had to wait to be asked up unless it was a Lady's Choice. The usual enquiry was: 'May I have this dance?' though sometimes it would be no more than a 'Ye goin' up?' I made a point of always accepting, even the poor dancers, only turning down the obviously drunk ones. Just once I was rejected for a Lady's Choice. 'No', he said; I had to cross the floor again feeling horribly small.

We were treated to really good bands. Usually an eight-piece outfit with saxes, clarinet, piano, a drummer, and they played the popular music of the day – Frank Sinatra, Bing Crosby, quicksteps, fox trots, waltzes. There wasn't any real trouble. Although the Palais did have a bar upstairs, there was never any serious drunkenness – at the first sign of bother the person would be ejected.

I don't think there was nearly the same amount of drinking in those days – we couldn't afford it for one thing. Do you know it wasn't till I was 21 that I had my first visit to a pub and my first alcoholic drink. A friend was celebrating her birthday and she suggested we pop into Ma Cameron's. I had one glass of sherry and that was my grand introduction to drink. I was only interested in the dancing, not wasting time and money on alcohol.

Margaret Leiper, b.1929. Locarno Ballroom. Interviewed 2014.

VISITING THE PARK

Union Terrace Gardens – Kathleen Porter's 'Trainie Park', a regular play spot for city centre children.

We'd wait for the stars

Our backie looked on to the front of the Spa Bar at the back door of His Majesty's Theatre, which was just across the road. At the end of the night, sometimes if it was warm inside the theatre, they'd open the doors at the side, right along by the church and up the steps, and we used to sit there when the doors were open and watch what was going on. We could see in and hear the music. Then we'd go down the back to the stage door and wait for the stars coming out there.

The Gardens were also frequented by the older generation – here playing at the giant draught boards and watched by all ages.

The 'Trainie Park' was our playground. Underneath the bridge; at the back door of His Majesty's Theatre and just round the corner underneath the bridge there, next to the railway. And then we had a playground in the Lower Denburn where there were swings. You never went to the lavvie when the 'Granda' was on because he used to peek over the top and watch you. In those days we didn't know what a paedophile was but he must have been something along those lines. They would say: 'Dinna ging in there 'cause the Granda's in his hoosie.'

The Belmont Cinema cost a penny and the seats were wooden forms. When anybody got up to go out, it alarmed the whole cinema because you pushed the whole form to get past. You'd see Betty Grable, John Payne, Sonja Henie. I liked that.

And music: the only music you got was if you went into the music shop for sheet music. It had the words written out and you'd listen to the radio and you'd have this bit of paper with all the words on it and sing along. Then you'd learn the words by heart.

Kathleen Porter, b.1932. The Trainie Park. Interviewed 2016.

All good pals together

But our best pastime was to walk up to Westburn Park. In the summer evenings we'd hold proper games of cricket. Ronnie Comber got a bat for his birthday and Jim Cardno's dad made us a set of stumps, complete with bails. We clubbed together to buy a hard composition ball from the Rubber Shop; with luck a 3/1d ball would last us through the whole season. We'd be up there in midsummer till 10 at night, playing out our Test matches. Then on the way home came the special treat of a twopenny poke of chips from the small chipper in Gerrard Street.

We were all good pals together. However, there was one incident which did rankle a bit at the time. Often, as we made our way back from the Westburn Park, we'd kick a ball around between us. Well, there was this small shop run by a firm called Tindall & Scott at the corner of Gerrard Street and we often stopped to play headers in the yard in front of it. The shop had a lot of stuff in its window and a bar to protect it. So when the ball hit against the window it simply bounced back, safe and sound. But as luck would have it on this occasion I headed the ball and somehow it went between the bars and smashed the window and ended up inside the shop. Trouble. We all took to our heels and rushed home.

But you can't make a noise of breaking glass in the city without other windows flying open and people gawping out to see what had happened. So it wasn't a surprise when the next day one of the lads came to tell me the breakage had been reported to the police and that they were coming up George Street making enquires. I realised the game was up and that my best plan would be to go to the police voluntarily and make a confession.

I went up to this bobby in George Street and told him 'I have something to report.' 'Oh, so you've decided to own up, have you.' He took notes and advised me to report

myself to Tindall and Scott. Fortunately I was now working at the Co-op and could afford – just – to pay for the breakage but I must admit that when I presented myself to them with all due apologies I half expected them to say: 'Well, as you've been so honest in coming forward, we'll say no more about the matter.' But no, what they did say was: 'You get a joiner to replace our window, pay his bill, and then you can get your ball back'.

So I had to fix up a joiner to carry out the work and then pay his bill, which came to 17/6d. I must say I was looking for my mates to help out with the money but none of them ever offered even to chip in with a half crown or so. So I had to pay the lot and this was out of my £2 wage from the Co-op. But at least I wasn't going to be charged with damage and at least we had our ball back and could carry on with our games.

Kenny Courage, b.1932. Westburn Park. Interviewed 2014.

Westburn Park on a warm summer's day and a mecca for Kenny Courage and his pals.
[PHOTO: ABERDEEN JOURNALS]

He was an adult in authority, so we did as he asked

Duthie Park was a great playground. In the 1950s it was a favourite attraction for Glaswegian holiday-makers with young children. The paddle-boating pond was especially popular. During my Primary school holidays I would occasionally hang around the pay point and offer my services to take children who were too young to go on

Sandy aged nine at about the period of his Duthie Park ordeal.

the boats unaccompanied for their 20-minute trip. The twopence per child (self included) was paid by grateful parents. I usually extended these trips to half an hour by just happening to be at the farthest point in the pond behind one of the two islands when the man in charge announced through his loud hailer that our time was up. The odd sixpence was my reward for safely returning these young Weegies to their anxious parents. My mug-shot must to this day adorn photo albums across the Central Belt.

But the park was also the scene of an unsavoury incident which occurred when my pal, Ronnie, and I (then aged nine and seven) were trying to get conkers down from a horse chestnut tree behind the large mound. To this end we were firing small stones from a catapult and this attracted the attention of the 'Parkie'.

He started to give us a telling off, a reprimand which we quite expected. But then he ordered us into the bushes, where he told us to take down our short trousers and our underpants. He was an adult and in authority; he had caught us doing something which we knew we shouldn't have been doing so we did as we were told. My seven-year-old knees were shaking with fright as we stood beside each other while he looked at our wee willies.

But that was it; after a minute or so he ordered us to pull on our trousers and go home. Now, whether he was afraid of being spotted or whether this simple peep at our willies was the limit of his needs I will never know. What I do know is that the incident is imprinted on my mind to this day and that I can still see that evil narrow pointed face, a cross between a rat and crow, as he stared at us.

This all happened 68 years ago and I presume the man to be long deceased but I swear I would still be able to pick him out in an ID parade even now.

The Duthie Park in a peaceful 1940s scene – but watch those bushes!

Since this time we have all become more knowledgeable about the practice of paedophilia but back then you simply went along with what an adult told you to do. However, I did know that something nasty had happened but because we had been caught doing something we accepted was wrong we considered it best not to tell our parents.

This was very much the same as when I was belted at school for something I had been told was wrong. I never would tell my parents even when, at the age of eight, it was for such a minor transgression as talking in the lines prior to going into the class. How times have changed!

Alexander (Sandy) Gallacher, b.1941. Nellfield Place. Interviewed 2015.

GOING TO THE PICTURES

Kathleen Porter cultivating her own film star look in the early 1950s.

He took her in his arms and gave her a kiss...

I went on to piece work at the net braiding factory. During the whole day after I'd been into the pictures the previous night, I was telling them how Sonja Henie had come skating along and fallen into the arms of John Payne... he took her in his arms and gave her a kiss. And they're asking what happened next, at the same time making these nets. And I'm telling them... then he did this... and then he did that. But, though my mouth was going, my hands had stopped. So when I got my pay packet at the end of the week I had no pay because I'd been too busy speaking. I remember this foreman, Jimmy, coming along, and I was furious. I'd no pay! I asked 'Why hiv I nae got ony wages?'

He says: 'Ye didna mak ony nets!'

Kathleen Porter, b.1932 Albion Street. Interviewed 2016

I can't sit here; my neck'll be broken!

I can remember going to the pictures when I was 14 and I had just enough money to go with this girl – I'd saved up fourpence. We were right in the front seat and she said 'Oh, I can't sit here. My neck'll be broken!' She changed her seat to sixpence to get further back and I sat by myself for four pence because I didn't have another tuppence. I wonder what the kids would think of that today.

The Globe Cinema, now closed and to let, but in Gladys Morrice's childhood a popular family outing.

[PHOTO: NORRIE M^c^NAMEE]

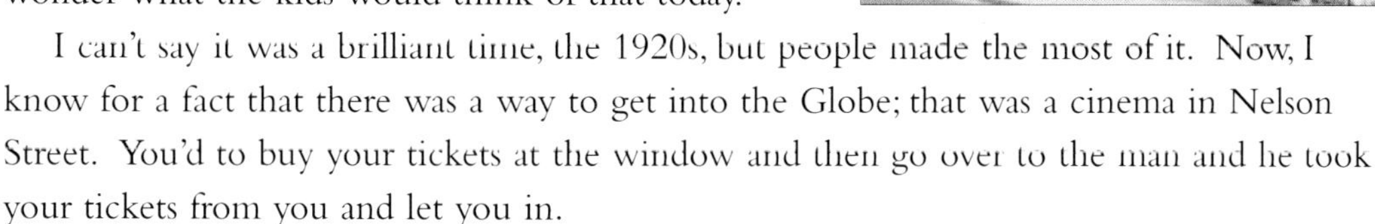

I can't say it was a brilliant time, the 1920s, but people made the most of it. Now, I know for a fact that there was a way to get into the Globe; that was a cinema in Nelson Street. You'd to buy your tickets at the window and then go over to the man and he took your tickets from you and let you in.

This family used to wait until there was a crowd going in and they didn't buy their tickets but they just moved forward with the crowd and then they gave the guy tuppence

MarionDouglas aged 18. As a young child, she was a regular at Northfield Community Club.

in his hand and they got into the pictures. As this chap said to me: 'I can let my fire out and take my bairns to the pictures and it's warm in there, for tuppence. And I canna keep a fire going at night for the kids for that.' So, although they were cheating, you understood that, in a way, they were doing the best for their kids.

Gladys Morrice, b.1920. The Globe Cinema. Interviewed 2016.

On Saturday night we went to the NCC

We used to go to the Northfield Community Cub – it was held in the school and you took sixpence and it was the pictures on a Saturday night. But if you didn't behave you didn't get to go. I must have been about six, seven, eight at that time and there'd be a black and white picture and a serial and a cartoon and then everybody had a card with a number on it and there was a draw and somebody would win something as well. It was brilliant and there were always loads of kids.

Marion Douglas, b.1948 Bucksburn. Interviewed 2016.

I saw films in all 17 of them

I must have seen a picture in every cinema in Aberdeen – and there were 17 of them back then. I was an avid follower of the Saturday morning children's performances at the Odeon. There we would be entertained to a programme of cartoons, a travelogue, the serial and then the big picture, which was usually a cowboy adventure starring such heroes as Roy Rodgers, Hopalong Cassidy or Gene Audrey. All this was accompanied by a noisy throng of excited kids.

Those mornings were the start of a lifelong pleasure for me. Of course, I watch television in the comfort of my own home but I still get a kick out of settling down in the dark with that large glowing screen in front of us all and having to focus on it alone in a way that is impossible amidst the distractions of the home.

Years later I was on one of those trams which used to run up Union Street and round to Holburn Street. This was on a Saturday morning and as we approached the Junction, the conductor turned to a passenger and asked him for the time. 'It's a quarter to 12.' 'Oh, no – we'll be gingin roon the corner an there'll be thoosans o' them Mickey Moosers swarmin aa ower us.' And he was right: within a few minutes his tram was bursting, full of excited young bodies crowding onto it. Absolute chaos – but for me happy memories of the time when I would have been one of them.

Hurrying off to the pictures? The young Mike Davidson caught striding along on Union Bridge.

Mitchell (Mike) Davidson, b.1940. The Odeon. Interviewed 2016.

There was luxury within: The Capitol restaurant, 1950s.

We had cinemas all over Aberdeen

My father was one of four sons, born to a local businessman called James – J.F. – Donald. He was a dance teacher who ran his own ballroom in North Silver Street: 'Donald's Ballroom.' During the interwar years, ballroom dancing was something of a craze among all classes. He would offer lessons in all the latest dances like foxtrots and the Charleston. He actually taught Prime Minister Asquith the Black Bottom when Asquith was up in the region, staying at Slains Castle.

Then in the 1920s J.F. realised that the cinema was going to be the really big leisure pursuit for all social classes and so he decided to enter the business. He bought the Cinema House at the bottom of Skene Terrace and then took over the Grand Central in George Street. But privately he would tell his family: 'This is just a passing craze – the cinema can't last!'

So he insisted that the sons all had to learn a trade to fall back on. My father became an optician and for many years he had an optical shop in Back Wynd.

Despite J.F.'s fears, the cinema flourished. People would incorporate it into their

When Donald Cinemas ruled the Aberdeen scene. A brochure designed to celebrate the opening of the luxurious 'Capitol', 1933. [PHOTO: ABERDEEN LIBRARY SERVICES]

weekly routines; it became a common habit to go as often as twice a week when programmes would change. The attitude was to pack them in and this applied most notoriously to the Saturday children's matinees. They actually employed a guy with a long pole who would tap the kids on their shoulders and order them to move up and make room, often to the extent that they would end up perched on the armrests.

So the cinema business caught on very well indeed. This meant that the sons were able to join in. In 1931 J.F. bought His Majesty's Theatre, which had newly gone bust. He did it up and reopened it in 1933. When he died of cancer later that year the four sons – including my father – had a flourishing business to inherit. It was shared out so that each of them got their quarter share. The eldest son, James, ran the ballroom and later theatre, my father, Herbert, took on the Union Street cinemas – he was the second son – while Dick, the youngest, became a professional footballer and then later managed the ice rink and the remaining cinemas. They proved to be good opportunists: whenever rivals ran into trouble, the Donalds were able to step in and buy them out; they acquired the Capitol and the Majestic in this way. These were the jewels in the crown but now, of course, the Majestic has been demolished and the Capitol is now a façade for a gigantic office development.

My father's role was to run the Union Street cinemas and they included the Queens and the Playhouse in addition to the Majestic and Capitol. At its height the cinema empire comprised 13 establishments with outposts in Inverurie, Torry, Kittybrewster and Stonehaven. During the war people continued to flock to get their weekly cinema fix and as the cinema was a reserved occupation – for morale purposes – the Donalds had rather a fortunate war. Father also ran the Beach Pavilion during its summer season, while the Capitol was often used for big variety shows with stars such as George Formby and Guy Mitchell appearing.

You couldn't call the Donalds an intellectual lot. They had bags of business knowhow but were pretty philistine in their outlook. I doubt whether my father ever read more than a couple of books in his life and I wouldn't say he really had much appreciation of the cinema either, except as a business. They were all solid Aberdeen businessmen rather than gentlemen of culture and refinement.

I looked on my father's business with a fair bit of pride. It was good to be able to walk down Union Street and think to myself: 'That's one of ours – and so is that one!' We had cinemas all over Aberdeen; the Donalds had a great presence in the city.

I would describe my father's interests as typical of his class of the time. It wouldn't be unfair to use the term philistine. The world of academia and that of the arts meant very little to him. His spare time meant golf or coffee at Isaac Benzies with his pals – who were drawn from the retail sector too. He mixed with his own kind, sharing their prejudices and narrowness of interests, no doubt.

My father worked long hours. He'd be there every afternoon and evening ready to greet his customers as they went into the Capitol or the Majestic, there at the top of the stairs, dressed in dinner jacket and bow tie. That's a ritual he kept up right into the 1960s.

Sid Donald as he is today, in retirement and enjoying the sun at his Athens home.

The four Donald brothers discussing plans for the Kingsway Cinema, 1938, with the architect Leslie Rollo (seated). From left: Richard, Herbert, James, Peter.

My father was a genuinely kind man but I must admit that the Donalds weren't exactly imaginative employers. They tended to take people for granted and hadn't much insight into them as individuals. For example, there was a marvellous old book-keeping lady who wrote everything down in longhand – no computers in those days – and yet she was almost ignored and was never very well rewarded. That was the sort of person, those who left school at 15, entered the firm and stayed there loyally and dutifully for the whole of the rest of their working lives yet left with scarcely a word of genuine gratitude.

And things could get quite spicy too. Not all was sweetness and light among the Donald brothers, believe me. More than once there'd be rows that would result in actual fisticuffs. I remember the day when one uncle hit another smack in the face and smashed his specs. They ended up rolling under the boardroom table, sibling rivals even into their 60s. It was occasionally a bit raw in tooth and claw in the Aberdeen business world of those days – screams and stand-up shouting.

Sidney (Sid) Donald, b.1942. Donalds' cinemas. Interviewed 2013.

Gladys Morrice: Taken on her 96th birthday, February 2016.

HOMELY DELIGHTS

Come and have your morning

It was a habit in those days where we lived in George Street; we had the top bit and these people had the middle bit and always on New Year's Day you invited your neighbour in for what they called a 'morning': 'Come and have your morning.' That was a nip of whisky.

Well, this year my mother couldn't afford to buy a bottle of whisky but they'd a little bit in an old bottle. She says: 'We'll have to ask John up for his morning; what are we going to do?' My Father says: 'I'll easy manage,' and he poured this little bit of whisky into a glass. Then he took the teapot, and he measured some tea into the other glass with a bit of water until he got them the same colour. My mother sweated blood in case my father got the glasses mixed up and she said 'Oh Philip, be careful! Philip, watch yourself!' She was in a terrible state.

John came up and my father gave him his whisky, and he stood and sipped his and never made a face, and everything was okay. When he went way, I can mind my mother said: 'Thank God for that! Oh, what a state I was in in case you gave him the wrong glass.'

Gladys Morrice, b.1920 King Street. Interviewed 2016.

Excitement of inside toilets and telephones

Whilst we were at No. 4, we got an inside toilet fitted, which my Mum still speaks about as being a major thing – which kids nowadays would find bizarre. I do remember when our first telephone was installed. That was really exciting. My dad worked for the Police as a cell block attendant. It was fitted on a Saturday morning and my dad was working a six to two shift. Obviously they knew what the number was in advance and my Dad phoned from work and Mum made me answer the phone and say the number. I remember being very excited speaking to Dad on this new phone, a big handset with a dial on the front. I remember it had your number on it and the number to dial for emergencies -'999' – was printed on your phone. I remember

The effects of one of Kathleen Porter's 'proper winters' of her childhood.

going shopping that afternoon and meeting my cousins in Littlewoods and telling them we'd had a phone fitted that morning and telling them what the number was – and this was a great thing. It was 575161 which has still stuck with me.

Dianne Morrison, b.1967. Rosemount. Interviewed 2015.

Proper winters back then

I remember when our neighbour, Charlie Cruickshank, built an igloo in the back garden. Winter back then was a proper winter, when snow was piled high like a wall on either side of the road.

Kathleen Porter, b.1932. Albion Street. Interviewed 2016.

Family picnics on the Cairn o' Mount

One of the lovely things I really remember from my childhood – when I was about seven or eight – on a Sunday we would leave about eight o'clock in the morning and there would be five cars: the grandparents to the youngest grandchildren, everybody went. The first car would take the pot of soup, next car they'd take the beef, the next would take the tatties and so on, and that's just how it went. We took a length of rope and a ball and we'd go away to the Cairn o' Mount or some other places, but the Cairn o' Mount was a favourite. We'd stop beside a wee stream and we had everything there for the day; we didn't need anything else. And we would stay there until maybe about six o'clock at night. Then our treat coming home was to stop at a chip shop. Somebody was allocated to go in: 'Can we get 14 fish, three pies, a black pudding?'

Marion Douglas, b.1948 Bucksburn. Interviewed 2016.

I can remember the decorations and seeing everything, and that's all we wanted. We didn't get anything; just being taken out to see the decorations was a great treat.

We hung up our stocking on Hogmanay

I'd got a half day from school because it was very bad weather and my grandmother said to me: 'Have you got a half day? Oh, that's fine. Peggy'll take you and Doris to see Santie at Isaac Benzies.'

Now, that was such a treat; I recall every bit of that. We walked round from King Street to Isaac Benzies. I can remember the decorations and seeing everything, and that's all we wanted. We didn't get anything; just being taken out to see the decorations was a great treat.

When I look at the kids today and what they get for Christmas! Now, I wasn't different; all the children were the same. You hung up your stocking – but we didn't hang it up on Christmas Eve; in Scotland you hung it up on Hogmanay night; Santie came on New Year's Day.

The men didn't even stop work on Christmas Day; they got New Year's Day off but Christmas was nothing up here. You hung up your stocking on Hogmanay and you got coppers in the point of the stocking – maybe even a sixpence – and you got an apple and an orange and a chocolate Santie. That was mostly what all the kids got; they didn't expect anything else except you got one present. I can remember my mother giving me sixpence a week to run down to a shop in George Street to pay for the Christmas presents.

Gladys Morrice, b.1920. King Street. Interviewed 2016.

Ye get 'em half price fae Harriet Street

I can remember there was a place in Harriet Street, off Schoolhill and that was Mitchell & Muil's shop for getting rid of their bakery that they hadn't sold the day before – and it was cheap there, half price or less. And there used to be great queues waiting there before eight o'clock in the morning.

The lady that stayed beneath us was a war widow and they had a hard time. She went out cleaning at E&Ms [Esslemont & McIntosh], away at six o'clock in the morning, and her two kids had to get their own breakfast and their own way to school. And she had a boy – he's done very well – and I can remember when he was a kid, his mother had some of her late husband's visitors down for afternoon tea. And there he was, Kenny Hunter, sitting at the table and she had a few nice cakes on the table.

This lady said to him: 'These are very nice cream cakes.'

Kenny pipes up and says: 'I went up for them. Ye get 'em half price fae Harriet Street if ye ging the day efter.'

Mrs Hunter says: 'I could have killed him.'

But the woman was gracious enough to say 'Oh well, whether you got them half price or not, they're very nice cakes and I am enjoying them.'

But that would have been Kenny Hunter, you see. And he came one time – he's travelled the world – to the Senior Citizens, and he gave us a talk and he had some slides on the Himalayas. I reminded him and he laughed and said: 'My God, those were hard up days, weren't they?' They really were; they were living from hand to mouth.

Gladys Morrice, b.1920. King Street. Interviewed 2016.

Grandma liked her fags

Grandma liked her cigarettes – Woodbines.

I don't know how the budgie in that house survived because it was like wading through fog.

Wendy Bradford, b.1972. Forbesfield Road. Interviewed 2016.

Just like grandma? The four-year-old Wendy Bradford trying a pipe for size.

Far did ye say Mam and Dad's awa till?

Back in the early days in Torry I would never have thought of us going foreign holidays. I must have been old enough to be left on my own but I was still a young lad when I got left for a fortnight and my parents went off to Torquay. They drove to Torquay taking something like three days.

Our neighbours couldn't believe that they'd gone on a holiday. The chap next door said to me, more than once: 'Far did ye say yer Mam and Dad's awa til?'

'Far did ye say....' In this case Arbroath. Alex with mother, early 1950s, on a family outing to the miniature railway.

So they were away down to the south of England and nobody could get over it. My father worked in Barry, Hendry & Cook, and again it's hard to believe, but in his early days there they literally locked the door for a fortnight; you didn't get paid. They had to give them a holiday so they just locked them out. They didn't get holiday pay or anything! It's just a different world now. You'd think I'm speaking about the 1800s but I'm not.

Alex Rae, b.1947. Torry. Interviewed 2016.

A close up of the 125cc BSA Bantam model Dennis Scott rode.

THE CHANGING SCENE

Once a biker always a biker

Just about the biggest development for young people in the early 1960s was the opening of the 62 Club in Summer Street. This was run by the Council and offered young folk the opportunity to practise a whole range of interests – sewing, photography, film, disco music, art. Some of us built up a motorbike section. At the back of the building was the old playground dating back to the days when it had been a school and in it stood the old bomb shelters. These became our workshops, complete with tools and a lathe, a place where we could tinker around with our machines, compare notes concerning specifications and any alterations we were attempting to make.

Always a biker: Dennis began his riding career as a telegram boy, buzzing about on a bike like 'AGF 156' depicted here.

We were for ever trying to perfect our bikes, not only to improve the performance but also the appearance. Those bikes could act as a great attraction for the opposite sex; I was now going steady and my girlfriend joined the club and became a member of the biking clique alongside myself. We were conscious of ourselves as forming a very special group. There were about a dozen of us and we would go out on runs together, usually out on the Deeside Road to the Coffee Pot at Culter. That run made for an ideal opportunity to try out our paces and to get up speed, sometimes being chased by the police. A whole swarm of us would also congregate at the Boulevard and ride up and down Union Street, all cylinders blazing. Our intention was to make something of a splash – we must have been a real noisy nuisance to the ordinary citizen.

We attired ourselves in leathers which sported various badges. Helmets weren't compulsory then so we could roar along with our hair streaming out in the wind and feel

His pride and joy: Following his spell with the Post Office, Dennis served as a fireman. A life – long fascination with machines has led him to work to preserve models such as this 1895 horse drawn Shand Masson engine.

ourselves to be the kings of the highway.

Once you reached the age of 21 you had to leave the 62 Club. But we bikers still continued our exploits and the sharing of memories. Since those days we've had a number of reunions. Though the helmet is mandatory nowadays – just as well as some of us would have difficulty in making our thinning hair fly out in the wind.

I still have a bike. Once a biker, always a biker, you see! Of course as you get older and have a family you have to graduate to a family car but I always return to my bike. It's in the blood. This is what the car driver can't understand as he sits encased in his metal box – that the motorbike is more than just a handy machine; it is a personal possession, a creature almost, which becomes part of you. As you sit astride it out there in the open, crouched over the handlebars going through the gears and making it roar into life, you can feel part of something that is alive. A motorbike can respond to your moods in a way that a car cannot. You can decide which aspect of yourself you're going to express today – whether to kick the bike into a high-speed race through the countryside or whether you are going to settle for a nice quiet spin, tootling about, taking in the scenery. Even now I'm at it, building up a machine, fussing around its engine, looking out for a new part here and there. I'm not ready to join the slipper brigade just yet.

Dennis Scott, b.1946. The 62 Club. Interviewed 2015.

That Marlon Brando look. A 19-year-old Alistair Brown sporting leather jacket, drain pipe trousers and a Tony Curtis DA haircut.

Marlon Brando was my role model

When I was moving through adolescence in the 1950s everything was beginning to change; the concept of the teenager was born and the notion of young people enjoying their own individuality in music and fashion began to take off. I must say I embraced it all. At Robert Gordon's College I had hated the whole regime of uniforms and conformity and couldn't wait to get out.

My role model became Marlon Brando – I had seen the film 'The Wild One' and I was hugely taken with his hair, his dress, his whole attitude. I was into a black leather jacket, blue suede shoes, drain pipe trousers and I had a Lurex shirt with sparkling threads running through it. I got a Tony Curtis haircut, with a DA at the back, and rode a motor bike. The result was that I was refused entry to Madame Murray's on account of this 'outlandish' dress.

This was the time when rock 'n roll first hit Aberdeen. I was at the very first dance to this exciting new music – 'Eddie Watson and his Alligators' in the Music Hall. I went along in the correct attire for the occasion: one lime green sock and one in shocking pink. I followed Elvis and Bill Haley and was deeply impressed by the film 'Blackboard Jungle.' When it came to the Majestic some teenagers were there, tearing up the seats in sympathy with the rebellious messages of the film. Musically, I was never into the Beatles and certainly not the likes of Cliff Richard; I much preferred the edgier sounds of Chuck Berry and the Rolling Stones.

You could describe me as a rebel but I never looked for trouble and certainly didn't indulge in violence or destructive behaviour. All I wanted to do was to escape the stifling conformity of the previous generation, the collar-and-tie folk, and assert our youthful freedoms to have our own identity. Really, what I was doing was to embrace the spirit of an age when rationing had come to an end, there was more money in our pockets and more colour entering our lives. In that way I was simply a creature of the time.

Alistair Brown, b.1940. Hilton Drive. Interviewed 2015.

A wonderful period to be young in

I didn't fully realise it at the time but the Sixties were a wonderful period to be young in. Our lives were so much easier than our parents' had been, what with their struggles through the war and then the austerity of the following years. But for us the age meant freedom. Yet the influence of our parents' sense of duty and of a properly organised community was still around us. I could go out into the town at night and never feel threatened. Oh, you knew not to go down to the harbour or to Hadden Street after dark for fear of being accosted, but everywhere else was considered quite secure. I'd go up to Northfield in the dark without qualms. I never heard of any of my friends running into trouble either.

The Fifties seemed like a sepia decade while the Sixties burst out into glorious colour.

The joy of being young. An 18 year old Meg Forbes at the Arts Ball, 1962. Future husband Gordon pays his homage.

At school it was a matter of strict uniform: skirts at a decent length, blouse with tie and a tunic. But whereas girls at the beginning of the decade had aspired to do no more than be dressed like their own mothers, later we could choose our own fashion statements. There was a craze for vividly coloured stockings, duffel coats, miniskirts.

I didn't think I was too way out but I do recall an incident where my father showed me he thought otherwise. I was in Union Street just by the Music Hall when I saw him approaching with a stranger at his side, deep in conversation. I prepared for the usual greeting but to my dismay he simply swept past me without any acknowledgement. When I got home I tackled him; at first he claimed not to have seen me but eventually admitted that, yes, he had. 'Then why didn't you speak to me?' I demanded. 'Well, I wasn't going to introduce you to anyone when you were looking such a mess!'

Margaret (Meg) Forbes, b.1944. Northfield. Interviewed 2015.

Things were different then... Joe Scott, aged nine, years before Gentlemen's 'clubbing' was part of the Aberdeen scene.

It's not like it used to be

We've been married 48 years. We started going out when I was 18; we got wed six years later when I came out of the RAF. It's not like nowadays: I was at a wedding two years ago; it was in April; by November they were divorced!

Social life has changed: there's much more going out and spending money; much more drinking. If you drive through the centre of town at night you see incredible goings on among the young people.

Over the Christmas period I helped this chap out with his one-man business. Afterwards he took me out for a meal. We had a meal at Café Society and then he suggested we walked down into Union Street, for some clubbing. I'd never been in a club before so he took me to 'Chicago.' The noise was overpowering; you couldn't hear each other speak; you had to shout at each other.

Then he took me to this 'gentlemen's club' in Chapel Street. A men-only establishment. It was full of these girls just about naked, with nothing to cover themselves but a couple of elastic bands. It was supposed to cost you £5 every time you danced with one. They all seemed to be foreign. I stuck to Diet Coke and refused to go up. One of them invited me for a dance behind the curtain; the deal is that she can touch you but you mustn't touch her – there are CCTV cameras to keep a check. I asked her age: 'Nineteen.' 'Look', I told her: 'I've got a granddaughter who's older than that.' Changed days.

Joe Scott, b.1933. Chapel Street. Interviewed 2005.

Not a hair out of place! A 16-year-old Louise Baxter is bridesmaid at a cousin's wedding.

My time at High came to a premature end

My time at the High School came to a somewhat premature end, and for that I blame the Rolling Stones. I had reached Year 4 and the Stones were coming to Aberdeen to play in the Capitol. I had a friend whose father was a policeman and who knew the route the group would be taking so some of us decided to go down and give them a welcome. My other friends all went home to change out of their uniforms but as my mother would be out at her work I wasn't in a position to do this so I had to go along in my High School regalia.

We all lined up, very excited, and sure enough along came the car carrying the Stones. It had to stop at the traffic lights, at which point there was a surge forward by the crowd and I found myself pressed up against the car. Its window was half open; I was pushed further forward and managed to get my hand in the window and grab at Mick Jagger's hair. A lock of it came away so there I was, standing at the roadside as the vehicle sped off, with a clump of Mick Jagger's hair in my hand.

For me this was a memorable moment and so it was too for Mick Jagger: 20 years later when he returned to the city and was interviewed about his previous experience here he recalled the day some of his hair was pulled out by a young Aberdonian female. But my

exploit had repercussions; I had been observed by a policeman who then grabbed hold of me, took one look at my High School uniform and promptly marched me back up the road to the school, lecturing me on my behaviour all the way.

The inevitable interview with Miss MacNab ensued. We came to an agreement that it would be best if I left the school and pursue my academic career elsewhere. I enrolled in Aberdeen College.

Louise Baxter, b.1948. The Rolling Stones. Interviewed 2015.

Safe in their dressing room, the Rolling Stones are being interviewed by P&J reporter Julie Davidson during their 1965 gig in Aberdeen. From left: Mick Jagger, Keith Richards, Charlie Watts, Brian Jones, Bill Wyman.
[PHOTO: ABERDEEN JOURNALS]

THE WORLD OF WORK:
The Public Sector

How it was: at the start of Doug Smith's long career. Here PC Hill, helmet firmly on, interrogates some lads in the Green, 1935. [PHOTO: ABERDEEN JOURNALS]

A life well lived:
Doug Smith in his 90s.

THE POLICE AND FIRE SERVICES

I would still rather have been a journalist!

My father was in the police. I came from a policing family: I had four uncles in the Force and heaps of cousins, too. But I never wanted to be a policeman myself. I was never impressed by my old man's way of life. He was a country policeman and was at the beck and call of everyone, night and day.

So I started out as a journalist on the 'Mearns Leader.' But this was only at 10 shillings a week and my digs came to 15 so in the end I felt I had no alternative but to join the police after all.

I did my police training in Aberdeen. Before you were let loose on the public you had three months learning the ropes. You studied police law, you learned to swim, did traffic drill and unarmed combat. You had to prove your physical fitness.

The pay started off at £2.10.4d a week – good for that period, in 1939. I was on the beat as an ordinary constable for 10 years. Over the following 20 years I got a series of promotions and ended up as an inspector. Most of the public were friendly enough and seemed to appreciate our presence but you did encounter some hostility. Some looked upon us as no more than a necessary evil and others as worse than that.

I've got a story which illustrates the point. It was my very first day on the beat. In those days when you first went out you would be accompanied by an experienced constable who would be showing you the ropes. It was over in Torry. So into the sub-station I went, trying desperately to make myself as inconspicuous as possible. There came a rap at the door. Someone had broken into the Maple Dairy in Victoria Road. He had been seen trying to make a getaway down Crombie Road; if we went at once we might be able to catch him. The two of us came running out of the station. 'Right', instructed my older colleague: 'you chase him on foot while I go to the top of the road on my bike and that way we'll trap him.'

So off I set, very conscious of my brand new uniform and my brand new helmet. By

Waiting for the clock to strike eight: A crowd gathers outside Craiginches Prison on the morning of Harry Burnett's execution.
[PHOTO: ABERDEEN JOURNALS]

this time a whole crowd was gathering, keen to see the fun. Someone shouted out: 'Bobby! He's in the wood yard.' Sure enough I could see his figure at the far end of the yard. So I went off in pursuit, having to clamber over piles and stacks of wood. He scaled the gate, with me in hot pursuit. I attempted to leap up after him but my helmet fell off and began to roll along the ground. Some kids began to play football with it. But the both of us landed on the ground more or less together and my colleague was able to apprehend him.

I returned to the crowd to retrieve my helmet and my dignity. Quite a mob of folk had gathered and were enjoying the entertainment. As I was picking up my helmet, I heard this shout from the crowd: 'Hey, baby-face! does your mother know you're out?' All rather embarrassing.

I had a spell in the CID, handling 'sudden deaths' – suicides and accidents at work or on the road mostly. This could be distressing. My task was often to go to the house and break the news as gently as I could – but that wasn't easy when you were telling a wife that the man she had said: 'Good-bye' to just a few hours before was now no more.

I remember once I had to go to this address with the news that the husband had been killed at his work. First I knocked at the door of a neighbour, asked her how well she knew the woman involved and if she could possibly go with me to help break some tragic news. I was in plain clothes so when I knocked at the door the woman inside promptly invited us in. I informed her of the sad news; all she said was: 'Oh! but I really must get on with the washing.' But when I returned later in the day I found her quite broken up. Some people react to bad news with hysterics, others quite stoically and some – as in this case – by going into a delayed shock.

Another big memory is the last execution to take place in Aberdeen, that of Henry James Burnett. I had been on duty at the High Court when Lord Wheatley passed

The Deputy Chief came up to me: 'I've got some news for you.' I replied: 'I hope it's good news.' 'Well, not exactly. You have to be present at the execution on Thursday.'

sentence on him. He had been found guilty of murder; he had been caught up in a love triangle with the wife of another man and had ended up shooting him. I was required to be in attendance at the actual execution.

But when the time came I had another thing entirely on my mind. It was the Friday evening beforehand and I had taken my wife and daughter to the circus. Half way through she turned to me and said: 'Oh, Doug! I'm not feeling at all well.' We saw the performance out and I took her home. But I was due to go on night shift so I had to leave her in bed, feeling quite poorly.

When I got back home the next morning I could see things had got worse. I called the doctor. I'll never forget what he told me after his examination: 'Your wife is gravely ill. I must warn you that in my opinion she only has a 50-50 chance of pulling through.'

I had to go again on duty that night but fortunately the family rallied round and helped out. When I reported back to the station the Deputy Chief came up to me: 'I've got some news for you.' I assumed it was about my wife so I replied: 'I hope it's good news.' 'Well, not exactly. You have to be present at the execution on Thursday.' Immediately the thought flashed through my mind: 'Well, that means two deaths for me this week – my wife and Harry Burnett.'

The next day I had to attend various meetings in connection with the execution. Then on the Tuesday the Deputy Town Clerk phoned me up. I would have to go and pick up a large case and take it to Craiginches. I was told that it contained a big bottle of brandy and several glasses.

On the Thursday of the execution I had to be at the prison by 7.30AM. A group of us were mustered to be in attendance: the Prison Governor, two prison officers, a minister of the church, a doctor, two magistrates, the Deputy Chief Constable and myself. At 7.55 we proceeded upstairs to the execution chamber. My task was to stand there and observe the party going into the gallows and to identify Burnett as the man I had seen sentenced at the High Court.

Burnett came out between a pair of warders and I lifted my hand to signify that it was indeed him. He appeared to be quite calm; he even had a slight smile on his face. He was then taken onto the scaffold and hung by the neck. Afterwards we all retired to the Governor's room. There the doctor got out the case with the brandy and announced: 'Well, gentlemen, we have had a harrowing experience so I suggest we all partake of a drop of brandy.' But I was on duty and not supposed to drink any alcohol. I looked at the Deputy Chief and he said: 'In view of the exceptional circumstances I am prepared to offer a dispensation. You may take your drink.' I am glad I did; I found that the tot did help to steady the nerves.

When I got up to the hospital that evening the news was much better. I found my wife sitting up in bed with a copy of the 'Evening Express' on her lap. She'd been reading the report of the execution.

Since my career began there have been many changes to policing. In the past you were still free to hand out summary justice to a young pest by giving a kick up the backside or a simple clip round the ear accompanied by the threat of informing the

'Our equipment was pretty basic' – but at least it was an advance on these pre-war bike radios.

parents, safe in the knowledge that the father would like as not give a slap to the other side of the face and would regard the whole incident as bringing shame to his family. Now it's more likely that the parent will report the matter to a solicitor and raise an action under the heading of 'human rights.' The only time you are allowed to lay a hand on anyone is when you are actually arresting them.

In my day any number wanted to join the City Police and we had little difficulty in enlisting a high standard. It was a good cross-section too, everyone from tradesmen and ex-Army to university graduates. And now there's a proposal to make all recruits university people with degrees. I think this is a mistake; you need to keep the doors open to people with life experience, not just book learning.

After all, police work encompasses a great range of demands: one minute you can be attending a murder, next assisting a blind person across the street and, in between, directing the traffic, chasing a burglar, attending an accident, helping an old age pensioner in distress and so on. That for me was one of the great attractions of the job – even if I still think I'd rather have been a journalist.

Douglas (Doug) Smith, b.1919. Aberdeen City Police. Interviewed 2015.

Equipment on the beat was pretty basic

I was PC 312. Back then in the early 1960s, walking the beat and maintaining a public presence was the leading strategy. The city was divided into four districts and one of them – in my case the south – became mine. Each district was supported by one car, which had a driver and a police passenger. You could call on the assistance of the car but basically you were on your own, pounding the streets, being visible to the public and

They look smart – but did they have heaters? The Aberdeen City Police fleet of the 1950s.

ensuring that everything was in order. Basic communication still relied upon the police box system; if you spotted an orange light flashing on one of the several boxes positioned on your beat then you would have to open it up with your key and find out what was what. Strict time keeping was essential.

The public still find the presence of the bobby on the beat reassuring but that belongs to an age which is more or less past. When I started out, walking the beat was still a practical proposition and a handful of bobbies could cover the whole city that way. This was because the population mostly lived in densely packed tenement buildings and a 50-yard walk would enable you to cover a large number of homes, shops and business premises. Nowadays the population is much more spread out; the individual house has largely supplanted the tenement block and many businesses have moved out to the estates and shopping malls on the periphery.

All this has meant that the patrol car is now the staple method of policing the city and the methods I was involved in back in the 1960s seem quite primitive. Yet at the time our transport was considered state of the art. We used Humber cars, big strong vehicles. But their heaters were stripped out because it was thought to be pampering the police to give them the same standard of in-car warmth that the public had. Being a policeman is a serious business; you don't go around in a car for a warm up.

The equipment of the bobby on the beat was pretty basic: radio, truncheon, handcuffs and whistle – and the all-important notebook. You were expected to keep meticulous records, fit to be used as evidence if necessary. You would go around looking out for any sign of things not being in order, trying door handles to ensure premises were tightly secured and so on.

I wouldn't claim to have been the bravest of officers; on a night patrol you could feel a spot of apprehension at the sound of a rat scuttling across a dark lane or a cat clanging into a bin. I was never one for rushing into trouble. One of my colleagues did go in to deter a robbery and got badly beaten up with his own truncheon; you were always aware that something similar could happen to you. But the work was interesting; you were serving the public and you were doing something worthwhile.

The work had its funny moments too. I remember one evening as I was on my beat in King Street at the time when the Kingsway bingo came out. One moment everything would be calm, the next the pavements and the roadway itself would be swarming with punters, so much so that the traffic would be brought to a halt. I was determined to demonstrate my authority and to show that matters had to be brought under control. So

I marched into the middle of King Street and began to direct the traffic with a fine flourish of policeman-like power. Unfortunately, a sudden gust of wind got up, blew my hat off and sent it bowling along the road. So I had to abandon my post and get down on my knees in an attempt to retrieve my hat from under the wheels of a bus – much to the amusement of the very crowd I had been attempting to discipline.

Society as a whole back then seemed to work on a basis of mutual trust. There was give and take on both sides; the public understood how we had to go about our business and on our side we would offer them a certain flexibility by focusing on the important wrongdoings and tolerate those minor breaches which tick over in any community. If you went to a house in pursuit of a theft then all you needed to say was: 'Can I just give the property a look over?' and you would be let in to do it. Nowadays the likely response is: 'Have you got a search warrant?'

In the past there were recognised important and respected members of any community – the minister, the doctor, the head teacher and, yes, the police too – the so called pillars of the community. There was an acceptance that there were certain people in positions of power which society depended upon for its welfare, that though mistakes might be made, on the whole, these powerful people were on the side of keeping society going.

What I am talking about is not confined to the police; it's a general feature of modern society and the way it has developed. In the old days, people were joined together by common experiences, by the grapevine of gossip and daily meetings. People stayed in the one place, worked together, visited each other's homes, knew what their families were up to and where people went to work. Now society is much more scattered and subject to constant comings and goings. The door to door exchange of local news has given way to the virtual reality of the social media.

With this the nature of crime has changed too. In the past, if there was a robbery, you could be sure that the culprit was to be found in the neighbourhood and you could make your enquiries by knocking on doors and asking: 'Where were you last night?' and so on. Or the detectives would pay a visit to the local pub where, from past experience, they knew there would be gossip and leads to pick up. Now the miscreants are just as likely to be driving into the district from miles away. Take the latest series of ATM robberies at spots like Newtonhill, Portlethen and Inverurie; they are probably the work of gangs from Merseyside or Glasgow, so where do you start your questioning now?

Alistair Ritchie, b.1944. Aberdeen City Police. Interviewed 2015.

...supplemented by the Panda car fleet which came into service 10 years later.

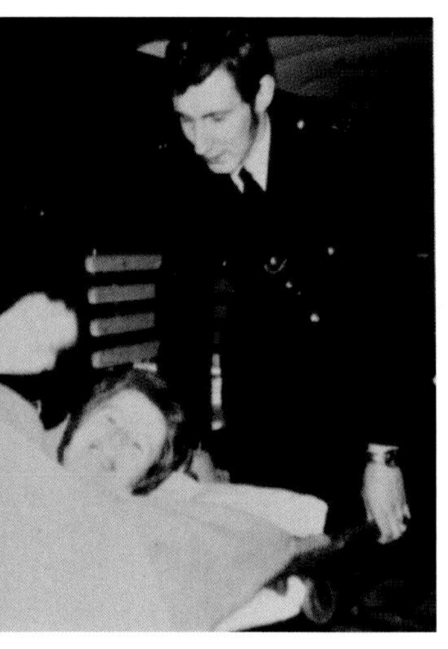

Off to give birth, in a Black Maria, with siren sounding and lights flashing.

Off to hospital in a Black Maria

I mind when my son, Chris, was born. It was time to go to the Matty and there was an ambulance strike on. So they said they hoped I didn't mind going off to hospital in a Black Maria; there's a picture of me waving as I'm being lifted on a stretcher into the back of it by a bobby. I said that I didn't mind but hoped they were going to put on the flashing light and the siren.

Marion Douglas b.1948, Bucksburn

When did you last see a policeman in the street?

After National Service, I applied to join Aberdeen City Police. My first day at Lodge Walk was quite amusing: measured for uniforms, sorted out your pay and getting things organised. Then in the afternoon each of the four of us who joined that day was seconded to somebody in plainclothes from the General Enquiries Department. I was put along with this chap and I didn't know where we were going or what we were doing. However, we got on fine, having a walk up Union Street where we turned left at Holburn Junction and then into the Justice Mill Lane toilet. We took observations in the toilet from behind the screens for an hour and a half. I booked off at five o'clock and came home. Naturally there were questions over the tea table: 'What were you doing today?'

'I got measured for my uniforms, I saw the doctor, we had our dinner and then I was allocated to this plainclothes officer and spent the afternoon in the toilets.' 'You did what?' asks my Mother. 'What were you doing in the toilets? What was going on there?' It was a very interesting tea-table conversation.

The focus of police work in Aberdeen changed greatly over my years in the Force. When I'd started in the early Sixties, we were told that to 'Guard, Watch and Patrol' was the mainstay of the job. It was a fine job for meeting people, and helping them if you could. You'd have to remember that at that time, in the early Sixties, we didn't have radios. We just had the lamps on boxes along the street that would flash and that's when you knew that somebody was needing you. You had to report in to hear if there had been an accident or a fight or so on.

Outside of the city centre, you got a police bike. When I was at Brierfield sub-station in Stockethill the bikes were kept through the back and one day the sergeant came in, complaining that they weren't being put to use. He said: 'There's a spider there leaving webs on the wheels so you can see they're not getting used.' So one of the boys spoke to the Sergeant the following day and said: 'Well, Sergeant, I've solved your problem with the bikes. There'll be no more webs – I've killed the spider!'

On the beat on a nightshift back then, after the pubs shut at half past nine or 10 o'clock, everybody went away to their beds, more or less, and then you had to check

properties: the windows and the doors and the back of the tenements. That took up a fair bit of time. You had to do that between 10 and one o'clock in the morning; then you got your piece between one and quarter to two. After 45 minutes for your sandwich or whatever, you'd to go back round the properties again. On the likes of George Street beats, for example, there's lots of property there and every door, every lobby would have to be looked into – quite often disturbing courting couples.

The Lodge Walk police HQ where Ken Raitt began his career in the 1960s. It was demolished and rebuilt in 1972.

Eventually, I became Inspector. As such I was in charge of a shift looking after a number of men at a time over the whole four districts of the city. In my time we were still hands-on to some extent and hopefully knew what was going on – but no longer checking that the bobby on the beat was in the right place at three o'clock in the morning. That had long gone by then; the boys didn't have time for that. They were busy all the time. When did you last see a policeman in the street? They just go from call to call to call and there aren't enough of them. The administration has become an ever-greater part of the job.

Our boys got overtime if they wished on a Friday or Saturday evening for a special patrol, or an extra patrol along Union Street. It's different now. To see Union Street now or Justice Mill Lane or Belmont Street, I'd be frightened to go down there myself late at night at a weekend. The biggest effect on that is due to the licensing hours, with places open until three and four o'clock in the morning. I've got grandchildren who go out at 10 o'clock at night. When I was courting, I had to have Sheila home by half-past nine at

The changing face of the Aberdeen bobby: left 1903 Police Constable; centre, a 1935 PC; right, 1972.

night; her father's last words as we went out were always: 'Don't make it late.' I can remember him saying that. If you'd gone to the pictures you'd have to run for your bus from Kittybrewster down to Gairn Terrace. It's so different now – everybody has cars and their own flats, and loads of money to drink. I don't believe there's any good in it.

There were a number of distressing things that happened during my 30 years in the Police. What affected me badly was whenever I was involved in cases of cot death. When still a constable, there was one instance where the baby was taken down to the mortuary and the Police Surgeon – Dr Hendry at that time – asked if I would go back to the house and retrieve the cot, the blanket and the baby's bottle. So, on his instructions, I went back to the house and obviously the parents were very upset and it was quite a task to take possession of those items. The distressed parents put up quite a fight to stop us taking items from the house so that the doctor could complete his examination and inquiry. Those sorts of things certainly left their mark on my mind.

One morning, when I was in uniform and sergeant in charge of the MSU [Mobile Support Unit], I and five PCs were called to the Royal Darroch Hotel in Cults; that was in October 1983. We went right out there and were met by this horrific scene. There was a mess of fire and rubble and three or four bodies lying in the forecourt of the hotel. The Fire Officers and ambulances were already on the scene. That was a Major Incident that I'll never forget; seeing what was waiting when we arrived.

Kenneth (Ken) Raitt, b.1939. Aberdeen City Police. Interviewed 2016

You can't do 30 years in the Fire Service without a few narrow escapes

By the time you'd done your 30 years in the Fire Service you're saying to yourself, that's enough. Well, I mean, it's not a normal job – that's why you retire at 55, because it's a pretty hard job. My fire service was all in the City and there were two stations: first King Street and then Anderson Drive opened. I was sent up there when it was brand new. It was a lovely station; now it's gone.

It's teamwork in the Fire Service; you had to work together. There was a certain amount of pride in being in the Fire Service. And the camaraderie was good. It was an unusual job, I enjoyed it; I had some good laughs – and some dodgy times as well.

I was at a few of the big incidents in Aberdeen – paint shops, paint stores, paint

factories. I was at that big one in the harbour, Isaac Spencer's. That was a big gut-out. And then I was at one in Flourmill Lane – another paint factory. That was gutted as well. There were a lot more that I went to. There were a few dodgy ones as well. Isaac Spencer's was explosions all the time because of chemicals. There was a big tank of spirits that we never knew was there and the guy came down who worked there – it was through the night – and he told us we were working where a tank of spirits was. So we got out.

You can't do 30 years without having a few narrow escapes. I once got electrocuted at a fire. This place was gutted out, the fire was out and there were a lot of wires hanging down like bunches of spaghetti. One fireman let out a yell when he was caught just as I came round the corner. He should have shouted 'Stop! Some of the wires are live!' – but he didn't. I thought he was stuck, or he'd collapsed, and as I tried to reach him, I just grabbed these hanging wires, thinking they were wires they'd used for wrapping up firewood. But there was one live wire among them and I was electrocuted as well – while stuck in water. So that was two of us electrocuted. I shouted: 'Cut the power!' at the top of my voice and somebody heard it and cut it. But this first guy never did that; and I asked him: 'Why didn't you shout to cut the power?' and he said: 'I dinna ken.' You meet them.

James (Jim) Butler, b.1923 Aberdeen Fire Brigade. Interviewed 2015.

'A big gut out'. The 1960 fire at Isaac Spencer's paint factory which Jim Butler helped to fight.
[PHOTO: ABERDEEN JOURNALS]

THE MEDICS

'Nae ticklin ma feet!' The message which Harry Gordon – in his famous panto dame guise – wrote on the back of this photograph he gave Isobel in thanks for her good care, not to mention some nifty acting.

The Nurse:
It's all about people

When I got to my Fifth year at Turriff Academy I thought I would like to train as a teacher. A lady came out from the Training College in Aberdeen to assess me. She took one look at me and said: 'Oh, you're left handed. That will never do – such a bad example to the children.' My attitude was: 'Well, if that's what I'm going to be up against then I'll look elsewhere.'

There was nursing in the family; three of my older sisters had gone in for it. A cousin suggested I write to Foresterhill and see what came of it. Their response was: 'Come in with the next batch.' So that was that. I'd had some doubts; I'd visited my sister when she was Assistant Matron at Woodend and seen how she made everyone jump to her bidding. She was my own sister but in this role she seemed so strict and formidable that I thought to myself: 'Is this what nursing does to you?'

But I went along – and I've never regretted it. I like people and nursing is all about people. I love listening to folk, love observing their body language and trying to work out what they're about. The great thing about nursing is that once people fall ill and have to get between those sheets they all become the same – and they all need you. However grand or poor they may be outside, get them in your ward and they need the same things: comforting words, someone to take notice of them, to listen to their problems, to show a personal interest.

So I was off to Foresterhill in autumn 1952. The Matron was Florence Kaye, and she was always on the ball. She had a terrific memory that meant you couldn't get away with anything. You'd be a wee bit behind and might break into a run down the corridor and suddenly there she'd be, sticking her face round the door to her office, barking out: 'Nurse Morrison. Remember: haemorrhage or fire. Those are the only two things that you run for – the rest of the time you will walk like a lady. Walk like a lady and you'll be treated like a lady.'

She was strict but fair and the training as a whole was like that. We had to wear a formal uniform: blue grey dress, white apron, bib, starched cuff, starched collar. You had a tag on your belt so that everyone knew your year and position. All this was laundered on the premises; you weren't allowed to take anything away into the outside world.

You had to stay in the nurses' home. This meant indoors by 10.30 although you got one late pass per week – till 11PM. But there were ways and means: there was this window downstairs that led into the ducts and you could crawl through it, make your way

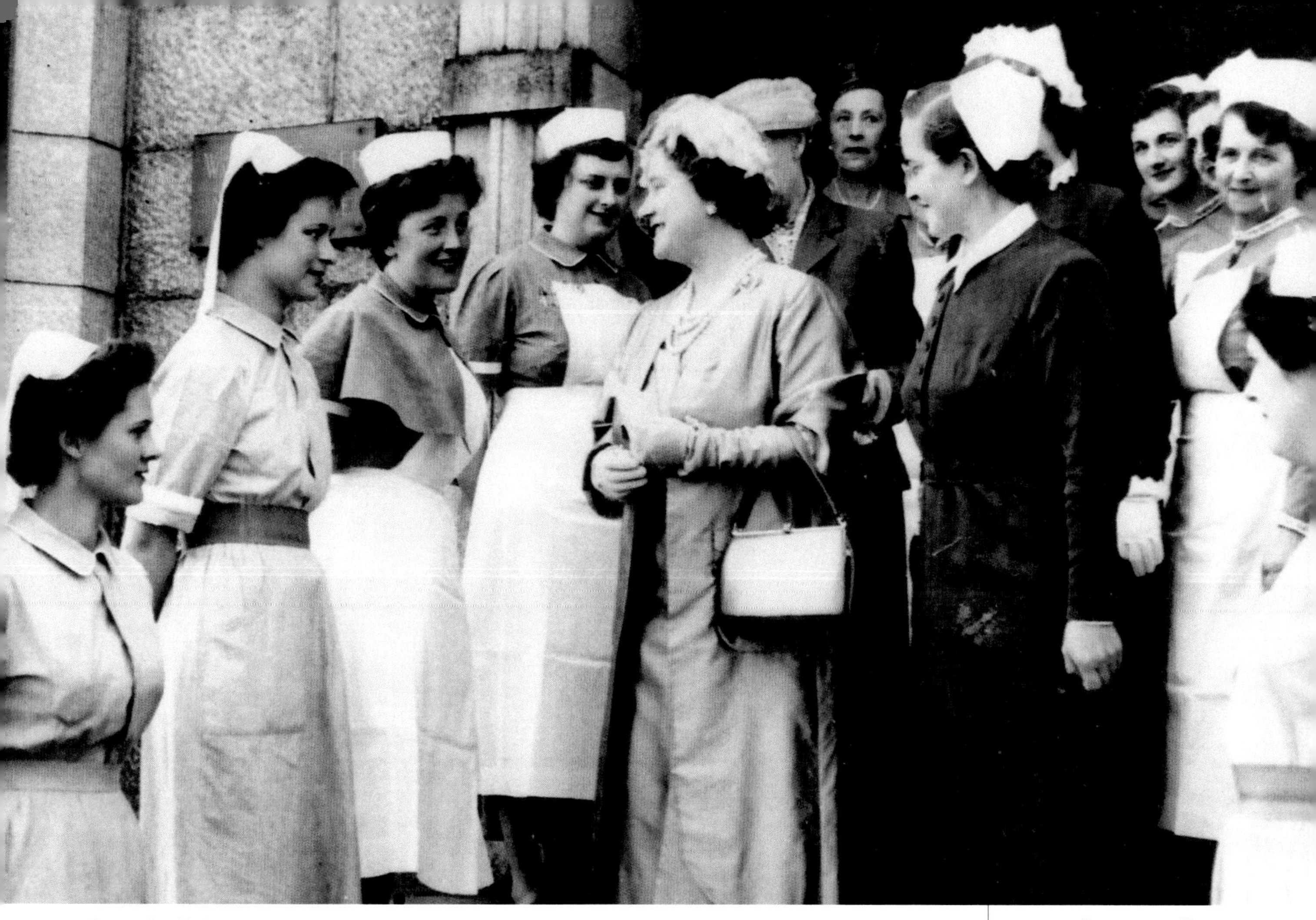

'How do you talk to a Queen?' The Queen Mother picks out Isobel for a few words at Foresterhill, 1959.

through all the pipes and then get up a back way into the floors above. I suspect the Matron knew what was going on but turned a blind eye to it. No doubt she'd done the same when she was in training.

Living in like that was actually a godsend. It meant that if you'd had a horrible day and were stressed out then there was always a friendly room you could go to and let it all pour out.

Mistakes to begin with were inevitable. On my first ward, I remember when I gave a diabetic patient too much insulin: 'Quick, give him a banana to eat!' That was the cure in those cases.

Then I had to confront my first dead patient; I remember standing looking down at the body and seeing it as just a shell, an empty vessel. It was in the gynaecology ward and we were nursing this lady who appeared to be doing fine, but then complications set in and we lost her. It happened while I was on night duty; I was devastated. I nearly packed it in there and then. But I got some strong advice from the sister: 'Look here, if you let yourself get emotionally involved like that then you'll be no good to anybody. You might as well pack your bags and leave right now if that's what's going to happen.'

We got up to some pretty mischievous ploys. There was this rather posh girl who would go out in a fur coat. She would then bring a boyfriend back and they would stand under the window, locked in a passionate goodnight while we could peep out at them from up above. One night we got a bucket of cold water and poured it over the top of them and quickly ducked back into the room. 'After all, she's wearing her fur coat so she won't even notice.'

And when we went out into the town it wasn't always true romance that we were

Were we allowed to take men back into the Nurses' Home? You must be joking.

after. We'd go to the Douglas Hotel where the young farmers tended to go and hope you'd end up with a partner who had a car and could give you a lift home, up to Foresterhill. The food at the hospital was truly awful, so stodgy, so tasteless, that another consideration would be to find a new boyfriend rich enough to treat you out to decent meal.

Were we allowed to take men back into the Nurses' Home? You must be joking. At the end of our course we had a coming out ball at the Home and for this you had to submit a list of male guests so they could be properly vetted beforehand. It was our responsibility to organise the evening; I managed to book a dance band from Inverurie. I remember looking around towards the end of the evening and spotting a pair who didn't seem to have been up on the floor at all. So I felt I had to invite one of them to dance. Well, I could hardly get a word out of him but then he graciously informed me: 'I might give you a phone call, sometime.' 'Oh no you won't!' I thought to myself. But he did contact me – and I ended up marrying him…

In 1959 I was presented to the Queen Mother. She was visiting the Provost, Tommy Mitchell, who was a private patient and, as the night staff and going off duty, we were lined up at the entrance as she came in. There were all these consultants at the back, anxious to be introduced to her; we nurses were at the front. To my astonishment she stopped in front of me and asked: 'And what has brought you into nursing?' My first thought was should I curtsey? And how do you address a queen? But she was very nice and easy with us. I was struck by how tiny she was and how much make-up she was wearing. It gave her face this creamy, smooth complexion. And she had very elegant high heels on; I was sure she would trip going up the steps and become one of our patients.

One of my most memorable patients was Harry Gordon, the famous entertainer. He had had a heart attack and was recuperating at Foresterhill. It so happened that I was attached to his medical unit so I got to know him quite well; he was such a cheery, friendly character. As it also happened, I had taken on the responsibility for organising our nurses' Christmas concert for the patients. The challenge was always to go one better than the previous year so I was becoming a bit preoccupied by the whole task. I knew we had plenty of talent among us but where to get the material?

Well, I was in Harry's room one day with the thoughts of this concert at the back of my mind and he must have noticed that something was up. 'My, but you're lookin' awfu' glum the day.' So I told him my problem. Immediately his eyes lit up: 'Have you got anyone who can play the piano or can dance and sing?' 'Oh, yes, we've got plenty of that sort of talent,' I answered, 'but we're short of material.'

'Oh, if it's material you're needing then I can help.' So he began to write out a script on odd pieces of paper, the words and the music together, and I would try it out, there in front of him. So there was I, prancing about his room, terrified all the while that somebody would come in on us. I knew what the question would be: 'What on earth do you think you are doing, Nurse Morrison. You're here to nurse, not to play around!'

Here's some of what he devised for us, all set out in his own handwriting: 'We are the nurses on parade/ To entertain we're not afraid/ If it's laughter you're after/ There's nothing could be dafter/ Than nurses on parade.' Then he did a version of the hokey-cokey for us, which began with us holding a finger up and ended with us sticking our tongues out. He was the real professional; he would lie there in his bed and make me do everything over and over till it was just right; he would hum the music and insist on getting the correct tempo. And here he was, supposed to be observing a quiet regime. I was terrified that something might happen to him because of all these efforts.

The concert was great fun and went down a storm. We pushed a piano around from ward to ward and I played it while another nurse accompanied me on the accordion. Afterwards Harry asked: 'How did it go?' and I was able to tell him: 'It was the best concert yet.' And Miss Kaye, who would have sacked me on the spot if she'd known what had been going on, remarked: 'Well, that was a jolly good concert. How did you manage it all?'

Harry Gordon was such a nice man and a terrific patient, never complaining, always cheerful and bright. He told me: 'You know, getting involved in that concert was the best medicine I could have had. I was getting so bored just sitting in bed all day with nothing to do.

He had a thing about having very ticklish feet. The young nurses used to play up to him and tease him mercilessly and he them. After he was discharged he gave me a photograph of himself in one of his famous pantomime dame's roles and on the back he wrote out: 'To Isobel with all good wishes – and nae ticklin ma feet!'

To some extent Harry Gordon's approach to life has been mine too: keep busy; get involved; enjoy people – and let them enjoy you. Life's too short to waste it sitting back and acting as a spectator.

Isobel Corrigall, b.1934. Foresterhill Nurses' Home. Interviewed 2011.

The Haematologist: A marvellous privilege

I saw it only when we were spring-cleaning – a chipped, crazed plate with 'A present from Swanage' on it. It turned out that it had been given to my father, then a GP in a poor mining area of Yorkshire, by a young woman who had had a lump on her breast but who couldn't afford to have hospital treatment for it – there was no NHS then. He arranged for her to be treated and she gave him the plate in gratitude. I was six or seven then and had been appalled by this but he said: 'The way you can help is to do something about it when you grow up.' So the idea of helping as a doctor, as someone who could make a difference to people's lives, began.

I embarked on my course, aged 17, in 1950. There was still discrimination against women in medicine then. The attitude was that female students would work for a year or two then leave medical work to get married and have children. The result was a quota

The photograph taken to commemorate Audrey Dawson's becoming the city's first female Deputy Lieutenant.

When I became a consultant, several doctors disapproved of me and my gender – some would walk past me in the hospital corridor

which allowed no more than 25% of medical school entrants to be female and this lingered on till the Equal Opportunities Act was passed in the 1970s. By that time we had found that the proportion of women still working in the NHS 10-12 years after qualifying was actually the same as men as at that time many of them had emigrated.

I encountered little sexist discrimination during the course but later, when I became a consultant, several doctors disapproved of me and my gender – some would walk past me in the hospital corridor without acknowledging my existence. This type of prejudice was not confined to Aberdeen: one lecturer at Edinburgh around that period always addressed his students as 'Gentlemen'. So when the men in the class all agreed to absent themselves so as to force him to say' Ladies', he entered the lecture theatre, looked around, and said: 'As there is nobody here today, I will not deliver my lecture.'

The lecture course was old-fashioned, based on 19th century principles; for instance we spent 900 hours being taught Anatomy – highly useful if one were to become a hand surgeon but over the top for the rest of us. But when we encountered patients that was when the course really came alive. I can remember the thrill – and the panic – of speaking to and examining my very first patient. But I knew that this is what I wanted to do, to deal with real people, and become of service to them.

I loved dealing with North-east patients, especially those from the country. They were, and are, so stoical, so forgiving and so anxious to help you help them, an attitude that seems to be common in a region where climate, the nature of the land, and the attitudes inherited from a farming or a fishing background have grown people with a firm grip of reality.

It was not always straightforward. Early in my career at Outpatients with several medical students present, an elderly lady told me that the prescribed pills were 'nae yeese', so she was taking her husband's pills, which were also round and white. As I was explaining to her how dangerous this could be, she leant forward, cutting me short, with a withering: 'I kent yer grannie.' This put an end to the argument – much to the amusement of the students.

I lived very near Foresterhill. When the patients required bone marrow transplants and had to spend some time in isolation from others' bugs, the single rooms used for the purpose happened to look over my back garden; several times, a patient would ring the bell to inform me it was raining and that I had better go home to take in my washing. Typical of Aberdeen.

Most people seemed to cope with the stress of having a serious illness so well and sometimes we, who are healthy, underestimate the capacity for endurance. Dealing with people with severe blood problems can be very worrying but also very rewarding. Two weeks ago a lady came up to me and said: 'I know you – you treated my son.' This had been more than 40 years ago, when he was a lovely wee boy of three. Now, she told me proudly, he was 45, and a scientist in Switzerland, with two daughters of his own.

In medicine it is vital to deal with the whole person and his or her family and not just see him or her in terms of a disease; to get to know the person and something of the

With family and friends, celebrating her award of an Honorary Doctorate of Laws, Aberdeen University, 2013.

strains and stresses in their own lives. I sometimes fear we have regressed from that human understanding and forgotten that the person in front of you is not simply an amalgamation of ticks on a check list.

Haematology has advanced hugely since I started working in that speciality. Then a lot of conditions such as acute leukaemia were often rapidly fatal but advances in treatment have been swift and are continuing. To be able to watch a young, acutely sick patient move on to a healthy life is a great privilege. I have had a young man come up to me and say: 'You won't recognise me, because I'm five feet taller than when you last saw me.' That sort of encouragement makes one feel that at least you have done what you could to help people. That is more than enough reward.

Audrey Dawson, b.1933. Haematology, Foresterhill. Interviewed 2014.

Audrey Dawson has also done important work overseas. In 1976 she was invited to Iran to advise on the setting up of a medical faculty at the city of Ahwaz. Ten years later, following the explosion at the nuclear reactor at Chernobyl, she had several spells in Gomel, Belarus, to lend her expertise to the ensuing cases of acute leukaemia in the area.

The physiotherapist: The buzz you get makes it all worth while

My career has given me many opportunities to meet different sorts and in a range of locations too. For example, I've had spells offshore on the rigs. I would fly out in the helicopter for three days at a time – and find myself as the only female among 200 men. Most of the problems I had to deal with were the result of physical stress. The men would be working a pattern of 12-hour shifts and be involved in

The freshly qualified physio, 1972.

heavy work so back and neck issues would arise. I would give treatments and also offer talks on how best to look after the body in such a work environment.

I found it a great experience. I mean – flying over the Old Man of Hoy, who would want to miss out on that? I was given my own little room with a bunk in it. The medical facilities were state of the art; they have to be because when you're miles from the nearest landfall the company will want everything possible to be done out there.

The attention paid to health issues is meticulous. There's a zero tolerance approach to alcohol and to drugs. They carry out surprise spot checks and if there's even just a trace then that's the end. Survival is the name of the game out there so absolutely no chances can be taken.

I mixed in well and was made to feel welcome. That's an aspect of my work I really appreciate – the opportunity to be independent and to work in a range of situations. Every community needs a physiotherapist; you can take your skills anywhere.

There's no shortage of work to be done. The emphasis has moved from straightforward physical issues to do with intensive labouring tasks to the modern age of the desk-bound worker. After all, our bodies were made for movement – we're basically hunters and gatherers – so to sit hunched up over a screen for hours on end doesn't come naturally to the human frame. Neck problems and all sorts of repetitive strains have now become a major issue. I remember attending a patient who worked in a warehouse and I assumed that I would have to give advice on how to lift loads correctly. 'Oh, bit I dinna hae to dee ony liftin. It's aa deen by pallets,' he told me. All he had to do was to sit at a PC and press buttons to carry out lifting by remote control. The only movement he would be making during his working day would be to turn to pick up a coffee cup.

That's now typical. So many jobs nowadays are PC-orientated. Even in an old fashioned office there would still be the opportunity to do some moving about if only to walk over to the filing cabinet or to move to another desk in order to hand something over. The modern office worker can now pass a whole day sitting at a desk, then sitting at a steering wheel to get home and then pass an evening slumped on a soft couch watching TV. You find that the real manual worker, where he still exists, rarely has problems because he learns how to set about his tasks properly and has a body which is used to being in motion. No, it's the sedentary office worker who presents the real problems – and more and more of us are having to become one.

Because these changes have crept in gradually we aren't really aware of how the rhythm of our physical lives has altered to an extent where a whole range of movement has now been replaced by sedentary habits. Think about meal times, for example. When I was at school I would catch the bus and travel across Aberdeen just to go home for my lunch. Fathers would often do the same. Offices would close for an hour or two just so that their workers could go out and eat at a café or restaurant. All that involved some moving about – but now the office worker will regard lunch as something to be taken on the wing; he or she will rummage around in the desk for a bought-in sandwich and eat it while still at work. The big meal will now be in the evening – following which people

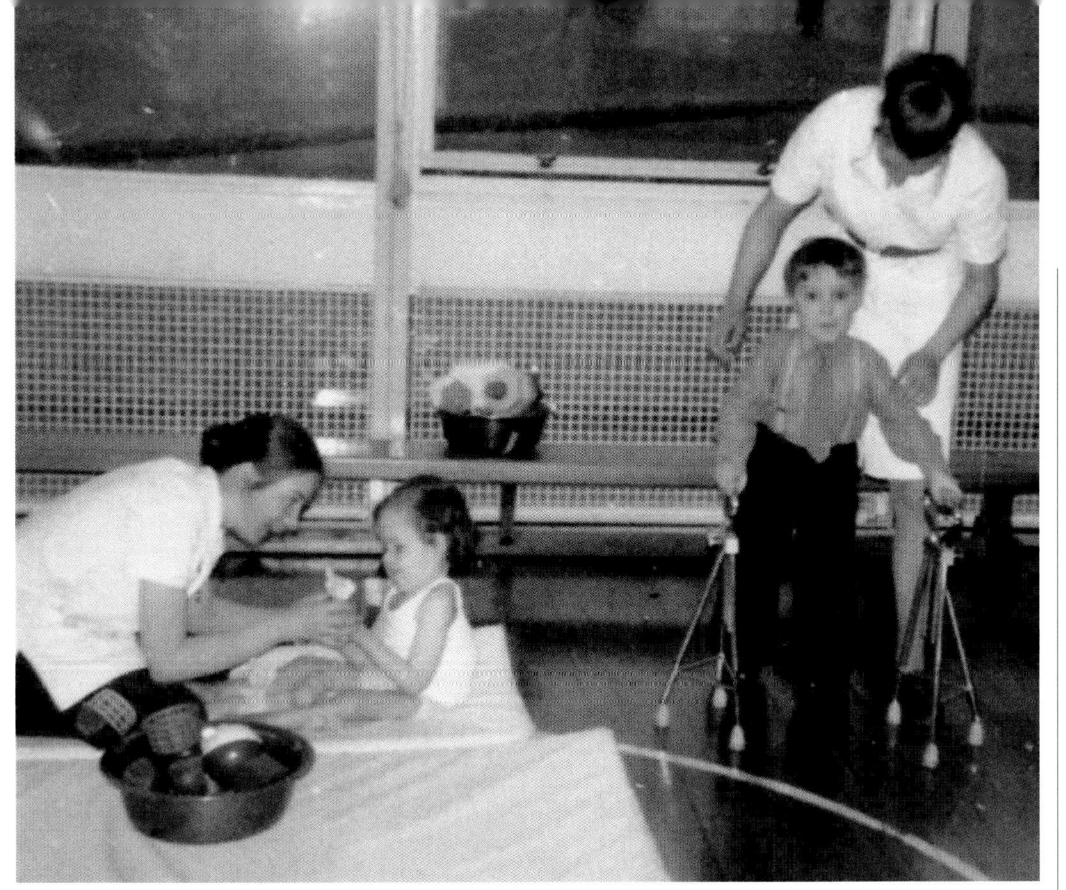

Working with a group of 'sick children', Woolmanhill.

will pass the rest of the day sitting and not give themselves a chance to work the food off.

Housework itself has also become much less physically demanding. Think of what wash day now means compared to the days when the housewife would spend hours, transferring clothes from one place to another, squeezing and wringing out the wet clothes, followed by a trip to the line to hang them all out. Now we simply pop a load into a washing machine, press a button and that's it.

So modern life takes as well as gives. I often think of the revolution that occurred during my grandfather's lifetime, the way he started off on the farm following the horse at the plough and ended up in the age of the combine harvester. He lived through a mechanical revolution and now we are in the midst of the electronic one. In his day if he wanted to make a phone call he would have to walk to the nearest phone box; now his grandchildren carry their own mobiles around in their pockets – and are developing strange new injuries as a result. Towards the end of my career I was seeing more and more patients who came to me complaining of sore thumbs. Why? It's because of their use of the mobile: nature has given us index fingers for pushing buttons but people have developed the technique of sitting with their mobiles in their laps and relying on their thumbs to send messages.

Modern life has a lot to answer for. Take the problem of obesity. So many people were coming to me with arthritic knees and lower back problems because of the extra weight they were carrying. I know that if I'm struggling upstairs with a load of shopping I will start to feel my knees – and yet some folk are lugging around that sort of extra 20 pounds or so all the time.

So many people were coming to me with arthritic knees and lower back problems because of the extra weight they were carrying.

But it's certainly not all bad. During my career physiotherapy developed all the time. We now have so many more techniques than we used to have. The great enemy for today's physiotherapy is time, rather than lack of tools. I've worked for both the NHS and for myself in private practice and I know the difference. It's not so much techniques or expertise as the simple pressures the NHS practitioner is under to work through an ever-

You've got to keep moving! Linda in action at the Hogmanay Fireballs, Stonehaven.

expanding referral list. Often the patient will have to wait six weeks or so for an appointment and when it comes they only get a big enough slot to have a quick examination and then be handed an exercise sheet. But really, the earlier you see the problem the better and when you do you want to take the time to explore the patient's whole lifestyle and get a sense of their temperament and likely attitude towards making the necessary changes in their daily routines.

And time to touch is also important. It's such a deep-seated natural urge that when we are hurt as a child we run to mummy to have it rubbed better. I did a lot of massaging. Although this does take more than the usual time-constrained NHS slot in the end it's cost effective. We can actually make such a difference to people's ability to perform their necessary daily tasks efficiently that in end we are saving the Health Service as well as the wider economy money.

What does a good physiotherapist need in addition to time? Well, obviously having a good pair of hands, a sensitive touch, is basic. So too is stamina – manipulating a patient's body and keeping up a spell of massage does impose heavy demands on you. But underlying all that are personal qualities. First must be enthusiasm, the personal ability to communicate a spirit of optimism and trust. After all, you are asking people to do arduous and uncomfortable things and to do them as exercises day after day. So you need to give them the feeling that it will all be worthwhile and definitely something they can manage to do.

Then I would say teaching skills, the ability to explain procedures clearly and to show empathy with people. What you are really trying to do is to put them in a position where they can manage their own conditions. You're not a doctor handing out a pill to be swallowed down twice a day; you are entering into a sort of partnership with folk who have come to you as complete strangers; you are getting to understand their situations so that you can explore with them the best way to work for an improvement. You are not just a dispenser of medicine: you are part of the treatment. And when things do work out and people come back to report how they have been restored to full function then, believe me, the buzz you get makes it all worthwhile.

Linda Duncan, b.1951. Aberdeen Physiotherapy. Interviewed 2014.

The medic: Bit they're weel paid fer it!

In those days Medicine was a rather leisurely course; in the first year all we did was to go over the sort of chemistry, physics and biology which we had already covered at school. Year Two was packed with endless Anatomy lectures. We'd have day-long series of lectures, broken only by sessions in the dissecting room.

I graduated in 1955. The career which then followed was rather different from the usual. After House posts in Aberdeen, I did my National Service in the RAMC, working

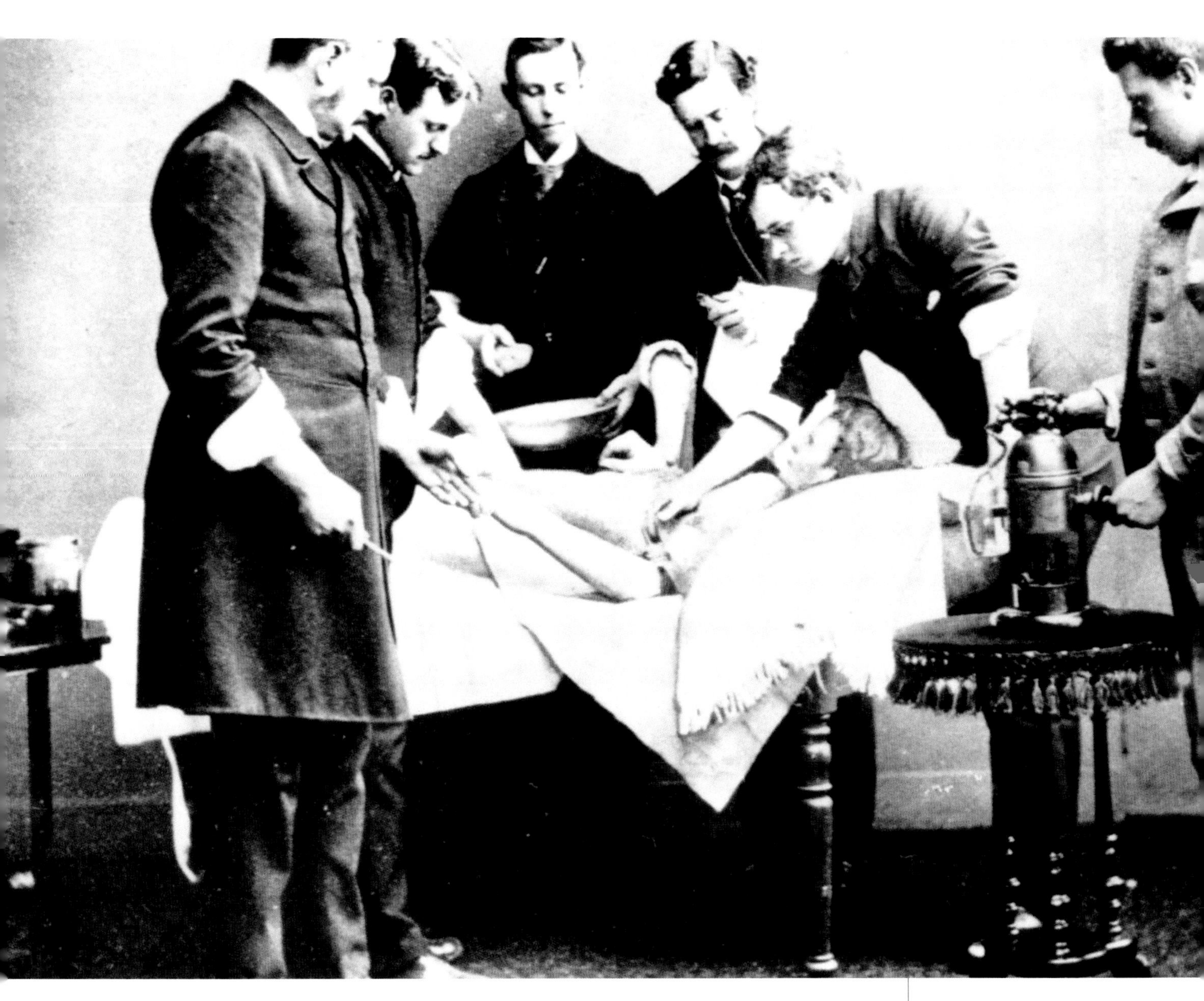

How it used to be: A late 19th century operation at Woolmanhill. [PHOTO: ABERDEEN LIBRARY SERVICES]

in a military hospital. I returned to Aberdeen where, after a spell as a trainee physician, I went to the University Student Health Service, which provided care for students and nurses at ARI and Woodend Hospital. I continued a clinical teaching role in a medical unit in ARI for a further seven years. In 1967 I took charge as Chief Medical Officer of the Student Health Service. Then came a seven year spell with the Scottish Home and Health department. By 1981 I was back at the University, this time as Dean of Postgraduate Medical Education and Executive Dean of Undergraduate Education.

Being involved with young people in the 1970s did pose a dilemma for me as this was the period of the pill and the growth of available abortion. What I did was to initiate psycho-sexual talks for new undergraduates with an input from psychologists and gynaecologists. When I had begun as a student in 1949 attitudes towards extra-marital pregnancy were still very disapproving and the University chaplain had held a particularly rigid attitude. It was rumoured that a student had been sent down for falling pregnant.

Another issue at that time was drugs. As a member of the Grampian Committee on Drug Misuse I can recall that scare stories became so intense that the football pitches at

When I was engaged in my surgical house job and I could find myself at post for the whole of a Sunday and a Monday.

Inverdee were spayed to obliterate the magic mushrooms growing there. But although this problem has undoubtedly grown in recent years a certain amount of drug taking, at least in the form of stimulants – for example taking uppers to assist in all-night revision sessions before exams – has always been with us.

My career covered a period of medical advancement greater than any before it and those developments have continued apace since my retirement. I was brought up in an era when service to the public was the paramount value; I can't understand the current nine-to-five attitudes which have taken root since then. There has also been a huge spread of female practitioners since the days when their entrance into courses was pegged at a 20% quota. Now with the quotas lifted the figure is more than 50%. Many of them will go on to become excellent doctors, of course, but what their influx has led to is a great increase in part-time working and family leave absences. This militates against continuity of care for the patient. It leads to the need to train more and more doctors to ensure a sufficient pool to cover the absences.

Yet back in the 1980s the fear was that we were training too many new doctors. Now there is a difficulty in attracting and holding on to the required numbers to maintain an efficient and caring health service. This applies to junior doctor posts in hospitals. We have all become aware of the controversies and the strike action over the imposition of seven days a week contracts in England - so different from my time when I was engaged in my surgical house job and I could find myself at post for the whole of a Sunday and a Monday. I remember once overhearing a pair of women in the waiting room. 'Ach, that peer doctor's bin up aa night.' To which came the ready reply: 'Ach bit they're weel paid fer it!' This encouraged me to work out my pay on a per hour basis; I found it came to all of sixpence halfpenny.

Being a junior doctor was a hard slog, no doubt about it. On the other hand, the long hours demanded did give you an enormous amount of experience, gained in a very short time.

Patients expect more now. The assumed deference to the superior wisdom of the doctor has more or less gone. Nowadays, patients are likely to come armed with a battery of information which they have googled up on their computer. And of course when they do see the doctor, it's quite likely that he or she will be staring at a computer screen as much as at the face of the patient.

The spread of electronic technology has led to a much more mechanised and bureaucratic system. The days of the traditional family doctor who would know not only the patient but all about the family circumstances have given way to the large group practice with consultations by appointment only and a receptionist who sees her job as acting as a vigilant gate keeper.

All this means that much of the old personal trusting doctor-patient relationship has been eroded. The days when the doctor could regard the patient as very much his or her patient have given way to a system where it's a large team of doctors, heavily reliant on their computerised records when they encounter a patient. Why, I can recall the time

The young doctor's other role: As a leader at the summer camp in Crathes of the Second BB, Aberdeen, 1947.

when a GP would try to pop into a hospital where one of his patients was being treated, both to check up on the progress of the patient and to have a word with the consultant. There were also doctors who would make a habit of popping into their older patients once a month simply to monitor their general welfare. Can you imagine this level of personal care today?

This means that the sort of warm bedside manner which a doctor could cultivate has now had to give way to a regime of quick, 10 minute, in-and-out consultations.

I was the first doctor to handle a case during the typhoid epidemic of 1964, when I was involved with the Student Health Service. My patient was in the sick bay at Crombie Hall; none of us had ever come across a typhoid case before but I realised that there was something unusual about this case and so sent specimens off. When the lab report came back with the diagnosis it was quite a shock.

For a few weeks in that early summer Aberdeen was almost in lockdown as the cases mounted and the isolation wards at the City Hospital became fuller and fuller. The city's Chief Medical Officer, Dr McQueen, later came in for a lot of criticism over his uncompromising approach to broadcasting the need for vigilant hygiene precautions. But in my opinion he did a great job. Of course there were accusations of his spreading an alarmist atmosphere and this did lead to some over the top reactions, such as examiners at the University donning gloves when handling student scripts, but it should be remembered how effectively the epidemic was contained. There were no secondary cases and only two fatalities and they were elderly people with underlying health issues.

My career in medicine was a long one. It covered a period of unprecedented advancement in the field even if that advancement was also accompanied by a decline in the human aspects of my calling I have never regretted giving all those years to such a worthwhile profession. What can be better than curing people's ills and healing their pain?

Campbell Murray, b.1931. Aberdeen Royal Infirmary. Interviewed 2016.

It was on the job that you learned most

When I started working as a junior doctor that was an eye opener and a half. Until you have to experience working nights and being tired you're never prepared for it. Chest medicine was my first job and I remember thinking that the men were so much fun. I think I'm much better at talking than doing; I'm not a very practical person in that way so the surgical side of things was never my forte. The men were so much fun in terms of the stories they told you. A lot of them had been in the war.

Our practical skills and experience had been limited; there were no simulations to practise on then like there are nowadays. It was on the job that you learned most. The men would be betting Maltesers whether my colleague or I were going to get the blood sample first time, and they were shouting across the ward to one another; it was hilarious. There was real camaraderie. You knew the patients like the back of your hand and they knew a bit about you as well. So that was when I decided I wanted to do hospital medicine.

I've loved all the jobs I've done. I feel lucky and very privileged that I've been able to do all of them. So how did I end up specialising in diabetes? I really enjoyed one of the jobs that I did and that was maybe a lot to do with the people and the patients I worked with. I think that a lot of diabetes care is about knowing the individual; I really liked that and the engagement with people at different points in their lives – dealing with the same questions but thinking how you can motivate the patient to change things.

Now I think a lot of junior doctors have to rotate through a lot of clinical areas too quickly so that they don't know whether they're coming or going. I suppose that for part of my core medical training when I spent six months in one department, I think that had a huge bearing on where I went and why. Also, I think you are always spurred on by people who are good role models and that's how you end up doing a lot of the things you do – because you like the way these people do things.

I've loved all the jobs I've done. I feel lucky and very privileged that I've been able to do all of them. So how did I end up specialising in diabetes?

Wendy Bradford, b.1972. Foresterhill. Interviewed 2016.

HIGH-PROFILE BACTERIOLOGIST

Aberdeen expert with a national reputation

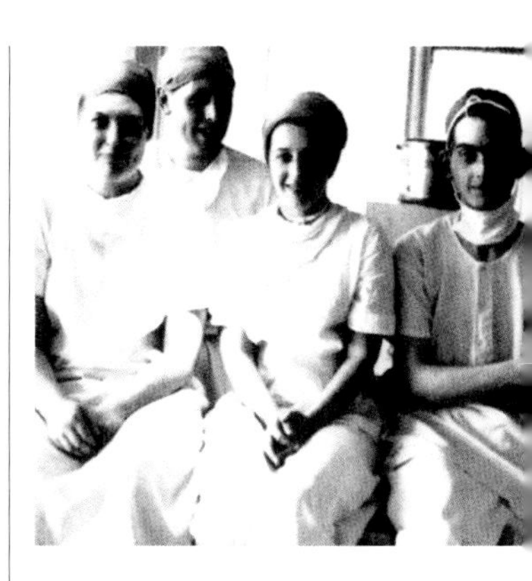

Hugh Pennington, far right, at the Lancaster Royal Infirmary, 1957.

In the right place at the right time

I am an Aberdonian both by adoption and by inclination. In some ways I arrived here by an accident of career. I had been working for 10 years in Glasgow and was anxious to progress my career; the post at Aberdeen came up, I applied and got it. But it could have been almost anywhere that was offering a suitable opening. However, I came, I liked what I saw and so here I am. Now that we are thoroughly settled here I wouldn't seriously consider moving anywhere else. I even like the climate.

I regard Lancaster as my native town; I spent the first meaningful 20 years of my life there. Lancaster was the home of two huge psychiatric hospitals, one of which had been built to serve much of the north of England.

The hospital had close family connections for us. Several of my relatives had their careers there and rose to high positions in it. I had a great aunt who was a matron while my grandfather was the Chief Male Nurse.

Just after I left school I did some work in the labs there and this gave me a great insight into the work of medical laboratories. I had decided to go into Medicine while I was still at school – Lancaster Royal Grammar School.

I also did some work in Lancaster's second psychiatric hospital where a relative held an administrative post. Its official title was 'The Royal Albert Institute for Idiots and Imbeciles for the Seven Northern Counties' – no PC mincing of words back then. It had been set up in the 1870s as a training centre for those who were mentally incapable of supporting themselves in the outside world. This hospital had 700 patients, many of them with severe learning difficulties. My time there had a powerful impression on me.

I saw a good deal of forensic work: post mortems ordered by the coroner. My time at the Royal Albert finally killed off any religious faith that might have been lingering on. In this I was very much going against the family grain. Both my parents were extremely religious and my father acted as a lay preacher. But now I was overwhelmed by the spectacle of all these wretched, suffering people who were allegedly the creation of a merciful God. But I never discussed my doubts with my father, knowing that this would have been a futile and upsetting clash.

Anyway, after school I did go into Medicine. I attended St Thomas's in London, in their buildings just opposite the Houses of Parliament. I did well there and got the chance to be involved in pathology work, something which interested me deeply. In those days you were thrown in at the deep end so you got plenty of hands-on experience from the very start. However, I knew that General Practice as opposed to lab work wasn't for me. I doubted my ability to interact effectively with the general public and I had too much scepticism to be able to offer the front of certainty that the patients usually require. Bacteriology appealed precisely because it was a field in which there was a host of issues which demanded investigation.

I got a post as Medical House Officer to Professor Sharpey-Schafer at St Thomas's. He proved to be an inspiring figure to me and to some extent I have modelled myself on him. He was very rational, very academic in that he was a detester of pomposity and was highly sceptical of any practice which couldn't be confirmed by hard evidence. He could be very sharp with colleagues and didn't suffer fools gladly. However, he was always highly considerate to his patients and was an excellent bedside man to them.

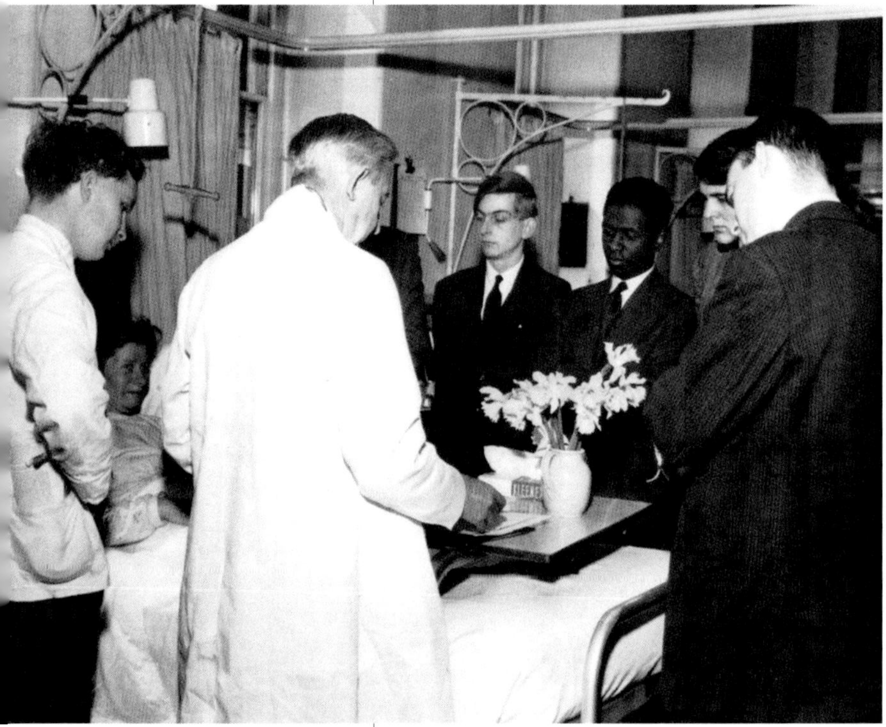

This I found to be the right sort of model especially as at that time so much medicine was based on tradition and mythologies and not the sort of evidence-based approach which he advocated. For example, one of the consultants rejected penicillin and for no better reason than it was a new-fangled notion which had been introduced after his own time.

I emerged from my stint at St Thomas's with a medical degree; I had done well in pathology. Following that I was then offered a post in bacteriology. I swithered for a while; my first wish had been pathology and the pull of being a dead meat pathologist is something which I can still feel to this day. When you open up a dead body there's a sense of excitement about it; you never quite know what you are going to find.

But there didn't appear to be any openings there so I decided to settle for bacteriology. Maybe that was always going to be for the best although pathology had a glamour about it which the hard slog of examining bugs in a lab could never possess.

On a ward round, as part of a group of medical students listening to the words of Professor Sharpey-Schafer, at St Thomas's, 1960.

When I joined the field, bacteriology was in the doldrums. But I was now working with an expert who had been a close colleague of Alexander Fleming at the time of the discovery of penicillin. This was Ronald Hare. He was an excellent bacteriologist in his own right and had done important pioneering work on influenza vaccination just before

On the Front Line of the never-ending war against food born disease.

I spent 10 years in Glasgow. Life in the city proved to be, shall we say, colourful. The very day we arrived we were greeted with the news of a murder by stabbing.

the Second World War. He was now running the department at St Thomas's and was my mentor. Our working conditions were pretty ramshackle, consisting of rooms more or less on the roof from which you could hear Big Ben booming away. Actually, this quite suited Hare because he didn't really hold with lavish equipment – rather as Fleming hadn't either.

Ronald Hare was succeeded by Tony Waterson and he introduced a fresh energy. He was a virologist and contact with him made me begin to think about the possibility of advancement. He got in cash and with it new equipment. I became absorbed in the investigation of a major issue surrounding viruses: why is it that some are killers while others remain benign, and how do you classify which are which?

I spent 10 years in London and emerged from them with a PhD and as a more or less fully-fledged bacteriologist and virologist. But I was keen to progress in my career. I spent a year in Madison, Wisconsin, doing work along the lines of what I had been engaged in back in the UK. I was a year there but realised it would be unwise to turn my temporary visa into a longer term one since the Vietnam war was at its height and the U.S. Government was keen to enlist any medic they could legally lay their hands on.

So I began to investigate posts back home. I had always been interested in entomology and had the notion that I could combine this interest with bacteriology and specialise in tropical medicine. I knew the Medical Research Council had posts in Gambia so I sent out feelers. The reply came back: no, there were presently no vacancies in Africa but they did have one in Glasgow.

So there I was, at the Institute of Virology at Glasgow in the 1970s, working on smallpox. In some ways it was a golden era. The pressure was on to complete high quality research so as to satisfy the Medical Research Council and there was no shortage of money. I had my own private lab, my own technician, good equipment, a brand new electron-microscope.

The consequence was I spent 10 years in Glasgow. Life in the city proved to be, shall we say, colourful. The very day we arrived we were greeted with the news of a murder by stabbing; I encountered sectarianism and gang-related graffiti; I learned that on certain match days the wearing of either green or blue could get you into bother, according to which part of town you were in.

On the other hand, Glaswegians proved to be a lively and friendly lot so it was by no means all bad.

My arrival here in Aberdeen was simply a matter of career progression. I saw the post advertised as the 'Chair in Bacteriology' and thought it looked an attractive opportunity. Although I was not fully aware of it at the time, I was coming to a place which had built up a considerable reputation in the field of infection control. Its great unsung hero was John Smith of the City Hospital who in the 1930s had conducted powerful work on perinatal sepsis. He was a man who had the gift of being able to get to the heart of the matter by asking the right questions.

The city itself struck me as a nice, tightly knit community, one where everyone seemed

In his laboratory at Foresterhill, 2003.

to know everyone else and where it was impossible to keep secrets. The very first day I arrived at Foresterhill, I was greeted with: 'You've been seen in Union Street.' But I quite liked that sense of strong identity. And the camaraderie in the Department was very strong, with none of the rivalries or backbiting you found elsewhere.

Compared to Glasgow, the city had the appearance of a neat and tidy place, one which prided itself on keeping things in good order. If you saw a notice stuck up in an Aberdeen shop window then you could be sure that it would be all square and neatly positioned whereas in Glasgow that same notice tended to be at an angle, shoved up anyhow.

How I came to develop something of a national profile is partly due to an accident of bacteriological fate. I had been conducting research on E-coli 0157 for the Scottish Health Service who had appointed us as the reference laboratory for the disease. So when a severe outbreak occurred in Wishaw in 1996, it was natural that we would be called in to carry out an investigation. I chaired the committee set up to make recommendations as to future conduct.

We were also fortunate in the character of the Scottish Secretary of State of the time, Michael Forsyth. Whatever your view as to his strong Tory politics, there is no doubt that he was an effective minister in that he could ask the incisive questions and make the right demands in terms of a crisp reporting of the findings. Yet he respected the need to utilise expert views too.

The never ending crusade for hygiene standards.

So we were given a well-defined task and as it was a highly dramatic outbreak, having been started in the familiar setting of a local butcher's shop and which went on to incur 21 fatalities, the media took an intense interest so that I found myself having to make regular appearances on TV and before the press. For me, that was a quick learning curve.

The press and TV have an insatiable appetite for sensation and can be easily fed it. Take the example of Aberdeen's typhoid outbreak in 1964. Back in the 1940s there had actually been an outbreak of E-coli which had carried off 100 babies in the city but that didn't make the headlines simply because in those days perinatal death incidence was so much higher than it is today that the story wasn't considered extraordinary enough to command that sort of attention. But 20 years on and the dreaded word 'typhoid' simply leapt out of the news reports. The journalists quickly got to work and the famous phrase 'the Beleaguered City' was coined.

Most scientists instinctively distrust the media simply because their training is in precise analysis and an awareness of complexities, whereas the press tends to search for the quick headline response and will happily simplify and yank words out of context. But fortunately the Wishaw outbreak was one of those events where the issues were relatively straightforward so I felt able to handle the media with some confidence. This experience put me in good stead for other occasions when an epidemic has thrust my work into the spotlight once more.

Because of these experiences, I have come to adopt a role as public educator, an expert whom the media and the Government now tends to turn to whenever, as is inevitable, the prospect of a disease outbreak rears its head once more. I am aware of the number of scares and misconceptions about. Take the current fear of running out of effective antibiotics and a reversion to the pre-penicillin days of mass deaths at the hands of everyday infections.

But this is an issue which has been around since the earliest days of penicillin. Fleming was warning us of it right back in the 1940s. In some respects the fact that it is now being dramatised is useful in that it should point us towards the necessity for responsible usage. But the equally important issue is prevention of the spread of disease in the first place and that can be greatly assisted by raising an awareness of good hygiene practice. Something as simple as hand washing will do as much for the control of infection as any brand new antibiotic.

It is therefore a scandal that not enough is done in terms of basic hygiene. That Wishaw butcher's shop knew full well what was required of it but negligently failed to do it. The medical profession is as guilty here as anyone. The lesson appears to be that unless you can institute a rigorous regime of instruction and surveillance then human nature seems to encourage people to cut corners and become lazily complacent. It's really an anthropological problem rather than a simple medical one – to change our everyday culture

I do see myself as something of a crusader for higher standards of personal and institutional hygiene. Every one of us is a walking continent of bacteria which inhabit our bodies; indeed, we all of us possess more bacteriological cells than we do of our own. I have to nag at people to beware the multi-used tea towel which has become a thriving colony for bugs; I have to tell them that cleaning can actually make things worse.

Absolute vigilance is the price we must all be ready to pay so as to make our hospitals and surgeries safe; it is a scandal that people can actually emerge from a ward suffering some infection they have picked up there because the bugs have come to regard the humid atmosphere of the average hospital as a happy breeding ground. This is a situation which can only be counteracted by scrupulous hygiene. It's a scandalous irony that I, a medical man, have to feel wary about the prospect of ever being admitted into a hospital as a patient.

My career has taken me to high spots which would have seemed unthinkable in the days when I was slogging away in the distinctly unglamorous area of micro-biology. Then, back in the Fifties, it was thought that antibiotics had more or less sorted out the problem of infection. But what we have learned since is that nature is sufficiently restless to continue to evolve new strains with which to threaten mankind, whether it be BSE, swine flu or Ebola.

I regard myself as a fortunate man to have devoted myself to a field which has proved to be so resilient to easy answers. Really, it has been a case of being in the right place at the right time. Nevertheless, I still have a wistful feeling that maybe dead meat pathology would have proved to be an even more exciting proposition…

Hugh Pennington. b. 1938. Aberdeen University Medical School. Interviewed 2016.

Professor Pennington frequently appears on the media as the go-to expert on infectious disease outbreaks and their prevention. He has also published widely, including the book: 'When Food kills: BSE, E-coli and Disaster Science'.

Meeting Prince Andrew in a line up at the Gordon Highlanders' Museum.

LOCAL AND NATIONAL GOVERNMENT

The Secretary: It was a great discipline

I started work as a shorthand typist at the Scott Sutherland School of Architecture – pleasant work in lovely surroundings. Then I decided I had to make a step up and so I joined the County Council in Union Terrace. I was in the County Clerk's office and then with the Legal Department. That was a real education, helping to handle all the deeds for housing grants and improvements.

The offices were very old fashioned, a rabbit warren heated by coal fires which a caretaker, who lived up the stairs, saw to. There would be huge board meetings with the table carefully laid out beforehand and a tea trolley going around half way through.

It was a strict and formal environment; if a councillor happened to see you slacking or reading a book at your desk, you were liable to be reported. You had to ask the typing pool supervisor for new supplies of paper whereupon the response would invariably be: 'What, have you been eating the stuff! You didn't dare make any mistake – that would mean typing out the whole page again. And as they were legal documents, you weren't really permitted to rub anything out. Bosses would have to think carefully about what they really wanted to say when they were dictating. Now the word processor makes us all slapdash and lazy. On the other hand, I didn't miss the days when everything had to be copied on carbons – dirty inky things. We had to wear nylon overalls to protect our clothes.

It was a demanding work environment. The attitude from the older staff was: 'You come in here, thinking you're proper secretaries and you know nothing. Well, we're not telling you – you'll just have to work it out for yourselves.' And we did. It was a great discipline.

Then I went over to the North East of Scotland Development Authority (NESDA). That's where I found myself working for Malcolm Bruce who, in the days before he

The NESDA days: Moira working with Malcolm Bruce, then a young research officer and later a long-serving MP.

entered Parliament, was a research officer fresh up from Liverpool where he'd studied Politics at the university. I was a typist for what became NESDA, which was an offshoot of Aberdeen County Council. This was an exciting time because the oil had now arrived and there were trade missions and Offshore Europe Exhibitions to help organise. I had to type up a comprehensive directory of oil companies from A to Z, a fascinating task.

For NESDA this was a period of rapid expansion with money seemingly no object. I think the results for Aberdeen have been mixed. The oil has brought prosperity and an influx of people from all corners of the world to the city but the cost of housing has shot up and the traditional trades – the granite, the fishing, the shipbuilding, the textiles – have been neglected.

Moira Mapley, b.1950. Aberdeenshire County Council. Interviewed 2014.

The job carried a bit of glamour

Just after the war, I embarked upon three happy years as a telegram delivery messenger. The job was a bit more varied than you might suppose – it wasn't all flying around from door to door, delivering telegrams. For example, in addition to us ordinary delivery lads there were also the fish market messengers who would wander about the fish market, handling telegrams as they came up as part of the business of the merchants.

A lot of the trade in fish selling and buying was carried on by telegrams in those days. A merchant at Peterhead might want to discover the price that hake was going for in Aberdeen so the quickest way of doing this in those days before mobile phones and email

'Camping' again? With colleague Ian Murphy in Union Street.

was to use the telegram service. It was a fast service; a query from Aberdeen to Peterhead would arrive within the hour and could be replied to on the spot.

Another aspect of the job was work in the Instrument Room. This was a huge open-plan space on the second floor, to be entered through the Dee Street doors of the main post office in Aberdeen. The room maintained immediate links via teleprinter to some 20 main centres throughout the UK as well as more local ones to North-east centres such as Fraserburgh, Buckie and Peterhead. We would act as 'indoor messengers' to keep this flow of work going.

There was the sorting section where telegrams came through which had to be allocated to their various destinations. We'd sort out the messages and then put them in their respective pigeon holes. From there as they mounted up, a messenger would then take them to the appropriate teleprinter. There was a whole bank of teleprinter operators always hard at it and they would have to handle a nonstop flow of messages to be sent down the line; they seemed to be tapping away furiously all day long. Thousands of telegrams would pass through the system each day. The service back then was not simply a useful way for people to get in touch with each other speedily: some 80% of businesses used it for their essential day to day work.

We messengers would be involved in all of these operations: receiving, despatching, sorting, allocating and delivering. It was a round the clock activity worked by a shift system. When you arrived you would sign in and then consult the duty roster for the day. As telegrams arrived for delivery in the city they would be enveloped, put into a tube and sent on to the delivery room.

Then you might spend the afternoon outside carrying out deliveries all over town. You'd start off by reporting to the delivery room where the Delivery Officer would shout out your number then hand over a bundle of messages. You had a docket with the number of telegrams for delivery written on. He would examine this and then work out how long it should take you to complete the task and when you were due back. This was calibrated to the exact five minutes and you were required to keep good time.

Unfortunately I just missed the motorbikes which came in in 1950 so had to rely on the standard push bikes they supplied you with. These were red framed 'Roadsters', pretty robust machines as they had to be to handle all weather conditions and also the many cobbled surfaces which still abounded in Aberdeen. If conditions were bad such as heavy snow then you'd be given some plastic tokens for use as fares on the trams and the buses, and then you had to trudge the rest of the way to the individual addresses. Whatever, the mail had to get through.

We had a uniform: blue serge with red stripes down the trouser legs and red piping round the collar. On our heads we had to wear a pillbox cap with a small peak rather like the French Foreign Legion. Round our waists we carried a pouch with a brass buckle and this had to be kept gleaming and polished. After all, we were representing the Post Office to the public and were expected to be smart and well behaved. We were a disciplined service, open to inspection at any time. We each had our own badge and

The Crown Street HQ of the Post office, where Bill Smith set out as a telegram boy in the late 1940s.

number such as 'GPO 9' on it, clearly displayed.

But as you got to know the ropes there was scope for a few little ruses. Once we found we could carry out a delivery even more quickly than the given schedule we might indulge in a spot of 'camping.' If another lad was leaving the delivery room at the same time as you then you might ask him: 'Where are you going? Mannofield area? Well, I'm doing Broomhill Road – fancy a bit of "camping"?' By this we meant that the pair of us would carry out the deliveries together, partly for a bit of companionship but also for the sport of seeing whether we could make it back in the time allowed. Another trick was to fly round the addresses so as to get back 10 minutes or so early. Then you didn't report back at the earlier time; instead you might use the bonus minutes by visiting 'Andy Birnie's', which was a small sweetie shop across the road, and take a bottle of lemonade.

You might get the odd tanner tip from a customer but even at Christmas I wouldn't say they were overgenerous – and, of course, you might be delivering bad news as well as good so the public could be a bit wary of our arrival on their doorstep.

I'd been happy to enter the Post Office service back in the 1940s when it was seen as a job for life. Parents would push to get their kids into it. The messengers were seen as quite a proud set. There were about 80 of us but far more than that had attempted to get into the position. It wasn't fantastically well paid – about four shillings a day at the age of 15 – and was regarded as a job for young fit lads up to the age of 18. But now that you were part of the Post Office you could consider yourself to be on the rung towards future promotion.

Receiving a presentation to mark his retirement after more than 40 years with the PO, 1987. Sylvia, his wife, is with him.

Besides, the messenger service carried a bit of glamour as we could be seen buzzing around town in our smart uniforms, delivering important messages to both the public and to business concerns. The tram system also had a network of what they called 'Tramway Boys' who delivered messages using the tram system – but we always thought of ourselves as superior to them. After all, we were the Post Office, representatives of His Majesty's Government.

William (Bill) Smith, b.1931. Aberdeen GPO. Interviewed 2014.

London? Hanoi? Brussels? Kabul? I'll give it a go!

My father didn't see much sense in me staying on at school if I wasn't going to university so at the age of 16 I attended Aberdeen College of Commerce and was trained in secretarial skills. This led to a career in the Civil Service.

My first job was at the Marine Laboratory, Victoria Road, Torry. I entered as a typist and left as the PA to the Deputy Director. Altogether, I was there for almost 20 years and enjoyed it. My boss thought I needed a new challenge and that I was stagnating and that I should find new tasks within my job but this suggestion led me to spreading my wings and moving on (not what he had in mind). The personnel officer at the Laboratory suggested I apply for a transfer to the Foreign and Commonwealth Office (FCO), who were on the lookout for secretarial staff.

I applied, was accepted and so began life in the FCO in the Gibraltar Section of the European Union Department Internal which also gave me my first involvement in a UK Presidency of the EU. (The presidency of the Council rotates every six months between the EU Member States and that Member State takes its turn in chairing all the meetings in the Council). This was the start of a FCO career that was to see me first in London and then posted to Hanoi, Brussels and Kabul.

Easier to stay in for a drink! Anne-Marie Meconi with colleague Helen Henderson, living it up in the British Embassy bar, Kabul.

To an outsider my progress might seem rather exotic and exciting but to me it has simply followed a natural course of events. I have been in one place, liked it, but whenever I was due to bid for my next posting I have thought: 'Why not? I'll give it a go.'

I took to London. For me it was an exciting place to find myself in and the fact that I was working right in the heart of Whitehall in a Government office, near the centre of events was amazing. I would leave the office and catch sight of Big Ben and immediately feel a thrill as though I was there on holiday. I also got a buzz from the fact that our offices overlooked No. 10 Downing Street and you could see all the comings and goings as well as hear the various crowds of demonstrators' protesting voices at the gates.

I never encountered any difficulties in being an Aberdonian at large in a Government office in the capital. Nor did I ever find the FCO environment to be at all stuffy or aloof. We all got on well together and except at formal occasions would be pretty relaxed in our dealings with each other and with the senior staff too. Any differences never went beyond routine banter and the good-humoured tribal insults traded at football or rugby times. Once when I was in the Embassy in Hanoi, England had had a win at football (the Vietnamese love football no matter who is playing). One of the Vietnamese staff remarked that I must be happy. I had to put him right: 'England/Scotland same as North/South Vietnam – when it comes to football.' We both laughed.

I loved my time in Hanoi. It proved to be a lovely first posting, so safe, so peaceful,

Sorry to be leaving? Anne-Marie's spell at Kabul comes to an end . Taken by the Embassy plaque just prior to her departure from Kabul.

just like a large village. It was a place you could walk around and feel perfectly safe. I was there in the British Embassy as PA to the Deputy Head of Mission for just over three years and then I was off to the UK Permanent Representation Office to the EU in Brussels, where I acted as PA to the Legal Team (and encountered my second UK Presidency to the EU). This gave me an insight into how the EU worked and especially the European Courts and the process of legislating the laws that would affect us. I was also lucky enough to go with one of the FCO lawyers (who was also a Scot) and see a case before 15 Member State judges in Luxembourg, which was very interesting and a great privilege.

I didn't really appreciate Brussels as a place as much as I should have done. I saw it as a sort of European London rather than for its own sake. But after my next posting, which was Kabul, Afghanistan, with the dry dust and sand, I must admit it did grow on me rather and when I went back to Brussels on a visit to stay with friends I appreciated the greenery, the beautiful parks and the everyday living.

The usual pattern was that after two postings you would return to London but by now I had the travel bug and was keen to go for another overseas posting. Most staff love an overseas posting because you not only see a bit of the world you also experience different cultures. That applied even to a trouble spot like Kabul. I was there from February 2006 to March 2008 as PA to the British Ambassador. Over the two years, I ended up working for three different Ambassadors. There were five Royal Military Police teams who looked after the Ambassador and so I got my introduction to the military and its workings and ranks. I also had my first experience of not being able to go outside without private security, armed bodyguards being with us at all times, and travelling in an armoured vehicle. The bodyguards, the Ghurkas and the local Afghani security had the job of keeping us all safe at different stages and this enabled us to get on with our jobs. I am grateful to them for keeping me alive.

Kabul was very much a trouble spot of course. There were a few incidents that reminded you of the dangers. On my 47th birthday I was working when we heard a loud bang outside. A bomb had gone off in the Serena Hotel and six people were killed and a number injured. I had arranged for a few friends to go there for my birthday celebration. If we had gone there 45 minutes earlier and not been working, we and the bodyguards travelling with us would have been caught up in it. Needless to say, I will never forget my 47th birthday.

Getting out and about in Kabul was difficult but could be arranged unless we were on 'lock-down'. So I personally never really got to see the real Afghanistan and that was a loss. I had a friend from my St Margaret's School days whose father worked in Pakistan in the Sixties and they had gone on their holidays to Afghanistan. She told me how beautiful the country was. Flying over it you could see spectacular mountain ranges. Kabul had four seasons so in winter we would have lots of snow, which was a relief from the heat and dust in the summer. But Kabul, by the time I left, unfortunately, was becoming a dangerous place in that at the beginning of my posting where you could once walk was now either a vehicle manoeuvre or out of bounds.

On my visits home I always made the effort to take some Scottish foods back with me to wherever I was posted and let my friends and colleagues have a taste of Scotland – Aitken's rowies, Dean's shortbread, macaroni-cheese pies, oatcakes have all been around the world with me. In Kabul there were a few friends/colleagues from the Grampian area and they definitely appreciated the rowie run.

I often wonder whether my travel lust was something in my genes, inherited from my Italian forebears. I've been to some pretty adventurous places but that's nothing compared to the courage my grandfather (Amadeo Meconi snr) had to summon up when he made the decision to quit his little Tuscan village to journey to a strange country where he didn't speak the language all those years ago. My father (Amadeo Meconi jnr) was a great believer in 'travel broadens the mind' which I think is very true.

Now I'm back working in Aberdeen. In the end I've returned to my roots – people tend to do that eventually, don't they? – but with many wonderful experiences to look back on.

Anne-Marie Meconi, b.1961. Foreign & Commonwealth Office. Interviewed 2016

I let my friends and colleagues have a taste of Scotland – Aitken's rowies, Dean's shortbread, macaroni-cheese pies, and oatcakes.

ABERDEEN
FC
FOOTBALL CLUB

THE SPORTING LIFE
Winter Pursuits

One of the crowd which acclaimed the triumphant Dons. Arthur Wyllie, second left (just by the hand). Alec McLeish is holding the cup aloft, 1990.

WINTER PURSUITS

The Primary Select player: He didn't look much of a footballer to me

Whenever we could we played sport – above all, football. At dinner time there would always be a game in the playground. I would rush home, gulp down my mince and tatties and then run back for the game. We also played on some open ground at the back of the school in the Denburn. This was by a very convenient lane where a concrete bollard kept the prowling police cars out. We would lay down the traditional couple of jackets for the goals.

Of course we had no referees but we tried to adhere to the rules and to keep up some sense of fair play. Usually this worked well enough though there would be the occasional heated dispute as to whether the ball had actually gone between the jackets for a goal or

Aberdeen Primary Select, 1950/51. Keith Taylor is back row, second left. 'Tubby' Ogston is the goalie; Alec Dawson the captain, flanked by Ian Burns (later of Aberdeen FC) left and Bill Lornie (later Luton Town) right. The spectacled wee lad is the great Denis Law.

A decade further on and Keith is turning out for Aberdeen University – back row, second right, 1960/61.

simply passed over one of them.

Sometimes we would take a 'ha'penny half' and catch the tramcar up to Hazelhead to play on the pitches there. Usually we had to use an old leather casing, which was so well used that it had sprouted hernias and had cracks all over its surface. If necessary we would stuff old newspapers in it; occasionally the ball would burst and then the papers would go flying all over the place. On Friday afternoons in the school they would come round to hand out the jerseys for the next day's School League match.

I was centre half. We had a very good team; the kingpins in those days were Seaton but we did manage to reach the final of the Primary School Shield and get beaten by them. The final was at Pittodrie and that was a great experience. I remember they had a free-kick about 35 yards out which bounced a couple of times before trickling through our goalie's legs and creeping six inches over the line. I just about managed to go up to him and mutter something about 'Hard luck, Jim – you did your best'.

I then got into the Primary Select team for the year. Tubby Ogston, later of Aberdeen and Liverpool, was our goalie; at left back there was Eric Fraser, then there was Ian Douglas, who went on to play for Dundee United, Ian Burns, later of the Dons, Jack Lornie of Luton Town and the great Alex Dawson. His father was a trawlerman who later went down to Hull; Alex went on to play for English Schoolboys and, post-Munich disaster, to star for Manchester United.

This little pipsqueak crouching down by us all, wearing his ordinary clothes and his

National Health specs wasn't actually selected but came anyway. My recollection is of how he would pester Frank Singer, who was running the team, for a game and of his being told: 'Look, you'll get your game next year.' He didn't look much of a footballer to me; I assumed he must be Frank's son and had come along because Mrs Singer was busy back at home doing the family wash and wanted to get this pesky little lad of theirs out of the way. He was, of course, Denis Law.

Keith Taylor, b.1938. Aberdeen Primary School Select. Interviewed 2008

The Sports Reporter: To think I'm getting paid to do this!

Writing has always been part of my life. As a kid I lived in this little fantasy world of football and writing about it. When we had our own little football team over in Torry I would make up hand-written programmes, even as a seven-year-old, and distribute copies among my friends.

I would also get together with a friend, Gordon Bathgate, who was very good at drawing, and we would produce a comic: I did the stories and he did the artwork. We would make up adventures that involved our friends. At secondary school I got into the way of writing ultra-long essays; they would ask for three pages and I would find myself turning in 30. Writing like that has always come naturally to me. Even now I will turn out a couple of quick pages to mark an occasion like a friend's birthday. As long as I have something to hang it on I can usually come up with 500 words or so in a quarter of an hour.

Even now I will turn out a couple of quick pages to mark a friend's birthday. As long as I have something to hang it on I can usually come up with 500 words or so in a quarter of an hour.

Journalism is, of course, different but it still means turning some real-life incident like a football match or a meeting with a player into a story. I've always done that; I'm still waiting for them to find me out. To think I once used to spend a fortune on going to watch Aberdeen FC and now they're paying me for the privilege.

But what I am really is a frustrated nurse. I've always enjoyed being around people and got satisfaction out of trying to help them.

However, after 14 months at the Nursing College I began to feel frustrated. I could see that a lot of my old pals were now out in the world earning good money. They were able to afford to enjoy themselves and go off on foreign holidays. My brother was a roofer and he offered to fix me up with work at that. It was a mistake: after a few weeks I realised that this was never going to be the life for me. The money was good but there was little satisfaction in the work, so I re-applied to get into the Nursing College.

I had to prove myself by taking on work as an auxiliary at Glenburn Wing, with the geriatrics. I can say that of all my working life those two years there were the happiest and the most satisfying. I was on the night shift a lot but many of the patients didn't really know what time of day or night it was so you had to help them get through by being by their side and chatting to them. That could be quite fascinating. One of the patients was

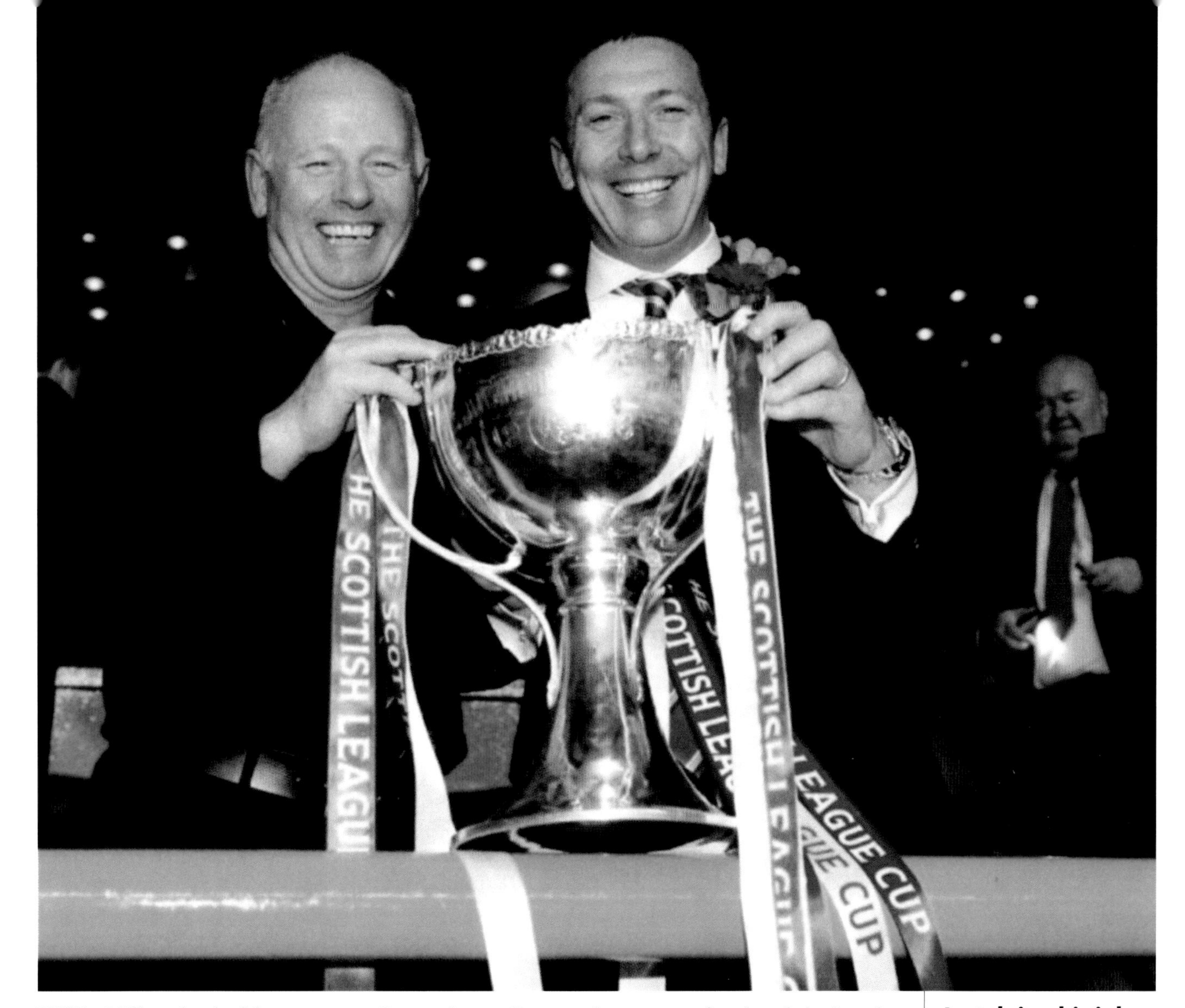

Just doing his job... Charlie Allan, searching out an interview, but also photo bombing Derek McInnes and Stewart Milne, holding the League Cup, 2014.

Willie Mills, who had been a great Dons player. By now he was confused and during the day would hardly speak but at night he came into his own. He was supposed to be bedridden but you'd spend half the night chasing him up and down the corridor. His short-term memory was gone but his recall of the 1930s and the old matches was fascinating.

However, I'd now met Janice, my future wife – she was a staff nurse – and wanted to get married. Economic reality now took over. At that time a nurse's pay was disgracefully poor and I found I couldn't afford to carry on. So for six years I was a postie, walking the streets of Torry and delivering mail there.

But all this time I had been running an amateur football team. The league secretary was Joe Paterson – sadly dead now – and he would moan that our games never got any coverage in the press. I asked him whether he had ever approached Aberdeen Journals about it and he said no. I offered to get onto them. When I did the response was: 'But we never get any copy'. I offered to supply it, starting off, as they advised, with results and scorers and any little interesting story I could come up with. I got into the way of dropping off a hand-written page or two into Aberdeen Journals each Sunday night and they would publish it midweek.

How I came into full time journalism is this. In 1990 the Journals had a lot of industrial problems and the journalists were on a long-term strike. By now my part time efforts for them had advanced to covering some Junior fixtures and even the odd

I like the company of older footballers but I find the younger ones are rather wary of me. That's because I criticise them and they don't like that.

Highland League match. I was invited to replace the striking journalists and cover local football. I can't say I'm proud of the circumstances under which I joined Aberdeen Journals. My wife and I spoke long and hard about it but in the end we decided that if I passed up the chance then I would regret it for the rest of my life.

I started with a good deal of trepidation. Here I was, trying to turn what had been a hobby into a full time career. To begin with I was doing the more straightforward stuff like handling the results and getting the team-lines together. But then came another break. The sports writer at that time was beginning to suffer difficulties and the paper needed a second writer as cover. My job was to be ready to step in as a second reporter and cover the significant matches that Aberdeen weren't involved in. For me this represented quite a jump. Here I was, being sent down south to cover Old Firm games and the Edinburgh Derby. I'd travel by train and take a taxi to the ground so as to prepare a report for the 'Green Final' with a follow up for the Monday issue. I could no longer watch the Dons but this was high level football. Then the problems for the chief reporter became worse and I was being asked to step in and cover the Dons.

Basically that has been what I've been doing since 1992. In that time I've been abroad; I've seen World Cups, covered matches in England. I've been doing all this – and they still haven't found me out. And now I'm the 'Evening Express' Sports Editor. Yet I've never lost the feeling of: 'Does what I write make any difference to anyone at all?' Surely, it's the opinion of the players and the manager which counts, not some hack like me.

I like the company of older footballers but I find the younger ones are rather wary of me. That's because I criticise them and they don't like that. You learn very quickly that you either massage their egos and get near them that way or keep your distance – and your credibility. I try to be honest; that's what I think I owe them. However, I have learned to temper my criticisms, to make them less personal. I remember being taken aside by Alex McLeish once for a chat: 'Look, you don't need to tell us if we've had a bad game,' he said. 'We realise you've got a job to do but there's no need to be vicious about it. Our families read the papers too, you know.' I've taken that comment on board and now I do try to be more positive in my approaches.

A gap has opened up between the players and the ordinary fan. It's not so marked in Aberdeen but even here the player will earn far more than those who watch him. It used to be that his wage would be little more than that of a skilled tradesman. Of course players can behave wildly, go out and drink and act Jack-the-lad. The truth is that football players are young men with a bit of money and something of a name and will always tend to run a bit wild. Things have changed in one respect however. I doubt whether many of them now have to claw their way up out of a deprived background. How many of them would have had the kind of boyhood we had when we spent hours playing on some waste ground behind a Torry tenement on a home-made pitch?

As a boy I used to cheat my way into Pittodrie. My mother would scrape the half-crown together to pay me in but I would spend that on comics and sweeties. At 10 o'clock I would go to the stadium and climb over the wall at the Beach End. I would then get into the bushes there and hide. I would meet up with a few others who did the same. We'd pass the time eating sweeties and sharing our comics. Once we heard the crowds coming in we'd emerge and join them just behind the toilet at the Beach End. That way I always got my money's worth however badly they played.

I try to maintain contact with my roots. I write as an Aberdonian football reporter, as someone who grew up following Aberdeen FC and who was an ordinary fan long before he became a professional reporter. I'm a football man first; a journalist second. I tell my wife that football comes first but she does come next. I once wrote that beating Rangers was better than sex. I thought it was quite funny at the time but for some reason it didn't go down well at home. In fact my wife detests the game. When we were courting she would come and watch the team and freeze for me on the touchline but once the ring was on that was that. At home we have two separate TV sets so Janice can go upstairs for her programmes while I enjoy the football downstairs in the comfort of the living room.

Charles (Charlie) Allan, b.1958. Aberdeen Journals. Interviewed 2006.

The Football Star: Did you really play for Manchester United?

My story begins in Footdee (known locally as Fittie), a quaint village at the mouth of Aberdeen harbour and where I grew up. It had a great community spirit with everyone looking out for each other and was like a big family. As Fittie is next to the beach, this was our playground. All day long we would play football. In the holidays it would be a quick breakfast then on to the sands or the grass for a game which would last until nightfall, sometimes 12 hours later.

We played with old-fashioned, heavy leather balls, which were not the greatest for passing and certainly not for heading but it made us all the better. The effort required did a lot for your development as a player. So there we were, day after day. In the evenings the kids were joined by the platers and the welders, just home from the Hall Russell and John Lewis shipyards. Rain, snow, sun – it made no difference; that was our life. We played with real commitment as if each game was an international. If there wasn't a game on at the beach, I would be outside working on my fitness and practising my skills.

Since I can remember I always wanted to be a professional footballer; it's all I ever thought about. Believe it or not, my team was Manchester United. The practice then was to pick an English team and a Scottish team to follow.

I attended St Clements Primary School, then Frederick Street. I was never much interested in schoolwork; all I ever wanted to do was play football. I was also a fast runner and won medals at school and went unbeaten for some considerable time. I played in the school football teams; the Frederick Street team was very successful and we won many trophies. Scouts would come along to watch although to begin with it seemed as if it was the other players they were interested in. I always knew I had the ability and if I

The young hopeful: John Fitzpatrick in his Manchester United strip, in his early days at the club.

The crowd was always behind me. In action at a packed Old Trafford, versus Leeds United, 1970.

continued to work hard my chance would come. I would throw myself into the games and training. By my last year at school some of the other boys were attracting interest from the scouts but still no-one seemed to be interested in me. Then at the end of the second last game of the season, Archie Beattie, the Manchester United scout, asked if he could call round to speak with my father. He had been a scout for Huddersfield and discovered Denis Law. Up until then I hadn't even been aware he was watching me.

The match had been played at Powis and afterwards I ran all the way back home to Fittie with the news. My dad's reaction was: 'Are you sure? Manchester United? Are you certain it's them?' The world's greatest club were enquiring after me.

Archie Beattie came to our house. So there I was in my living room, in my short trousers, listening to the representative from Manchester United telling my father that the greatest club in the land was inviting me to Manchester for a two-week trial that Easter. He told me that I would have to get a haircut and that I must never wear winkle picker shoes because they were bad for a footballer's feet. I would have agreed to anything. I was 14 years old and going to Old Trafford. I had never been further than Stonehaven.

The club arranged my travel and accommodation. I was met at Victoria Station by the Chief Scout, Joe Armstrong. I was quite terrified but I also knew this was my chance and that I mustn't let anything get in the way. I knew I would have to work really hard but I saw myself as a winner; I was always very competitive at sport and had to be first at everything.

I met up with two Irish lads: Jimmy Keilloh and a young lad called George Best. We became the best of mates. Another great support was Ian Moir. I was very homesick and would phone home to my dad every night. Coming from Aberdeen, Ian seemed to understand what I was feeling and took me under his wing. He would tell me to keep going and that if I worked at the game then I would be all right. Later on after he signed for United in 1962, Denis Law, also, of course, from Aberdeen, offered similar support.

At the end of the fortnight I came back up to Aberdeen and returned to school. Manchester United invited me back for another spell in the summer. I played a couple of B games and did quite well. I was then asked to report to Matt Busby, who we called 'The Boss'. I looked upon him as a god; he was a father figure to the young lads so when I climbed the stairs to his office I was very nervous. Manchester United wanted to sign me. The Chief Scout came back to Aberdeen to discuss terms. In those days at the age of 15 you couldn't sign full professional terms and had to sign as an amateur. I joined Manchester United from Thistle Lads Club in September 1961.

Once back at Old Trafford, George Best and I were called into the office and told as we were on amateur forms we would have to get a part time job. The club arranged for us to train as plumbers. Can you imagine it: George Best, a plumber! On the first day George took me aside and asked if I fancied this plumber business. As far as he was concerned he was at Manchester United to play football. The plumbing boss asked if we thought we would enjoy the work: 'Not really – what we're good at is football, not this other stuff.' 'In that case take the afternoon off.' The next day it was the same. 'Is it

always going to be like this, each afternoon off?' Yes, we were told, but we should keep the arrangement quiet from Mr Busby.

We were delighted. The workshop was half an hour from the Cliff (Man. Utd. training ground). We would run there and spend each afternoon of our plumbing career practising our football skills together. After a while, Matt Busby called us in to his office to ask how we were enjoying plumbing. 'Fantastic, Boss – we are really enjoying it.' said George: 'That's funny – you're never there.' said Busby. He wasn't angry at all, just pleased we had spent the time going back to the Cliff and working hard at our game. This must have paid off because we won the FA Youth Cup that year.

We stayed in club digs run by a kindly Irish lady, a real home from home. She would keep an eye on us as we were still young lads. We would spend our spare time at the YMCA playing snooker or at the bowling alley. We were too young to go to pubs and nightclubs. That all changed later.

I made my first team debut at the age of 18, in midfield, against Sunderland at Roker Park. I phoned my dad with the news and he arranged to come and watch the match. So there I was, in front of 50,000 people, in the same team as George Best, Denis Law and Bobby Charlton. We were beaten 2-1, but after the game Matt Busby said I had given a good account of myself.

If playing with Bobby Charlton, Denis Law and George Best wasn't going to inspire you then nothing would. I was a hard worker and played with great enthusiasm – I always

A great line up: United pose with the European Cup, 1968. John is extreme right in a front row which runs, from left, Jimmy Ryan, Nobby Stiles, Denis Law, Sit Matt Busby, Bobby Charlton, Brian Kidd. George Best is second row behind Charlton.

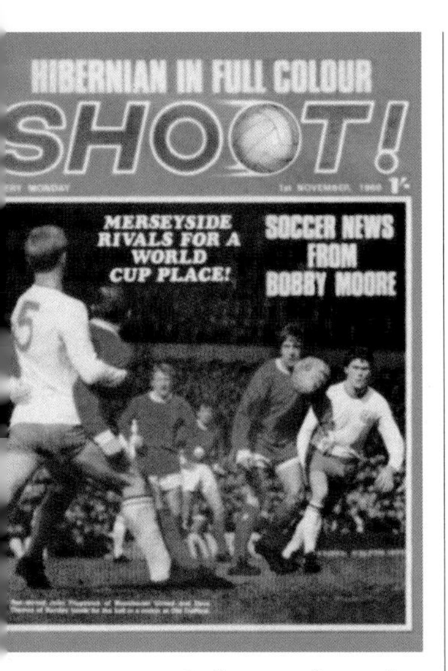

John makes the front cover of 'Shoot'; playing against Burnley, 1969.

gave 100%. I listened to what I was told; Denis Law would say the difference between a pass a yard from him and one to his feet could be the difference between a goal for the team and giving the ball to the opposition. I worked at my passing; I made sure I could pass the ball right to his feet. Matt Busby kept the game simple for us: 'Remember, pass, pass to the man's feet.'

The Manchester United crowd were always behind me. I was a competitive player; I never shirked a tackle, was always in the thick of the action. The crowd loved that and let me know it. Perhaps this was my Fittie upbringing, all those games with the older men on the beach. Above all, here I was playing for the team of my boyhood dreams.

The next stage was to get a regular place in the first team. I played for Manchester United's first team 147 times and played in all the qualifying games leading up to the European Cup Final in 1968. I was awarded a European Cup medal. I even made history by being the first ever substitute when this was introduced in 1965.

During one game at Blackburn Rovers which was going nowhere, George said: 'Look, John, what this match needs is livening up. Next time you get the ball in our half, pass it straight to me and I'll show them all how to score a goal.' Well, I did exactly that; it was in our half, there were plenty of players between George and the goal but he just went through them, beat every one of them, and walked the ball into the net.

George Best was a footballing genius; what a character! He had it all: imagination, dribbling ability, ball control, skill. Brave as a lion and alongside Denis Law and Bobby Charlton… When you ran out to play alongside that trio you knew the opposition would be saying to themselves: 'My god, there's not just one of them, there's three of them. If two of them don't do it, the third surely will.'

What happened to George was a tragedy. When I went to his funeral at Stormont in Belfast and saw the coffin my first thought was: 'Can George really be dead?' My wife Barbara and I were later invited to Belfast to see a moving stage production of his life and we visited his family home and grave.

My first serious footballing injury was during a match against Leeds United. I was up against Johnny Giles and he tackled me hard. I was barely 19 years old and had to have an operation to remove cartilage. This pattern continued for several years (in total I had five operations) until my injuries started to take their toll. I had always been a naturally fit guy who threw myself into training and gave everything that was asked of me.

The end came when I was 26. I had been playing well and improving all the time. I was coming in to my prime – I was being talked of for the Scotland team. But physically I was struggling. The club sent me to Harley Street, to see the best surgeon in the business, Sir Oswald Clark. I remember the consultation as if it was yesterday. Sir Oswald said: 'If you continue playing you will be in a wheelchair by the time you are in your 30s – retire now.' The decision was made for me.

By this point, Tommy Doherty was Manchester United manager and he offered me a coaching job – if I wanted it. After six months of trying to adjust I knew it was not for me and Barbara and I decided to return to Aberdeen.

Greeting the local hero: John is given a great welcome home to Fittie following United's European Cup victory in 1968.

My football career may have been relatively short (I was with Manchester United for 11 years) but was long enough to have experienced a lifetime of memories and emotions and I would not change that for anything. I travelled the world first class with Manchester United, visiting countries, some of which were quite inaccessible at the time.

When I retired from football I took some time to readjust so took a couple of years out and played golf most days. Then as time moved on I started to take an interest in wine and decided this could be the start of a new career. I worked for one of the big wine companies for a couple of years and then started my own business. I am lucky that I have a very loyal customer base; many are still buying from me 40 years later and are now good friends.

My injuries have continued to bother me and I have had several operations – hip and knee replacements. These were great successes for which I am eternally grateful and enabled me to get back to playing golf and gardening, which I love.

With friend and team mate, the great George Best, en route for another United match together.

Manchester United has a former players association and regularly have golf outings, dinners, autograph signing sessions etc., which is a chance to catch up with my team mates. I still receive letters from fans requesting autographs for their valued photo collections. I was also invited to the European Cup Finals in Russia and Barcelona. All unforgettable experiences.

I had an incredible time at Manchester United and was very, very fortunate to be one of the few players to get this opportunity. Every schoolboy's dream, I am sure. I played with the best – Best, Law, Charlton – and played against some of the greatest footballers of all time including Beckenbauer and Cruyff. For that I am forever grateful.

Nae bad for a Fittie loon.

John Fitzpatrick, b.1946. Fittie and Manchester United. Interviewed 2006.

The Football Coach: One bad apple can rot the whole barrel

Once I have retired from my post as Head Teacher at St Machar Academy, I'm moving on to a second career at Pittodrie, working in youth development for the club. I've found that the same qualities that are required in school life are necessary for success in football too. It's about setting standards. Alex Ferguson believed that. Whenever he was looking at a player it was character he would go for above all else. He would say: 'We'll watch this player. We'll watch him in fine weather but then we'll go back and see him again when it's heavy going and see how he gets on then. And we'll see him when his team is being thumped and whether he can handle that. And we'll talk to his parents and we'll look at his school reports too.' He would say: 'Unless he's as good as Pele, we won't take him if his character falls short. One bad apple can rot the whole barrel. You mustn't forget that we'll be taking on lads who will have to live in digs, miles from home. We must look after them and see that they have the character to handle that situation.'

Lenny Taylor, b.1945. Pittodrie Stadium. Interviewed 2005.

Aberdeen Grammar School FPs women's hockey section, 1990. Wendy Bradford is directly beneath the Rubislaw Pavilion clock.

The Hockey Player:
I see you scored a goal at the weekend

There were so many different activities that you could do after school but by the end of my first year and into second year there were teachers' strikes and all the extra-curricular stuff really stopped – except for hockey. We were the Rubislaw Jets and the lady who ran the team wasn't in the union and so she carried on with it.

I continued playing through school and university. A year after graduating I'd gone up to Elgin to work as a Senior House Officer. Geriatric Medicine was my first posting and there was a patient in the ward who found out that I played hockey. I would come in on a Monday morning and this old man would say: 'I see you scored a goal at the weekend.' He would have the newspaper out and he'd have looked out the report for me.

Wendy Bradford, b.1972. Aberdeen Grammar School FPs. Interviewed 2016.

The referee:
Without us the game can't start at all!

As a boy I drank in the football atmosphere right from the start. There were fewer cars around when I was that age so we could play in the street. And if I could find no-one else to kick a ball with I would invent my own games; hours were spent kicking a ball against the kerb to see if I could get it to come back to me or in using the garage door to hold my own matches.

I went to Ashley Road Primary School, which at that time was being coached by my father and was a really good team. By P6 I was the captain and we won the league. The next year we repeated this triumph and also beat Robert Gordon's College in the final at

Pittodrie to take the shield. We were able to celebrate by wallowing in the big communal bath where our Dons heroes relaxed at the end of their games.

For my Secondary I went to Aberdeen Grammar School, which at that time was exclusively rugby. I enjoyed all sports so didn't resent having to muck in on the rugby field. But football was always my main love and I came to an arrangement with the Grammar School sports masters that if I played for the school on a Saturday morning they would permit me to turn out for my football team – King Street – in the afternoons.

I was a pretty useful player and developed into a decent right back who could maybe have gone places but I developed fluid on my knees and when I was 16 I got into refereeing and that soon took over my football life.

Aberdeen's four Category 1 referees, of the 1990s: from left, Alan Freeland, George Simpson, Sandy Roy, Mike Pocock.

I just seemed to drift into refereeing. One thing simply led to another. When I was 16 I would spend my Friday evenings training with the King Street Sports Club. Neil Paterson, who was great force in juvenile and amateur football in the city in those days, would come along. One evening he invited me to help out by taking Primary age kids. To begin with this entailed little more than running the tuck shop but soon developed into taking some games of five-a-side in the gym.

I made a good impression so the Friday came when Neil approached me with the question: 'What are you doing tomorrow morning? How about coming up to Hazlehead with me and helping take charge of the league matches there?' When I got there he suddenly said: 'We need a ref – how about giving it a try?' At that point I had had no thoughts of acting in that position but I went on, enjoyed the experience and felt I was showing up well.

This led to classes run by the local association at Queen's Cross. Billy Knowles took them and instructed us in the laws of the game. The course lasted 10 weeks and in December we took our exams. The results came out on my birthday so that as a newly arrived 17-year-old I found out that I had passed and with flying colours. I actually won the Peter Craigmyle Trophy awarded to the highest entrant of the year.

I remember one day at Inverdee when Brian Bridgewater, who was two years older than me, was having a hard time of it. He came into the dressing room at the end somewhat distraught. The advice he was given has stayed with me as an important watchword: 'Look, just remember the spectators aren't shouting at you – they're shouting at the referee, not you personally – and for them the insults don't go deep; they are no more than a release of pent up feelings and will soon be forgotten.'

Sometimes you just have to do it. Alan Freeland sending off Motherwell's John Davies in a match against Celtic, 2000.

So I quickly learned that the referee can never please everybody. When I began, my hardest challenge was communication. I was very conscious of my young age and that I was now having to deal with players who were maybe 10 years my elder. Some of them seemed to tower over me and had more experience of the game than I could yet muster. I recall the time when I found myself having to deal with a huge burly defender who head butted an opposition forward and bust his nose. I had to force myself to put on a front of cool authority but inwardly I was fearful he would simply abuse me and refuse to leave the field of play. In the event he suddenly seemed to come to himself and greeted me with a 'Sorry, ref – I was out of order there.' He appeared to have accepted me as an authority figure; that taught me to respect my own position as the one charged with managing the conduct of players and not to shrink back from any situation that might arise.

I was very naive to begin with and was hazy about how a referee's career might progress. Back then Aberdeen had had very few top class referees so there was no model for me to follow. For me one step just seemed to succeed another. I began with Juvenile games at 17; four years later I progressed to the Juniors. I was with the Juniors for a couple of years and then I made the move up to the Senior grades. I had been serving my apprenticeship without fully understanding where I was going.

This was in the early 1990s and back then Scottish refereeing was still languishing in the dark ages. It was all rather amateurish: we had to buy our own uniforms and sew the badge on ourselves. There was little in the way of organised training or coaching. Fitness

My first Category 1 match was Arbroath v Queen of the South in the old Division 2. When I blew the whistle for the kick-off my mouth had gone completely dry and no peep came out.

tests had just been introduced but they were scarcely the rigorous demands they have now become; on the very first one the more elderly referees were actually able to walk the final lap.

It is all so different now. Although we aren't full time professionals, we are expected to show a professional commitment. I doubt whether the public appreciates the demands on time – they see the 90 minute performance without realising that behind it will be several hours of travelling, that the ref has to report another 90 minutes before kick-off, that he will be expected to train at least twice a week, to attend seminars at Stirling or St Andrews regularly. Fitness levels are most important and the referee is expected to keep himself in top class shape always. Not only must he keep up with the game, his apparent body shape and mobility must be such as not to attract derisory comment during his 90 minutes in the public eye.

Technology has revolutionised the way he goes about his business: his heart rate will be monitored throughout the game, he will be wearing a communication kit so that he can be in continuous communication with his assistants and fourth official and, of course, seminars will utilise video playback evidence for later discussion.

Above all the referee is now subject to an intensive system of supervision. When I started, all you received from your match observer was the bare mark; now he will get a detailed e-mailed report and have a feedback session on the phone. There has been a shift from an assessment that is content merely to score the performance to one in which the observer's comments are there to furnish material for development and a shared analysis. The observer has thus become a coach as much as an examiner.

All this is mostly unknown to the pundit on the terracing. The constant poring over decisions, which any televised game is now subject to, has put referees further under the spotlight than ever. But one thing the punter will never appreciate is the difference in perspective between what he can see from his elevated position on the terracing and what is available to the man who is in the thick of the action. The fan has the privilege of being able to take in everything; the referee will often have his view suddenly obscured by a player moving in front of his line of vision. With the best will in the world errors are inevitable.

My first match as a Category 1 was Arbroath versus Queen of the South in the old Division 2. I got off to a nervy start. It was a warm August day and when I came to blow the whistle for the kick-off I found my mouth had gone completely dry and no peep came out.

I got through the game but Bob Valentine, my observer, was moved to remark on my somewhat agitated demeanour. For the whole of the first half I was so intent on demonstrating my control that I kept blowing up and making dramatic gesticulations. His report informed me that Mr Freeland's verbal warnings were somewhat excessive: 'reaching epidemic proportions.' When he next saw me at a Raith Rovers match I was so keen to show that I had taken in his guidance of being calm that this time his report commented that: 'If Mr Freeland had been any more relaxed then he would have been horizontal.'

So my first season was a learning curve in which I had to develop the right balance – as all referees must – between unobtrusive calm and a demonstration of control.

By now I had become aware of the structure for Scottish referees, could see my way ahead and was determined to go as far as I could. In 1997 I got onto the FIFA list.

I have always been keen to control a game by man management rather than by sanctions and by fear. For me the priority has always been to help keep the game flowing and not punctuate it too often by dramatic displays of card wielding authority. You have to take into account the fact that in any match there will be a variety of attitudes among the players. Some will be more aggressive and ready to mix it than will others; some will accept your judgements more readily than others. So that insight becomes part of your decision making too.

You won't necessarily deal with a similar infringement in exactly the same way. Has this particular player simply made an honest mistake or is he the type to try and test you as to how much you are going to let him get away with?

Then again you have to develop a feel for the mood of the game at the outset. Some teams might have been roused up by their manager's pep talk and want to fly into tackles from the start; others might be carrying some sort of animosity from a previous fixture; the side battling against relegation will be up for the fight in a way that a mid-table side might not be and so on. You look for signals right from the kick-off, for the body languages and the chat that's going backwards and forwards. Hearing can be as important as seeing.

He could play a bit, too! Alan as part of the line up of Aberdeen and District Referees Association team which played against their Banff and Moray counterparts in 1989. Alan is second back row. The other Category 1 referees are, to his right: Sandy Roy and Mike Pocock while George Simpson is front row centre.

I was in John Lewis's buying Christmas gifts when I suddenly heard a voice in my ear: 'Freeland, you are the worst referee ever.'

Above all you must try to be crisp and positive in your decision making. It is important to make your presence felt from the very start yet not be too hasty with the cards – if you penalise a fairly marginal infringement in the first five minutes you might be putting down a marker but you might also be making a rod for your own back and find that you have to carry on dishing out the cards all through the game. Refereeing is a constant matter of fine tuning, of getting the balance right.

Of course you will make mistakes: just as a player will miss an open goal or scuff a penalty attempt, you can fail to spot a foul or you will misjudge a simulation. The vital thing is to put the error behind you and to save the analysis for after the game. If you dwell on your error then as sure as anything you will make another one or find yourself trying to compensate. No, just get on with it in the same way as a player has to. Believe me, you will have plenty of time to brood on your errors on the long drive home. That's the bit that the public don't see: they seem to think you just pack your bag and somehow disappear into the night without another thought in your head. But we care all right; many a time I have had to endure a wretched and lonely drive back home, tearing myself apart over some mistake or other.

Even though I have now been retired nine years I'm still haunted by the mishaps I've been involved in. I have been threatened by members of the public, been bundled out of the ground by the back door, had to get a police escort after a game – and that was just a Junior match in Dundee.

In that respect the date 13 September 2000 will always be engraved on my memory. It was a Hibs versus Dundee United match and I awarded a late penalty to Hibs under the most unfortunate circumstances. United had deliberately kicked the ball out so as to allow an injured player to receive attention. The convention in such instances is for the opposing team to return the ball to the injured side but it was late in the game and Hibs decided just to attack. I awarded the penalty but a crowd of players mobbed me. It was seven minutes before the penalty could be taken.

After the game and on my way home, the phone started ringing; I went to answer it only to hear a voice informing me that I was 'the worst f... referee on the whole planet.' The phone rang again; this time it was a guy threatening to kill me.

Even after the furore of the Saturday match has died down you are not immune from attacks. Once I was in John Lewis's buying Christmas gifts and standing at the cash desk when I suddenly heard a voice in my ear: 'Freeland, you are the worst referee ever.' I turned round only to see the figure of a man hurrying off, safe in the knowledge that he had planted his little insult and was now going to get away before I could react.

It's important to develop a psychological feel for the game and its players. Humour can be a great help here. You have to be philosophical about the behaviour of managers and accept that they will always have the ear of the press whereas we aren't allowed to indulge in post-match explanations. So when they moan that 'I can't see how on earth that was a penalty!' you have to realise that they are talking to their fans and attempting to justify their job, not offering up a rational analysis.

The line of vision isn't always clear... eyeing up the conditions prior to a European tie in a foggy Helsinki.

When I refereed a Celtic game with Martin O'Neill as their manager and had to send off two of his players I just knew he would go to the press with 'The worst referee ever.' I refused to rise to the bait and contented myself with the retort: 'Mr O'Neill, just tell me something I have not heard before.'

That is the downside to the job but it can't detract from the many memorable moments the game has given me. I'll never forget going down to Ibrox when Rangers were chasing the title and had to play Kilmarnock. As I walked out in front of 60,000 supporters the noise was deafening; I swear you could feel the grass bouncing up and down with it. Of course you get nervous beforehand and have to pay more visits to the toilet than normal but these are occasions that will imprint themselves on your memory for ever more.

Naturally I've had my disappointments. I was never given an Old Firm match or a cup final – the best I got was fourth official just before I was due to retire. But on the other hand I've travelled the world and been to places that I would otherwise never have been near. Even the time when my trip to Tbilisi in Georgia took five days of round trip travel with flight delays and a return to home late at night and then having to get up for work the next morning – no you wouldn't be without such experiences.

No, I don't regret my time as a referee, not for one minute. You accept the insults and the mistakes partly because refereeing has given you such a wonderful collection of experiences and partly because you know that your conscience is clear and that you have always strived to do the very best that good preparation, a clear head and a properly professional approach has enabled you to. Often the referee is the most abused person on the field but he is always going to be the most essential one too. A game can always go ahead without a player or a manager but it won't even start without a referee!

Alan Freeland, b.1961. Scottish Football Association. Interviewed 2016.

The Schoolboy Rugby player: Don't ever apologise!

It was the Hunter brothers who took Games. Naturally I found myself being introduced to rugby. I attempted to throw myself into this strange new sport but with the ball in my hands and me embarking on a run I received a hard tackle. I was upended and my boot accidently cracked into the head of my assailant with the result that he was felled and laid on the ground in agony. I bent down to apologise whereupon I felt my collar being grabbed roughly and being pulled upright again. A voice was hissing in my ear: 'Don't you ever apologise again to an opponent. This is rugby and it is a man's game.' All accompanied by a series of clips to the side of my face.

Somehow I never did take to this rugby.

Mitchell (Mike) Davidson, b.1940. Aberdeen Grammar School. Interviewed 2016.

The Rugby International: I always enjoyed the physical involvement

When people ask where I come from my answer is 'Bucksburn.' My father worked in the paper mills at Wiggin's Teape, Stoneywood. There he finished up as foreman in the cutting and rolling department. He was also an able sportsman; football was his game. He was good enough to earn a trial for Rangers.

It was inevitable that I would take up football too. I inherited my dad's ability and did well enough for the scouts to come sniffing around. A couple of professional sides showed an interest and Eddie Turnball, then the manager of the Dons, showed an interest in signing me.

After leaving school, I was working at a holiday job in the wages office at the paper mills at Stoneywood. I was debating as to whether I should sign on as a professional footballer when I received a letter from R.J.C. Glasgow, who had been my PE teacher at Robert Gordon's and who was a player and vice-captain of Gordonians. He got in touch, he told me, because he hadn't seen me at training for Gordonians even though I had been the skipper of a very successful school side, most of whom had gone on to join Gordonians. He informed me that Gordonians were stuck for a scrum half for the first game of the season owing to injuries. He could guarantee that if I were to play alongside Alan Leiper, who would be at fly half, then we would stand a good chance of making the District match for the North versus the Midlands.

It didn't take me long to make up my mind. I realised that I'd been drifting along and that I had really been waiting for some definite offer to come along. I had certainly been

He could have become a football pro. Bucksburn Primary School 1952/53. Ian McCrae is end of front row, right.

The school boy prodigy. On the run for Robert Gordon's College v Royal High, 1957.

flattered to attract the attention I had at football but I also knew that one game as a pro and my amateur status would be gone and with it my rugby prospects. I had six years of rugby at Robert Gordon's College behind me and had enjoyed the sport enormously, much more than my football.

I hadn't played rugby at all at my Primary school and my very first game wasn't till I arrived at Robert Gordon's College in 1953. I took to it straightaway. I reckon I got a special thrill out of being able to mix it with the bigger guys. Even though I was no more than a wee skinny kid, I could chop them all down and soon got a bit of a name for myself. From that starting point my skills developed quite naturally: sidestepping, passing, kicking. I began at full back and then in my Third year I moved up to fly half. The following year I was at scrum half.

Before I went to Robert Gordon's College I'd hardly been aware of the sport – it was all football in our house. I can't recall even seeing it on TV and I was certainly never taken to a match. But I came from a sporting background. There was Dad's football and Mum had been a top sprinter, even going down to meets in London. Then there was my uncle Alec Castles, who was a leading Grades cricketer. They all encouraged me at any sport right through my career; at Seafield I'd look over at the stand and knew I would see them sitting there, cheering me on.

Every Saturday morning in the season I had been turning out for some school team or other. I had actually started off as a full back for the Minors in my First year despite my small stature and lack of kicking power. But what I had got was energy, fitness and a natural love of getting into the thick of things. I was small and skinny but I could tackle and threw myself at everything and everybody.

At that point I wouldn't have flinched from any opportunity to get involved. My routine was rugby in the morning for the school, football in the afternoon for the Boys Brigade and then for the 25th Old Boys, then, when I became 16, BB Dance Club at night followed by seeing my girlfriend home – and, to cap it, my first girlfriend I met at the Dance Club lived in Kincorth, a full six miles across town from my home in Bucksburn. No wonder I was fit.

In the winter my rugby was also coming on apace. By Year 3 at RGC I was in the Colts and already setting my sights on the First XV. Occasionally we would find ourselves in the same coach travelling to an away fixture and I would look at them all and think that it wouldn't be too long before I was one of them. By S4 I was into the Second XV and the following year made the First team. I began to get noticed; my name would feature in reports in the papers and people were starting to talk about me. I realised that rugby was a game where I could go places.

But I never dreamed how fast recognition would come. With the encouragement of Ronnie Glasgow I found myself in the national trials, working my way up through the preliminary North v Midlands match to being scrum half in the combined North and Midlands teams versus the South, Edinburgh and Glasgow. I was picked as reserve scrum half for the final trial match. But with five minutes gone there was an injury to the Blues scrum half and I came on. So within three months of leaving school there I was in the

The all round sportsman: Taking the field at Mannofield as wicket keeper for Aberdeen Schools Select v Glasgow, 1957. Mel Edwards is first left (see chapter 8).

Demonstrating his football skills. North of Scotland v All Blacks, 1964.

final trial for the national team.

I was involved in trial matches for the next four or five years. My first cap came against England at Twickenham in 1967. My third was against France in 1969; I was only there as travelling reserve but three minutes into the game another injury and I was on. I can claim that my appearance represented a record for international rugby – that of being the first ever reserve in the Northern Hemisphere to take the field; up to then reserves were not permitted to replace an injured player. The French ran us ragged but we tackled like demons, with me in the thick of it, and we ran out 6-3 winners. And I played a part in the winning try: at a scrum close to their line, I hacked the ball out – as you were allowed then to do – I dribbled it towards their line using my football skills, had a stab at it, as their full back tried to pick it up, fell over their full back and Jim Telfer picked it up and got it over the line.

I was just below average height but I had the attributes of a good scrum half. I could dribble, I could pass, I could kick with either foot and I could tackle. Most of all, I revelled in the sheer rough and tumble of it all and was quite fearless about the possibility of getting hurt. In that position you are bound to get clobbered from time to time but I had the resilience to take it. If an opponent grabbed hold of you and threw you to the ground then you just picked yourself up and got on with it.

And I kept myself really fit. After a game I would have a pint or two and also a wee puffy – the only time I ever smoked. Then the next day would see me go on my Sunday run, four or five miles so as to get rid of any stiffness. Monday evening would be weights in the garage at home, Tuesday and Thursdays were club training but on the Wednesday I would go to the gym and take on a circuit which I had worked out for myself. Friday night was Boys Brigade – I was an officer in the 64th Company at Bankhead – and I worked at some gymnastics there. I would occasionally go out to Balmedie and spend an hour running a circuit round the sand dunes.

So I was in action seven days a week. I did this mostly by myself. Rugby wasn't then the highly professionalised sport it has since become and players were left to their own devices between matches. Even when I was reserve for the British Lions for the New Zealand tour in 1972 the preparations we received were no more than pretty basic. We

Captain of Gordonians, 1968/69.

went down to Eastbourne for a five-day pre-tour session and the only advice we reserves went away with was: 'Mind you keep yourself fit.'

This was advice I didn't need as I never failed to work myself hard during the week. Nor did I spare myself on a Saturday evening either. In those days the favoured après-game drinking den was the George Hotel and it was the norm to down up to a dozen pints during a Saturday session. I knew I would be sweating it out the next day or two.

The social side has always been an important part of rugby culture and the drinking was a valuable bonding exercise. So were the sing-songs we would hold on the coach coming back from an away fixture. We kept it up all through the journey and only

Passing out from the scrum on debut for Scotland v England, in the Calcutta Cup at Twickenham, 1967.

stopped when the coach let us off for a roadside pee.

It's probably true to say that being based in Aberdeen didn't help my international career and that if I had been playing for one of the Edinburgh or Glasgow teams I might have earned more than my six Scotland caps. It was suggested to me more than once that I should relocate to the south but I'm an Aberdeen lad through and through and never considered doing that.

It's true to say that I've never been a great spectator. For me sport has always been about action and involvement. In that sense I'm glad I played when I did. Rugby for me nowadays has become a total bore. They've tinkered around with the rules in order to make it easier to retain possession and the game has become stereotyped and predictable. Besides which, since professionalisation there has been more and more emphasis on sheer athletic strength and less on the kind of skills I used to relish. You sit and try to get interested in a match on TV and find it's always the same pattern: pick up-crunch-tackle.

I've always enjoyed the sense of physical involvement. Even now in my seventies I try to have a run a couple of times a week or, failing that, go on a long walk, maybe for two hours at a time. I love the hills and the mountains and I've scaled every one of the Munros, and the Corbetts as well as the 3,000-footers in England, Wales and Ireland.

Happy days. I also extended my rugby career by helping set up an Aberdeen 'Golden Oldies' side – we called ourselves the Aberdeen Strollers. There was a series of teams like ours all over the world of rugby and we appeared in a number of 'Golden Oldies' festivals – in places like Dublin, Toronto and London. There was no serious tackling – except by me, of course. We took it quite seriously and had our own logo and made up

Getting into the Gallic spirit: Scotland players before their match v France, 1969. Ian is in the beret. Among the rest are, from left: F Laidlaw, A Carmichael, I Smith, G Brown, W Steele, G Strachan, R Clark, R Hannah, H Bryce.

commemorative programmes.

I also had the great good fortune to be invited to represent Scotland in an ex-internationalists tournament in Bermuda on four occasions. These were wonderful trips; Bermuda is an exquisite island where one could enjoy the climate, the hospitality and the opportunity to renew friendships with teammates and opponents from the past.

In this way my rugby career enabled me to take part in the game till I was into my 60s. It was all great fun – and that goes for my times as a whole, both at rugby and as a cricket player. It's true that when you look back, you realise that although I've had the suggestions and offers, I've never been tempted to forsake Aberdeen and the teams I've played for there. Why should I? Aberdeen is a super city to live in and it's got everything you need for a balanced and active life. I feel blessed to have lived and played all my life here.

Ian McCrae, b.1941. Gordonians RFC. Interviewed 2015.

In addition to his distinguished career in rugby and early football prowess, Ian McCrae has been a gifted all round sportsman. For many years he represented Stoneywood Cricket Club, proving himself to be one of the city's leading batsmen during that time.

The 'greatest moment of his life': Arthur getting his hands on the European Cup winners Cup, Pittodrie Street, 1983.

The Fan: Over 50 years of unbroken attendance

Just about my most vivid memory of growing up in Aberdeen is my passion for Aberdeen Football Club. I caught the bug playing in the playground at Kittybrewster School. I was never any good at the game and didn't even make the school team but I had an uncle who was a stalwart of the Inverurie Supporters' Club and he encouraged my interest. The first game I actually went to, with my uncle, was on 31 March 1956 and that was a defeat to Raith Rovers, 5–3. Never mind: I was well and truly hooked and have followed them ever since. I have hardly missed a home game since I was old enough

Aberdeen F C Supporters' Club gathering 1967. Arthur is happily standing right at the back, left of 'Exit'.

to go by myself, starting in August 1964. Over 50 years of more or less unbroken attendance.

I now have a season ticket, Richard Donald Stand, middle tier, lower section, and from there I have a perfect view right down the whole sweep of the pitch. In my time I have seen a number of great players in the red but the one that stands out for me for sheer skill and artistry has to be the Hungarian international, Zoltan Varga. Sadly we only had him for a season and then he ended up at Ajax to be the replacement for Johann Cruyff. Of today's players my favourite is Jonny Hayes, so fast, so good on the ball.

I didn't actually go to the Gothenburg triumph of 1983 but a workmate did and he brought me back a programme. Well, the following Saturday the Dons were at home to Hibs so I took my camera and the programme with me in the hope of getting some autographs. As I was waiting in Pittodrie Street I got the shock of my life: there coming towards me were Alex Ferguson and Archie Knox, and they had the cup between them, swinging it along as they went. Better than that, they allowed me to hold the cup and to have a photo taken while doing so. Just about the greatest moment of my life.

Arthur Wyllie, b.1948. Aberdeen FC. Interviewed 2016

THE FISH

Fittie, Torry, The Harbour and the North Sea

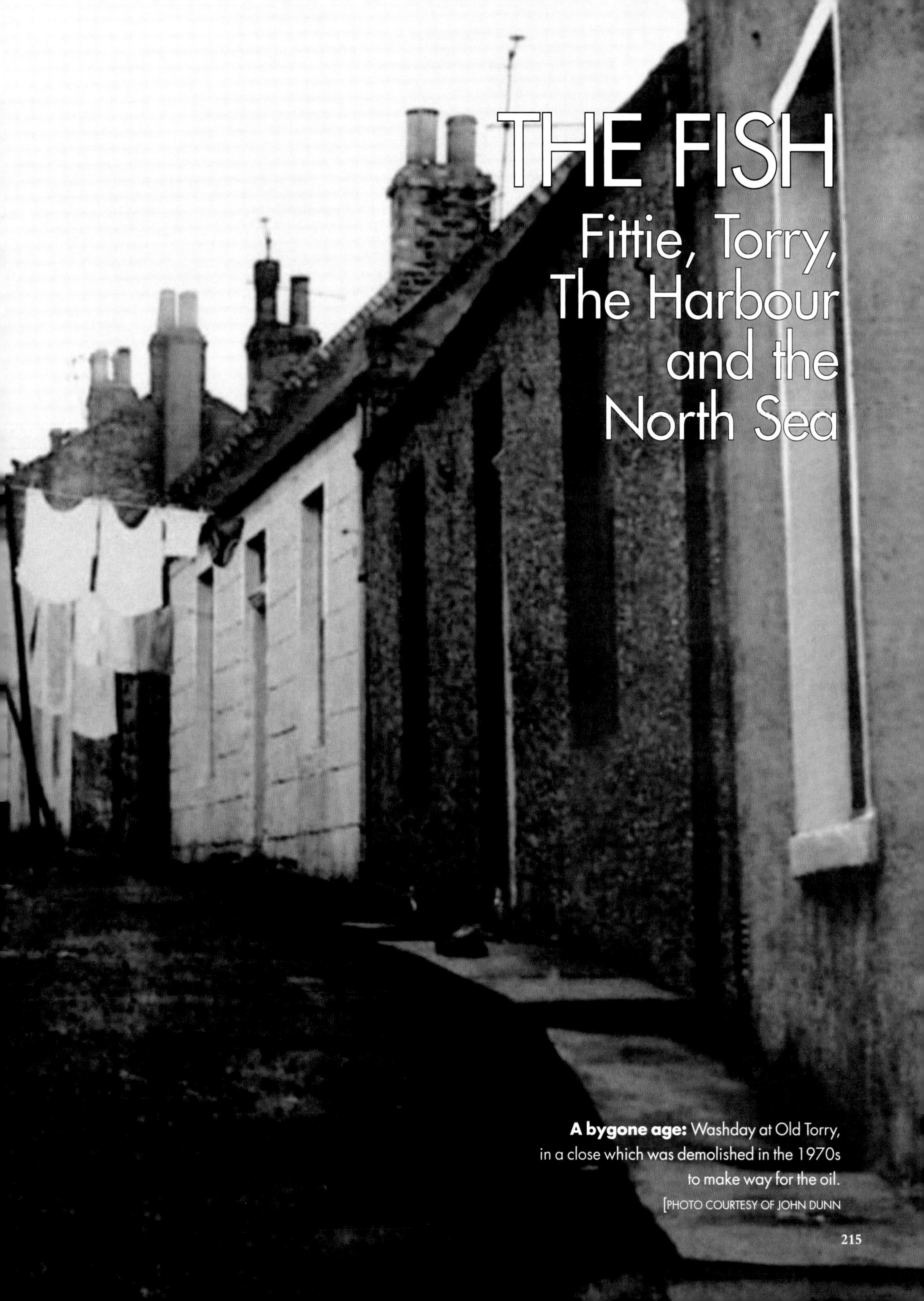

A bygone age: Washday at Old Torry, in a close which was demolished in the 1970s to make way for the oil.
[PHOTO COURTESY OF JOHN DUNN

The retirement, 2007: Ken finally takes down his Royal Warrants prior to closing up his famous Thistle Street shop.

THE FISH BUSINESS
Merchants, Canners and Filleters

Put down that knife, Kenneth!

I have always considered myself to be a Torry Loon although I was born in a top floor tenement flat on Regent Quay in 1935. In 1938, the year before the outbreak of World War 2, my mum and dad moved to a middle floor flat at 55 Menzies Road; my grandparents lived in a top floor flat at No. 57. This move was most convenient for Dad as he worked as a fish filleter alongside his father; the walk to work across the Chain Bridge was so easy. The firm on Riverside Drive was the Scottish Co-operative Wholesale Society, (SCWS), one of the largest fish processors in Aberdeen at the time. At their busiest times there were about 50-80 hand fish filleters, most of them women. Back then the workers had a lunch break of about 45 minutes to one hour and for those who happened to live a short distance from the 'fish hoose' they would walk/run home for a quick bite to eat – no grazing back then.

In late 1939, early 1940, my father was called up to do military service and he spent his six years in the Army Catering Corps including time as as a cook in Germany after the British invasion. On his return to 'Civvy Street' he returned to the SCWS, working in the 'fresh department.' This department processed all the fresh fish bought that day off the fish markets; the filleted fish was then dispatched to co-operative stores throughout Scotland and elsewhere; it was a very busy firm. I would occasionally help my father if he had to do overtime, helping to empty kilns of the smoked fish, pack them and put them into the large fridges, all ready for the next day's transport. On one evening there was a small squad of filleters working and one of the women was showing me how to fillet haddocks, and I think I was doing quite well. However, when my father spotted me with a knife in my hand he said: 'Kenneth put that knife down', which I did. 'You'll do something other than this trade.' And so I did.

On leaving school in 1951 I began a five year apprenticeship as a radio engineer with Miller Brothers, a very old established firm who were photograph processors, optical

The irresistible fishmonger: Ken Watmough shows off his wares.

experts, and radio and gramophone repairers. The family were relatives of the Bruce Miller family. Evening classes three nights per week for three years were required as part of the City and Guilds course, which I completed successfully by the time I was 18.

At the age of 21 I was called up and did two years National Service in the Royal Air Force. After the basic 'square bashing', I was posted to an RAF training school at RAF Compton Bassett in Wiltshire to be trained on all the RAF Ground Wireless equipment; I'm sure my civilian qualification was a big help here. After completing the seven month Ground Wireless Fitters course I was promoted to the rank of corporal and posted to RAF Cosford, a school for Boy Entrants. I was an instructor on the Ground Wireless Wing and had to train these young airmen to be ready for joining the man's service as fully qualified ground wireless mechanics.

National Service was a bit of a wrench for some 18-year-old young men but I enjoyed the service life and for me the whole experience was a valuable part of my adult life.

After my two years I was fortunate on returning to Aberdeen to land a super job as a radio and television engineer with Bruce Miller's. They were well-established music sellers in George Street: they sold sheet music, a complete range of musical instruments, electric guitars, amplifiers with all the gizmos needed to be a pop star. There was a department solely dedicated to the largest range of electronic organs in Scotland, record players, radio and television and a white goods department. I spent much of my time servicing TVs, and also in installing, servicing and tuning electronic organs. At that time sale of small electronic organs for the home was very popular in the North-east. The

Representing Scotland at the National Federation of Fishmongers. With chefs Ainsley Harriot and Rick Stein.

installation, servicing and tuning of these took me to hotel function rooms, private houses and many churches and mission halls throughout the north of Scotland.

I moved from Bruce Miller's in 1964 to DER (Domestic Electric Rentals), which was part of the Thorne Electrical Group, and was opening a branch in Aberdeen. This company, as with many other companies, rented television sets, this being very popular back then, and I was appointed as manager. In the course of next three years I had opened a further two new branches in Aberdeen. DER took over Radio Rentals and I was transferred to them as Aberdeen manager.

Throughout my life I have always had an interest in local politics and I was successfully elected in 1974 as the Conservative councillor for Hazlehead and Craigiebuckler. Also about then as TVs were becoming more reliable and the popularity of TV rentals was declining I intended to move and was invited to become part of an insurance company sales team. Much of the sales calls took place in the evenings and this gave me time to do my council meetings during the day.

How I re-entered the fish trade is a bit of a story. One of my clients had written off his Simca van and as my daughter had a small Simca car I bought the van for spares, not knowing how important this wee van was to become.

It was during a holiday in Ballater, 1978-79 that I noticed a wee van selling fish. This van came down from Portsoy onto Deeside, some distance. From this I saw an opportunity to provide this type of service from nearer Aberdeen. The Simca van was repaired and equipped and after making personal visits to the many Deeside hotels and restaurants the Ken Watmough fish delivery business started. To begin with I rented space in a railway arch in College Street and little did I think whilst preparing crab claws for an American customer that I would be reminded of what my father had said to me all these years ago, and, yet now, here I was in the fish trade.

One of my suppliers also had a fishmonger's shop in Thistle Street, which his sister ran badly and he was keen to offload; I willingly took over the lease in 1982. As a retail fishmonger I enrolled as a member of the National Federation of Fishmongers; membership was essential, as it is the main UK body and a great sharing network. I attended many seminars and trade meetings and in 1984 I was elected as the Scottish representative to the NFF Council. Council meetings take place in London at Fishmonger's Hall, the HQ of 'Fishmongers Company'. This ancient livery company gives us the use of one of their meeting rooms for our council meetings. Our meetings take place quarterly and as time passed I was elected in 1998 as vice-president and took office as national president in 1999. I remain a council member to this day.

But before all this could happen some serious trading changes had to take place and buying direct at auction in Aberdeen Fish Market was necessary. This was a completely new experience but a lot of generous help from trade friends was much appreciated. Also I had to get back to learning how to fillet and process all species of fish to my own high standard for my type of fishmonger shop, and it worked.

It was not too long, certainly after a lot of hard work and commitment, that the Ken

The net braiding team at the Enterprise Ship Stores, 1949 – an integral part of the fish scene at that time. This is where Kathleen Porter (ref. page 131) worked for a spell.

Watmough fishmonger's shop became well known for selling a wide range of quality fish and seafood. As proof of this I was invited in 1983 to be a supplier to HM the Queen Mother at her Birkhall home near Ballater. I also started supplying HRH Prince of Wales, (Duke of Rothesay in Scotland). I was granted the Queen Mother Warrant in 1986 and HRH Prince of Wales in 1987; both warrants I held until my retirement in 2007.

In retirement, I can look back on what has gone on in my life, along with the many associated activities and can honestly claim that my most enjoyable years were spent being a fishmonger.

Kenneth (Ken) Watmough, b.1935. Federation of Fishmongers. Interviewed 2016.

My speciality was filleting flat fish

I'd heard my friend was getting about £8 a week working in the fish. That was a lot of money. So I got a job in the fish and I was there seven or eight years. I started at J&J Phillips at Cabels Lane in Torry. We worked from eight o'clock until six, Monday to Friday, and a half-day on a Saturday. It was all fresh fish we worked on, bought that day from the Market. We smoked some of it on the premises. You started off by packing, then skinning, but once you graduated you would become a specialist in certain jobs; I

Kathleen Porter, the young filleter, November 1949.

ended up as a filleter. My speciality was flat fish – the big thing was being able to fillet a fish without leaving bones in and taking all of the fish off the bones. Later I got fed up working in the fish and was thinking it was getting beneath me. But I'd loved working there; it was a wonderful atmosphere. Everybody sang. One person would start whistling and then the whole 20-odd started whistling along.

It was good working in the fish but when you went to the dancing and any guy asked you where you worked, you'd never say you worked there. Never. I was engaged to a London guy and I was walking home from Torry one day and I had on my work boots. They were really nice boots with the white socks turned over the tops of them. He came past in his car and he saw me with these boots on. I'd told him I worked in an office. When he saw I worked in the fish that was the end of that.

You need to remember that in those days you had hardly any baths. If you wanted a bath you'd have to go to public baths like the Uptown Baths in Justice Mill Lane or the one in Hanover Street; otherwise, if you didn't go there, it was a metal bath or just a basin in your house.

Kathleen Porter, b.1932. J&J Phillips, Torry. Interviewed 2016.

She was an amazing character

Dad was in the fish business along with his mother and his brother: 'Barbara Nicoll & Sons.' In the fish market she was known as 'Babby Ann' but if I ever tried to call her that I'd get a clip round the lug. She was an amazing character. When she died it was just about the biggest funeral ever held in Aberdeen.

The hearse left from 56 Menzies Road and it was already arriving at the cemetery at Allenvale opposite the Duthie Park, well over a mile off, when the last car left the street. That's how many people attended. She was buried on a Sunday, the day she had fixed so as not to interfere with an ordinary working day at the fish market. The Salvation Army arranged it; the band and the songsters were there in the churchyard to play all her favourite tunes. The whole of the fish trade turned out. She was such a well-known and well-loved character.

She was a fish merchant. She'd go down to the fish market to buy the fish and then spend most of the day in her shop at the New Market, down the stairs there in the basement. She'd be there every evening till after six and she would have started her day in the fish market buying the fish at six in the morning. She was a very hard-working woman who lived on her own. She was widowed early. The fish was her whole life, that and the Salvation Army, to which she was devoted. If ever they were doing any fund raising she would be in the thick of it: any sales of work.

I loved that woman. When I pop my clogs I hope to be buried in Allenvale alongside her. She was such a great character. She sat at the table entertaining people, maybe the Major from the Salvation Army, and she would just take out her teeth, wrap them up in a

She would just take out her teeth, wrap them up in a hanky and then start handing the food around.

'A very big business': Aberdeen Fish Market in full flow, 1920s.

hanky and then start handing the food around.

Granny kept the best tenement in Torry; absolutely spanking inside it was. She wouldn't allow anyone to prop up their bikes in the hallways; everyone had to take their turn at cleaning the stairs. If anyone was late she would just go up to their door, give it a knock and cry out: 'Come on, Mrs —, it's your turn this week for the stairs!

Dennis Nicoll, b.1938. Barbara Nicoll & Sons, Torry. Interviewed 2006.

The fish was a very big business

The Fish Market was very busy with three sales on a Saturday morning. I went straight into the Fish Market at 15. I applied for one or two jobs as a clerk or for office work. I got this job in the fish with Robert Hastie & Sons. The fish buying and the office work were combined. You were out in the morning selling your fish and then you had to do all your books and accounts in the afternoon. You also had a fleet of trawlers so you had all their work to do as well – buying, selling, gear and so forth.

From the beginning, you went onto the Market as a trainee salesman. The salesman actually sold the fish and as the trainee you wrote down and booked every box of fish that he sold and you also noted the buyer and seller. Your book should tally with the book that he had – so it was a back-up for him as well. So if a buyer said: 'I only got nine boxes,' or 'I only bought nine boxes,' you could check up the different books and see who was right. It was my boss, the fish salesman, who conducted the auction; he sold his firm's trawler of fish. It was called 'a shot' of fish and you had the flats to start with – lemon sole or halibut and things like that, then you had your quantities of haddock, then your green fish – cod – and then your offals such as your skate, your roker, your turbot and such

The fish was sold a boat at a time; the boat's whole catch was landed on the quayside and the salesman sold that boat of fish.

lower stuff. And he sold down the rows, rows of 20 boxes. The fish was sold a boat at a time; the boat's whole catch was landed on the quayside and the salesman sold that boat of fish.

The boats could come in at any time after eight or nine o' clock in the morning right up until maybe five o' clock on the following morning of the sale. The boat that was in first had its fish sold first. The porters started at three or four o' clock landing the catch. I was never in at that time at all; sales didn't start until seven or half past. There were also salmon sales as well but that was a separate unit in the market and they happened at nine o' clock.

The company I worked for owned their trawlers and they had their own ship's chandlers who did all the ropes and the nets. They had a number of girls as well who made nets, up in the loft in Commercial Quay. They had five trawlers, all in Aberdeen. They went away for maybe eight to ten days; it depends where they went – sometimes maybe only three or four days. It depended where they were getting fish. So you didn't have fish to sell every day but you always had plenty of books to keep up with in the office, even on a quieter day.

Kenneth (Ken) Raitt, b.1939. Fish Market. Interviewed 2016.

On the assembly line – the worst of jobs

Financial matters eased when I went to university because I now was receiving a fairly generous grant. But I still had to take on part-time jobs, not only during the long holidays but every weekend too. The very worst job I ever had was on the assembly line at Marshall's Canning Factory over in Torry. This was where they received herring and packed it into tins to be sent to the Forces. It was a filthy, smelly job with no regard to hygiene whatsoever. The routine was for the dozen of us to stand in a line at a huge table; two would weigh out the herring and the rest of us would pack it into the cans and one girl would then pour a dollop of tomato sauce on the top of the fish.

Hygiene was non-existent: we wore welly boots and had an apron but there was no compulsion to wear gloves or to cover our hair. If a fish fell to the floor you simply picked it up and carried on. And the floor was wet and slippery and covered with debris. One of the women was suffering from running sores on her hands and face but still took her place on the assembly line. There was a loft above and from it new supplies of cans would come raining down on us, often without any warning. The result was that we often cut open our fingers and had to get an Elastoplast to cover the bleeding. But fish oil and Elastoplast don't mix and before very long the covering would slip off the finger and get lost, goodness knows where. If it had disappeared into the can along with its contents then that was too bad. I could imagine some poor soldier fighting for his country, opening his can of herring and having to spit out a piece of dirty Elastoplast off the finger of some Torry quine a couple of thousand miles away.

Graduation Day, 1959 – and a world away from Marshall's Canning Factory. Liz is second right.

The worst thing about the job was the language, that and the perpetual stink of fish about your person. The women workers were from a Torry fishing background and were the roughest of the rough. Talk was on a no-holds-barred basis, a mix of oaths, of obscenities and of naked sexual references. I think they took especial delight in enlightening this green young university student who had landed among them for the summer. When they discovered I was actually studying Mathematics then they concluded I must be truly nuts – I mean, why would anyone possibly want to go beyond the 12 times table and the ability to add up the shopping basket? There were two other students working alongside me but they were second year medics and so were revered by the workers, who could see the point of their subject. Even though they had four years of their studies to go, their colleagues would insist on addressing them respectfully as 'Doctor.' No such respect for me, however.

The smell was an even bigger problem. By now I was living in a house which had its own bathroom and when I got home I would make for it and wash everything including my hair. But however hard you scrubbed, the fishy smell seemed to cling to your very pores. I would travel up back home on the 17 bus and when passengers further along the line got on I could sense their reluctance to sit anywhere near me. That was the summer when I had no social life whatsoever.

Elizabeth (Liz) Strachan, b.1939. Marshall's Canning factory, Torry. Interviewed 2014.

Some of the boats would be out at sea for 30 days and when they landed, the porters would refuse to unload because of the smell.

We all trusted each other

In those days the fish market was full of hally-racket buggers who'd be up to all kinds of tricks. No harm in it, just fun, just taking the micky out of people. If a photographer was around they would hold up a notice behind someone's head with the message 'Pervert' or 'Idiot'. Of course, in the old days the fish was much more plentiful and there was more money around and they were all keen on enjoying it. We would all help each other, make sure nobody had to struggle. If someone had got some good fish in, from Faroe or Iceland, something you hadn't got yourself, they would sell you some and help you out.

We all trusted each other. Once you were known in the fish market no money was involved in your dealings. You'd go up to the box you wanted and just put your tally on it. That acted as your word of honour. You'd get the bill the following Monday to settle the account. They gave you till noon on the Tuesday to pay; if you failed then the salesman would tell you in front of everyone: 'Sorry, you can't have any more fish. You haven't settled your bill.' That would show you up, put you in a bad light. It seldom happened: in all my 40 years at the fish market I only saw it about half a dozen times.

In the 43 years since I went in, the fish market has shrunk cruelly. When I started you could have gone from one end of the fish market to the other, which would stretch round Blakie's Quay, a whole mile and a quarter, and do that three times in the day – three and three-quarter miles of fish in all.

The old steam trawlers would land their catch early in the morning and the sale would start at seven. All the fish was laid out. Once they were cleared, the next batch of boats would land their fish. You had 'second sales', then 'third sales'. There was a herring market at Blaikie's quay and at the main market there would fish of all sorts: ling, skate, cod, lemon sole, haddock, plaice, turbot, sharks, even the odd dolphin. You name it; it would be there.

I couldn't say that the quality was always of the highest. Sometimes the boats might be away for three to four weeks, right the way up to Iceland, and some of the quality would have become poor. You can imagine what the first fish they had caught, maybe 30 days before, had got like. That's why the fish had to be laid out so that you could always see what you would be bidding for. The best would be the ones which were at the top, caught last just before the boat had come in. You had to use your eye and your experience to get the best. What you would look for would be a nice fresh body, as stiff as a poker and a bright eye.

What I would look for when I went down in the morning was to come back with a good variety of fish. If the quality was right I'd take it – mullets, bass, rainbow trout, haddock, skate, plaice, ling – the lot. Every one of them has to be cut differently. I picked up how to do that when I was young. Even as a schoolboy I'd be down at the fish house, playing around but also keeping my eyes open to see how it was all done.

But the fish market porters ruined things. They would stop the sales for next to nothing. Some of the boats would be out at sea for 30 days and when they landed, the

On a basis of trust: Fish market salesmen at work, 1950s.

porters would refuse to unload because of the smell. That meant the whole fish market came to halt. They were looking after their own jobs – protectionism. They refused any flexibility. Boats had to be unloaded in strict rotation, however big or small their catch. Their union was very strong; they operated a closed shop. Jobs would be handed down from father to son and kept in the family.

They made good money but the fish market collapsed in the end. Boats began to move off to Peterhead where they could unload themselves or make their own arrangements and bring in their own casual labour. Aberdeen has never really recovered its old position.

I loved the fish market, always; I never got tired of it, the buzz and the people there. The hours were long but they kept you busy. I'd get up at 4.30, leave the house at five and down to the shop. The first thing I did was to get the yellow fish which had been cured the night before. They were pickled and had been hung up and put on trays to go into the big fridge so as to dry out. I would take them out, take them to the kilns in the basement, get the fires going. Only then did I go down to the fish market for the buying. I'd load up the van with empty boxes, go down, get my fish and return and unload. The last thing you did each day was to pickle the yellow fish and hang them out to dry. Next day, pile them up on racks and put them into the fridge to dry. Then the following day, when they were bone dry, you'd smoke them over the kilns.

I would do all my own cutting and filleting. I could get through 10 fish in under three minutes; two/three quick cuts are all that's necessary. That's something that takes about six months to pick up properly. The secret is ultra-sharp knives. That way the blade will slice through the fish nice and clean and you won't cut yourself. A blunt blade will bounce and go into you; a sharp blade never. It's like a razor. A good filleter can make a bad fish into a good one; a bad filleter and it's the other way around.

We'd shift about 2,000 fish a week. In the days of the wild salmon, and when I was the only fishmonger in town to have a licence to buy it, I would sell as much as I could get. Between November and the end of December, for the Christmas orders, I would produce in excess of 1,000 sides of smoked salmon, all smoked on the premises. I would sell it all over the world including Australia, America, and France. Now it's the farmed salmon that's sold mostly.

Haddock was the backbone of the business; the simple haddock, yellow, smoked, white, block fish. The demand for good quality fresh fish is still there. Once the quota system settles down then the trade will flourish as it ever did. We need to keep the foreign boats out. But I also blame the use of the beam trawlers, which sweep the sea floor with chains and churn up the sea bottom. That's where the fish feed and they've been frightened off. Go back to the old-fashioned way with one net to a boat, then the fish will return.

Aberdeen harbour has changed. The old fish market has been cut right back. The boats can't bring in enough now. The Government restricts our boats but the foreign ones can come in and fish our grounds. The Poles and the French use big net trawlers and go right up the West coast. These are the buggers who've messed up their own grounds and now they're doing the same to ours.

Dennis Nicoll, b.1938. Aberdeen Fish Market. Interviewed 2006.

THE FISHING COMMUNITIES
Fittie and Torry

'A great community spirit': Fittie neighbours pause for a chat, 1964. [PHOTO: ABERDEEN JOURNALS]

A Fittie childhood

Footdee is a community on its own, different from the rest of Aberdeen. The only other place like it is Torry, Aberdeen's other fishing community and across the Dee from us. In my mother's day a ferry connected the two and you had to pay a farthing to cross to the other side with a rope pulling it along. When I was at the Academy we had to write an essay on where we lived and that's when I realised how different what I was describing was from anyone else in the class. Everything about us was to do with the sea and with boats. They would describe playing games in the park; they would talk of going on the swings whereas our favourite was to 'ride the waves'. At high tide there would be just this little piece of sand left and we would go down to it and wait for the waves to come crashing in towards us. The idea was to get as close as possible before turning round and running back up the slipway, shrieking and getting a good soaking too. That was our fun.

The houses down in the old village had sheds at the back and some had no running water inside the houses either; you had to share a sink with others. But our grandmothers kept their houses spick and span. Everything was polished till it was gleaming. The lino

Still an attractive and special place. 'Welcome to my garden', 2017.

on the floor would be rubbed and rubbed so that you could see your own face looking back up at you from out of it. In the kitchen there would be a nice rug in its middle; there would be the black grate, all leaded and polished till it too shone out.

Footdee had a great community spirit; everyone was involved with each other's lives, young and old together. There was a close family life. On a Saturday evening we'd all go to the carnival together; then after the fun we'd walk up Justice Street and buy a bag of chips at Robertson's chipper. The children had their own games too. There would be beddies and for that we used proper wooden beddies made by my grandfather. Then there'd be skipping games and great games of hide and seek. This was much more elaborate than a simple matter of finding where somebody was hidden. We would lay a trail of objects like empty bottles and tins which led to the hiding place and the one who'd found the most clues would be the winner. We'd use the whole of Footdee as our playground so the game could take hours.

Children had their own games. There would be beddies with proper wooden beddies made by my grandfather. Then there'd be skipping games and great games of hide and seek.

We'd use the beach as our great playground. We'd play on the swings there or get up a game of tennis using a washing line. We'd got hold of an old netball stand and had games with it. A lot of activity was organised round East St Clement Church, which was right next door to us. We'd go to a service each Sunday morning, then Sunday school and, once you were old enough, to Bible class. During the week there were the Lifeboys, the Boys' Brigade and the Girls' Guildry. Then the school ran a play centre twice a week. There was always something on and the whole community joined in. In the spring and in September the church would hold its picnic; a train would be hired and we would set off to Torphins or Lumphanan and play in a field there. You'd come back with a goody bag filled with a cake, a couple of biscuits and some sweeties.

The community hung together. My mother could recall the times when doors were never locked and if you went to call on someone you'd simply throw their door open and shout up: 'Are you there, Granny Kelly?' or whoever. If anyone was ill or in need, then Granny would make some soup, pour it into a carrying tin and get you to take it round. She wouldn't make a fuss: just a 'Here, take this round to old Mrs Brown – she could maybe do with a bit of nice hot soup'.

The 1950s and 60s now seem a Golden Age to me. Our pleasures were so simple and never-ending. On a Saturday Granddad Kelly would take us down the fish market, a wonderful place full of smells and noises and excitement. The harbour would be five, six deep with boats, all stacked up against the quay and men having to jump from one deck to the next to get ashore. In the Fish Market you'd see the thousands of boxes laid out and hear the shouts and the din of the sellers auctioning them off. It was impossible to make out what was being said, it was so loud and so fast, but then you'd see someone going up to a box and sticking a label on it and you knew another one had been sold. Then the Fish Market porters would come to wheel the piled boxes away. There was something colourful about the whole thing; there was a romance about the old Fish Market.

The girls would play huge games of rounders; it was quite a challenge to get round

Now a conservation area: Fittie as it is today.

with anything up to 20 fielders going after the ball. There was a massive green space where the new carnival now is and that's where we were free to play away our summer evenings. The people from the town seemed to stick to the areas behind the Beach Ballroom so we could regard all this as our own Footdee space. It was the same with the beach itself. We would all stick to the sands up at our end and leave the stretches to the north to the rest of Aberdeen. Swimming was a huge part of my childhood, sometimes in the baths but usually just in the sea.

We would spend all day down at the beach. Twenty of us would set off at nine in the morning, armed with bottles of lemonade and a few biscuits and pick our spot. The older kids were expected to look after the younger ones and keep them out of harm. Back home, the mothers would be doing their cleaning; at about 11 they would appear with sandwiches and flasks. In the afternoon when the men had come off their shift they would be the ones to come down with fresh drink and food. It might be nine at night before we'd finally make our way home to bed.

At some point in the afternoon the older ones would go to the shop to buy cones of ice cream for us all. These were called cappies and the man would always ask: 'D'ye wint some juice on it?' If you said yes, then you'd get a nice squirt of raspberry over its top. By the time those who'd gone on this message had returned, the ice cream might be melting and running down the cones; they would lick them to keep the ice-cream from running onto their hands. When you got your cappy it might have been licked by two or the different tongues but you didn't care. Then there were the bags of Smith's crisps with their tiny twists of salt inside each packet. It was thought very lucky if you were the one who found two of those blue twists in your bag.

All around us in Footdee the men worked either at the sea fishing or in the shipyards. The yards were big employers in those days. It would take Hall Russell's 25 minutes to empty of its workforce each night; they would come pouring through the gates and onto the nearest bus. You'd see them piling on, crammed all the way up the stairs and hanging off the platform. The buses accommodated up to 56 passengers – officially – but there must have been what seemed to be 150 or so on some of them.

Footdee was that kind of place: full of colour and busy things happening. The SAI works could be seen from the windows. You'd go there at night, look out through the glass and see all these colours from the chemicals, flying up into the darkness, lighting it up with beautiful lemon, blues and red shades. You'd open the window and sniff the sulphur in the air. Then you had the little steam train every half hour puffing its way up from the harbour, where it had been getting another load of coal, right the way up Church Street on its rails that were built into the cobbles and onto the gas works nearby. I'm sure none of this was very healthy for us but it was all part of the noise and the colour of Footdee.

Footdee itself has changed. When the oil came a lot of the old families began to move out. The shipyards have closed; the fishing at the harbour is down to a few boxes. Footdee is now a conservation area; it's still a very attractive and special place, quaint and picturesque. This has made it a desirable place to move into. It's become a yuppie community mostly populated by incomers. I consider I grew up and left at exactly the right time. I'm very grateful for my childhood in Footdee. It was a wonderful time and in a wonderful place.

Norma Reid, b.1943 Footdee. Interviewed 2006.

It was a very close-knit community

Being brought up in a close-knit community. The two-year-old Alex Rae on the doorstep of his granny's home in Grampian Place, 1949.

Torry was a very close-knit community. The men coming home with their bags over their shoulders on a Tuesday – that was what they called a 'half-landing'. My grandfather had been amongst them; he used to come home on a Tuesday and take us to the Tivoli. Then he went away again in the early hours of Wednesday morning and came back on a Saturday and the process was repeated, week in, week out. Most people who lived in Torry at that time were trawler men or worked in the fish market; it was definitely a fishing community over there. Even in later life the older guys would have been the skipper of a boat or the mate. What I remember on a Saturday morning was people wandering up the road in the early hours. You looked out of the window and saw these guys with black oilskin bags – which I know now was their clothes – and they had a net bag in their hand, which was their fish, taking home a 'fry' to their families.

My grandmother never went much beyond Menzies Road. I don't think she ever went across the bridge over the Dee. She did all of her shopping in Torry, went to the

Descended from a line of Torry folk. Ron Caie's great grandfather, William, nicknamed Cheerie (possibly ironically), fisherman, with family, 1880s.

pictures in Torry, went to church in Torry. It's a changed community now but she knew everybody and everybody knew her. And within the tenement that she stayed in, in Grampian Place, they didn't call each other by their Christian names, always their surnames. There was the Wifie Forrest and the Wifie Garden and my granny just got called the Wifie Jeffrey and that's what everybody called her; I don't suppose anybody knew that her real name was Williamina.

Alex Rae, b.1947. Grampian Place, Torry. Interviewed 2016.

We were Torry folk

My parents were Torry folk and that's where I spent my boyhood. My father was a superintendent marine engineer for a fleet of some 14 trawlers. Torry had its own strong values. The old fishing community in particular held on to its close-knit, introspective ways. I say introspective but it's curious to consider how in many

Ron's engineer father, William, on board the Melbourne, 1928.

households there was at least one member who had travelled the high seas and been to places like India, Burma, China and Fiji, not to mention the regular seasonal trips down to Lowestoft, Grimsby and Yarmouth. My father was once on a job down in Dunedin, New Zealand, working in the engine room when he heard the unmistakable instruction of 'Haud on a mintie'. When he asked where the speaker had originally come from he was told, Torry' and when whereabouts in Torry: 'Victoria Road'. It turned out that the two of them had originally lived just 10 doors from each other and now here they were on the other side of the world together.

My father was frequently out at sea on a trawler and the ship to shore radios were often the only way to keep up with his whereabouts. Everyone in Torry would listen in and the comings and goings of the local vessels were a standard subject of gossip. I remember once when my father was out on a sea trial and, came his dinner time, was still 20 miles offshore. He radioed in to inform my mother that as it was now three o'clock he wouldn't make the meal table that day. My mother was furious and berated him over the radio in vigorous style – for the whole of Torry to listen in to.

As I grew older I got the chance to join my father on the occasional trial trip. Some of these maiden trips could be regarded almost as festive outings. I remember going on the trial voyage of the trawler: 'Loch Lomond', and there was a huge crowd of folk on board and a picnic-like atmosphere among them. When something went wrong and the brand new vessel bashed onto the North Pier, it was quickly shrugged off as just 'a wee dunt' and the trip continued on its merry way.

Torry was a good place to grow up in. We were conscious of it being a distinct community from the city over the bridge on the other side of the Dee. But by now there was three Torrys: there was the old and original fishing community clustered round the harbour, then the working class suburb, which had developed in the 19th century around Menzies Road and Victoria Road and full of 'toonsers' who had no connection with the sea. Lastly there was the Garden City, the new model council house scheme built by the city between the wars and of high-quality housing stock.

The old fishing community resented the toonser incomers and when my father married my mother, who came from the other side of the Dee, he was thought of as having married 'out'.

Father and son on board: Schoolboy Ron with his engineer dad.

Victoria Road hasn't changed so very much in the years since those days, not in outward appearance at least. There are still shops stretching up and down it towards the bridge though their identity has been changed. There used to be some real characters among them. There was a fine butcher called Horatio Robbie, and I used to love going in among the sawdust on the floor and gaze at the imposing pair of Highland cattle horns he displayed on his wall like some hunting trophy. Further down the road was another butcher, Willy Morris, and he would entice the ladies into his shops by holding up a string of his own shop-made sausages and thrilling them by describing them as his 'tubes of joy'. On the corner of Baxter Street there was a post office and stationery shop run by Willy Bruce, who had lost a leg in the First World War. Then there was Feel George, slightly

wanting and always wandering around, not to mention the notorious Snuffy Ivy, a 'lady of the night'; you'd see her climbing onto the bus a little the worse for wear and complaining in a loud voice about 'Aa thae snobs in Torry'.

My uncle had an interesting experience once with a pair of ladies who were in the same line of business as Snuffy. He was messing about in his uncle's boat down in the Torry harbour when he was approached by two young ladies. There was a trawler riding at anchor but stuck out there because there was some infection on board and it was having to fly the Yellow Flag. They asked if he would kindly row them out to the boat – there would be half a crown in it for him. Evidently they had calculated that there would be members of the crew sufficiently sex-starved to make it worth their while. When he got back to the shore it was to find the police waiting for him. He was bundled into a van and taken to his uncle, who was a pillar of the church. I think he was let off with a severe warning and a bit of a beating.

Ronald (Ron) Caie, b.1938. Victoria Road, Torry. Interviewed 2014.

The engine room of RMS Cedric when Ron's father was Second Engineer on the New York-Liverpool run.

Once a Torry quine, always a Torry quine

Once a Tory quine always a Torry quine. I have two sons; one of them says he will never ever leave Torry; he wouldn't dream of living anywhere else. But that's not surprising: Torry's in the family's blood. When we were newly married and looking for our own place to live in my father told us: 'Dinna ging onywye ower the watter. Ye'll niver settle onywhere awa fae Torry.'

And he's been proved right. We've gone looking for houses all over the town umpteen times but I still come back home and decide that, no, Torry is where I was born, it's where I grew up and it's where I want to live out my days. We came to this address in 1975 and here we still are 40 years later. You see, there's no place like Torry.

Margaret Wright, b.1950. Walker Road, Torry. Interviewed 2016.

The young Torry quine: a four-year-old Wilma Gillanders, taken outside the wash house in the backie.

It was fabulous when I was growing up

We lived at 118 Victoria Road, Torry. Until very recently this remained the old family home as my mother continued to stay there till her death in 2004. So I'm a Torry quine, through and through. I'm very happy and proud to be so. The house is still there; it's one of the large Victoria Road tenements.

My mother was the lynchpin of our family. She was so proud, hardworking and loyal – and, most of all, loving. Through our whole lives she was our champion and our supporter; she never faltered. She sang like a lintie and at our family gatherings we would all gather around her. She was never happier than when Dad was home and we could all be there with her. She was bright and had a wicked sense of humour. She was a small woman, only five-foot two, but she kept us all 'in-aboot'. She lived till she was 94, a grand old lady to the very end.

When I was growing up it was a fabulous place: the stairs shone and smelt of polish, always; the windows were kept gleaming and the stair landing spotless. All the women took their turn so that it was cleaned every day. All the children of the tenement played together. It was like living in one great extended family where everyone looked out for each other and knew each other intimately.

Dad was frequently away at sea, being a trawl skipper. When he came home the tenement would have this big fry up. He would appear with this huge pile of fish and I would race up and down the stairs, calling in at each flat to collect an enamel pie dish from each. I'd take them all back to our flat and then would come the sharing out of the fish according to the numbers in each flat. I would go back up and down the stairs with the pie dishes, now filled with fish and everyone would have their big fry up

We children would play in the backyards; we'd hold concerts in the backies with songs of the day like 'Put Another Nickel in, in the Nickelodeon' featuring loudly. To me 118 was a fabulous place. Our toilets were shared ones, half way down the stairs, and looked after with great pride. You wouldn't dare come in from the backie with muddy feet because someone was bound to have just finished cleaning the stairs.

For Mum, it was a place where everyone pulled together. She was full of stories about how, in the war when the sirens went, they would all first of all gather beneath the stairs in the lobby and then make a dash for it to the shelters when the going was good. She was full of happy memories of all her friends and neighbours. When I think back I am too. We children always felt safe and looked after. We were free to roam over the whole area without fear. Our playground was the Bay of Nigg. This was the spot for big family

Skipper father, Charles Lamb Buchan, shown centre, wearing suit.

picnics. There were always heaps of kids to play with. All us kids would hive up the lanes and dart in and out of the gardens, nicking carrots. But that was as far as the mischief went: everyone knew I was Wilma Buchan and I knew that if ever I got up to anything too outrageous my mother would know about it within 24 hours.

That's how I was brought up, in a framework of discipline, respect, sharing – and love.

My parents kept an open house. All five of us would take our friends back to 118. The flat was always full of folk. It didn't matter who, all were made to feel welcome. When my sisters worked at the fish they would appear with the other fish quines; when my brother was in the Army he would bring back the lads from the barracks; when my other brother got involved with the church, members of his choir would drop in and when I was at the college I would bring back my student friends. When my mother died we received dozens of letters and cards which recalled visits to number 118 and the bowl of soup my mother would instantly provide. I had so many happy times there: singing and telling stories round the fire, all together. When I was a student I would hold post-Torcher parties at home. I'd put a tarpaulin on the floor, all the furniture would be pushed back and then Mum would retire to her bed with a Bacardi and Coke, which she never actually drank, and let us get on with it.

My father was a lovely man, a great romantic. He would draw hearts on the steamed up windows and print out the message: 'I love you.' He was a skipper and occasionally people would come in to prepare for their mates' tickets. Then they would have to practise Morse code. He had these little tins with holes drilled into them, which once had held dried milk, and he would lay them out in the living room and then out into the

Wilma with her parents.

Wilma's sister, Olive.

Wilma with her brother, Charlie, in uniform, 1947.

kitchen and you could see the lights flashing on and off as they spelled out the messages. He also rigged up a microphone attachment to the radio and invited his mates to listen to us performing. I'd sing 'Ye Banks and Braes,' and Mum: 'Just a-Waerying for You.'

When I had my first leather school bag at the age of five the skippers all banded together to take me in a taxi off to the Equitable to get it. And when I was at the college I might meet my dad at the Silver Slipper where he was with his mates – and oh, the stories! Of storms and trips and big catches. Every birthday he would prepare haggis and neeps for us all. Then when I was 17 I put in a request: 'Not haggis and neeps again, please Dad.' When my pals and I got home to celebrate my birthday we found caviar and champagne laid out for us and Mum and Dad standing there, beaming away.

They were a lovely and loving couple. Father was born in Sandhaven; he came from a line of seamen. His father had been a skipper before him. He was one of nine and he would tell this story of how they were all supposed to have their own hymn book but the family simply couldn't afford it. When my father turned up without his own hymn book at the school he got belted.

The routine for Dad was a fortnight to three weeks on a fishing trip, followed by three or four days at home. A lot depended on the weather and the way the fish were running. He had been at sea since he was 13 and had started out on the coal burners. His whole life was spent at sea. He was a lovely, lovely man. He loved music and he loved singing. He loved cooking. He was a bright and intelligent man. He adored my mother and he adored all of us.

We were always conscious of what a dangerous life being out at sea was for him and the others in Torry. My brother went to sea and so did my uncle. My brother became a mate; he couldn't get his skipper's ticket because he was colour blind. My younger brother wanted to go as well but here my mother put her foot down; she couldn't face another family member going off to such a dangerous life. He had to settle for being a ship's rigger and a chandler; eventually he had his own fish business.

Each night we would listen to the Shipping Forecast: 'Rockall, Bailey, Dogger, German Bight...' You'd lie awake in the night and think about him out there on the open seas. I remember the time my father lost a man overboard, off the 'George Robb', and how devastated he was over it. The atmosphere in the house was heavy for weeks after.

The telegram he sent me on my first day as a teacher, at Smithfield, was typical of the man and of the way he thought of us all. I've got it framed up there on the wall: 'From the "Scottish Princess", wishing you every success and a happy classroom. Love Dad.' He had a wealth of stories; he'd obviously had a hard life. Sometimes, when he had to go down the harbour to settle up, I would accompany him. We'd go to this big warehouse and I'd be taken up to the loft where they made nets and they would show me how they did it. I can remember sitting there with these women and the sunlight coming through the high windrows, making these lovely dark nets glisten in their hands as they worked with them. They would sing and tell stories as they worked away.

When Bob and I were courting we would take the car out to the harbour entrance

Off on another trip: 'The Scottish Princess' leaves port.

whenever we knew his boat was coming in and when we saw it we would flash our headlights and he would then put all the lights on the 'Scottish Princess' on for us so that we could watch the boat gliding back home, all ablaze with light. Then we would drive down to take him home, with his sea bags and those little oval tins for sweeties and nuts.

Kids today complain of being bored, of having no amenities, but we never seemed to be at a loss as to anything to do. The beach at Nigg gave us rock pools and buckies; we could row the boaties on the Dee. There was roller-skating in the street. We were never stuck in the house; we were forever out and about. Even late into the evening in the summer my mum had no worries about us. Now I'm constantly on the lookout for my grandson – he's seven. When we were young, my mother would simply say: 'Now don't wander off too far' and she would know we would be all right but now I'd be terrified to let him out of my sight. We now have this whole culture of fear for children's safety.

But then the area has definitely changed. In her later years I would take my turn with my sisters, Olive, Helen and Margaret, to go across to look after Mum. She would go to bed at eight but I would sit up till late. You'd look out of the window and see the Amadeus [popular nightclub] bus come into the street. Mum lived opposite the police box and the bus would debouche there. You'd see all the young people stagger off it and then… the language, the violence, the drunkenness. What they got up to in the phone box, well! And then there's the drugs.

It's no longer my Torry. The social fabric has broken down. Oh, there are still some of them left but these tend to be the old residents, who are now dying out. These are the ones who even at the end would stop me in the street and ask 'How's your mum? I haven't seen her at the window the last day or two – I hope she's all right.' When she died they were the ones who sent in the wreaths and the cards. It would have broken her heart if she had realised how rare all that was now becoming. She was born in 1909 and died in July 2004.

Well, perhaps it's not all bad: there has been an effort to revive interest in Torry as an old and proud community. There's the sign on the bridge which lets people know just how old Torry is; there were the 500th year gala celebrations; hanging baskets are put out in the summer. But it's difficult – and of course the fishing's gone into severe decline too.

Wilma Gillanders, b.1944. Victoria Road, Torry. Interviewed 2006.

The young people stagger off the bus and then… the language, the violence, the drunkenness. What they got up to in the phone box – well! And then there's the drugs.

The demise of Old Torry: Mrs Charlotte Simpson surveys the site of her old home, 1974. [PHOTO: ABERDEEN JOURNALS]

The village was like a ghost town

So much has come out of Torry. It's not a big or grand place but it's produced a heap of folk who've worked hard and got on in their lives. When I heard that old Torry was to be demolished to make way for oil development, I walked from my home in Ferryhill over the Chain Bridge with my dog to take a last look at the place where I had spent my childhood.

The village was like a ghost town; there was nobody to be seen. We wandered around, going upstairs and downstairs, looking into the abandoned houses including the one I had lived in. We also saw the one on Pier Head where my husband's grandfather had lived – now appearing as a tiny cottage in a row of other tiny cottages. What amazed me as I looked on at all the abandoned buildings was how small everything seemed. To think that whole families were brought up and to good lives from such tiny homes.

It was all very sad but I was glad I had been able to see the old Torry before it disappeared for ever.

Gina Gove, b.1923. Ferry Road, Torry. Interviewed 2016

I can remember the great big barrage balloons at the harbour to protect the yards

Grandfather's route march to Girdleness

My Torry grandparents lived in a cottage at the bottom of Baxter Street and I can remember the great big barrage balloons at the harbour – to protect the three shipbuilding yards down there. My grandfather would take us for a walk and he was an ex-RSM in the Gordons and he would make us walk in front of him on a route march to the Girdleness Lighthouse and back again. He would say: 'Get those shoulders back! Get those stomachs in!' But he always sent us back the last bit to the cottage because he went into the Nineteenth Hole.

Martha Alexander, b.1937. Baxter Street. Interviewed 2015.

TORRY MARINE RESEARCH LABORATORY

One of Aberdeen's best-kept secrets

At the Lab I started off as a Research Assistant: 'Unestablished', which basically meant I was on probation. I was in the plankton section and there I was initiated into the methods of plankton analysis – learning to categorise types, understand their place in the marine food chain, have knowledge of the ways in which they could be caught, what plankton's longer term prospects were, and how to measure such things by an accurate use of statistics and so on. I seemed to spend hours, peering down a microscope with an older colleague beside me tutoring me in all the ways of plankton.

I must admit I got wearied of this after a while. I was more interested in the ship side of the Lab's work, the actual venturing out to sea to catch the plankton. The older guys in the Lab began to recognise me as a safe pair of hands and also that I had a strong mechanical bent. So they put me on to looking after the equipment. This was vital work since the nets to catch the plankton had to be spun from a very fine silk which tended to rot in the salt water and so required constant inspection and maintenance.

Aberdeen's best kept secret'. The Marine Research Laboratory, Torry.

I made good progress and was invited down to London for my interview to rise to the rank of an Established Assistant. This was an extraordinary exercise in Civil Service bureaucracy. I had to be interviewed by Dr Ron Wright, who actually worked at the Lab and who accompanied me down on the train and then back again. Why all this couldn't

'A vessel with quite a history': The SS Explorer on yet another research expedition.

have been seen to back in Aberdeen is one of those Civil Service rituals.

The Lab was a leading research institute of its type, a place with a worldwide reputation and I was proud to become part of its work. Its director was Sir Cyril Lucas, a man of decidedly fixed habits. His home was in the West end and he would arrive at Falconer's department store, there to have his morning coffee and then pop round to his tobacconist to purchase his pipe tobacco, then visit R.S. McColl's for a newspaper. You could fix the hours of the day by him – but he was a true giant in his field.

In Scotland we had no rivals and in the UK only our twin institute at Lowestoft could challenge that position. When I started, the Lab employed maybe 100; now it is more like 300. Its work in amassing and advising on marine activity in the North Sea has become even more vital in this era of oil extraction and fish conservation. We have given crucial information on how the North Sea functions and have carried out a series of measurements along the Faroe/Shetland channel that offers invaluable evidence of climate change. We hold analysis data stretching back to the 19th century and so can show patterns and developments over a lengthy period of time. We have offered advice on fish stocks and the fixing of quotas.

In my time associated with the Lab the North Sea has become just about the most industrialised stretch of water on the whole planet. It is now stuffed full of oil rigs, of wind turbines, of gas and oil installations, of platforms and storage units. All this must affect the fish stocks; EU quotas have played their part in attempting to attack the issue. They have also been a contentious matter, the subject of annual negotiation and horse trading, so the work of the Laboratory becomes more and more central.

A lot of my Marine Laboratory time was spent at sea, some on our very own research ship: 'SS Explorer'. This vessel has quite a history. It was launched in Aberdeen in 1955 and was built by Alexander Hall's shipyard in the city. Its role was to investigate breeding and feeding grounds so as to establish fish levels and species types. We also monitored pollution and diseases.

It was built to very high standards of quality. It was old fashioned even at its inception in that it was a steam-driven boat and its hull was of riveted steel, constructed to withstand arctic ice. The phone system utilised heavy Bakelite instruments. Many of the instruments on board ran by clockwork and had been put together by ourselves in the Lab. On the other hand it carried the very first computer ever to appear on a similar vessel and this at a time when Aberdeen could only boast two others – one at ARI, the other at the University. It was by today's standards a massive machine and required its own cabin – and probably had much less power than the phone in your pocket. Internally the ship was a thing of some beauty. The officer's mess had a lovely sideboard of rich mahogany and comfortable chairs, made by Galloway & Sykes of Union Street.

We carried a total complement of 28 crew, seven scientists and 16 officers. As was normal a clear hierarchy prevailed on board; the officers and we scientists enjoyed the relative luxury of our fine mess but the ordinary crew had to make do with benches and a basic table. Trawling has always been a tough and dangerous way of life and as such has

On deck of The Explorer. John Dunn is third right.

attracted men who were themselves tough. Unfortunately, then as now, government ships didn't pay well and we tended to get older men or guys with colourful pasts and, on some occasions when we were short of crew members, a call would be made to the local prison for suitable recruits.

One thing you quickly learn on board is the identity of the most important man afloat. That is not the Captain or the Chief Engineer – it is the cook. Out at sea, food becomes very important to the morale and wellbeing of the men. They will put up with the rustiest old bucket as long as they can look forward to four good meals a day. They expect three-course breakfasts, three-course lunches, three-course dinners and supper too – you eat far more at sea than you would dream of consuming at home. Fortunately we normally had excellent fare on 'Explorer'.

The 'Explorer' did noble service and was finally withdrawn in 1984. 'The SS Explorer Preservation Society' has been set up. She now rests at Leith, awaiting full restoration.

I would describe the Marine Laboratory as one of Aberdeen's best-kept secrets. Here, the city has a world class research establishment, one that has been doing vital work for over a century and yet very few of its citizens are more than vaguely aware of its existence let alone its significance

And yet the work of the Marine Laboratory is more important than ever. The world is running out of resources on its land surfaces and yet a huge wealth of matter lies beneath the oceans just waiting to be properly researched and exploited. It's an irony that we now know more about Outer Space than we do about the inner space of the world beneath the waves. New species and fresh opportunities for foodstuffs, for energy and for medical development, await us down there and yet we pursue the glamour of space exploration and are willing to pump billions into it while that inner space lies largely neglected. Reverse that order of priority and our Torry based Research Laboratory could yet have a future equal to its glorious past.

John Dunn, b.1948. Torry Marine Research Laboratory. Interviewed 2016.

During his career at the Laboratory, John Dunn became deeply involved in schemes like Nuffield projects, designed to engage young talents in marine related developments. This has resulted in success at national level, with students gaining awards in several competitions.

Many of the instruments on board ran by clockwork and had been put together by ourselves in the Lab.

Safely on shore: A 17-year-old Bill Gordon, right, with mates Ron Ironside and Billy Still, Union Street, 1957.

OUT AT SEA
Trawlers, Riggers and Naval Recruits

The Marine Engineer: All at sea

I went to the Trades College and just hated it: I'm not a practical person in that way. I got expelled but my mother got me back in. Then a job came up at Mugiemoss paper mill. I quite enjoyed it there. However, I was a useless engineer. I had absolutely no aptitude for it or any interest. When my time was finished I signed up for the Merchant Navy, onto the Ben Line. I always remember my father singing: 'Those faraway places with strange sounding names...' and the notion of going off to see them had stuck in my mind. In fact I have always enjoyed travel and seeing new places. I enjoyed that aspect of the Navy but I was still a hopeless engineer and I kept being found out.

I was always on edge at sea, frightened of being landed with the next job that I wouldn't be able to do. I made some hellish bloomers. Once I succeeded in shutting the whole ship down in the middle of the night. Everyone had to go around in pitch black. They wouldn't speak to me for a week; they threatened to abandon me on some desert island. Another problem was being attacked by homosexuals. I was quite a pretty boy in those days: black, thick hair and slim. Nearly all the catering staff on board would be homosexual. This was before homosexuality was tolerated on shore and so they would join up to get away from that.

One night the Chief Engineer invited me into his cabin for a drink. I was sitting there and he started asking me about my own sex life, about any girls on shore and so on. Then he invited me to use his toilet – and still I didn't realise what was up. It was warm on the ship and I was wearing just my boiler suit and a pair of y-fronts. He started to grab at me to haul my suit off. I couldn't believe what was happening: 'No, no – you've got this all wrong!' I was yelling. I tried to get through the door but he slammed it shut on me. I was in a real dilemma – he was my Chief Engineer and I could have been charged with mutiny. I just hit out at him – on the face but not too hard. However, he fell back on the bed. Then he came at me again and this time I hit him really hard, right in the stomach. He fell back and started vomiting, doubled up. I rushed out back to my

Bill Gordon, right, with friend Ron Ironside and bike, Tillydrone, late 1950s.

cabin. I went to bed with a great big pair of scissors under the pillow, ready to defend my honour. I couldn't sleep; I didn't know what to do. It was nine o'clock and I was due on watch. Then came a knock at the door. It was the Chief: 'Ah, I think there was some mistake last night. Let's just forget it, shall we?'

Two weeks later I got promoted, even though I was the worst engineer in the world. But he wanted to get rid of me and out onto another boat. I liked going to all the different places, to Djakarta, to Hong Kong and so on but the boat would take so long to get there. Day after day it was eight hours on, four hours off, and only the empty sea to look at. The highlight of the week would be getting curry on a Sunday.

The best time was when the ship blew up in the Malacca Straits – not my fault, for once – and we had to stay in dock for 10 weeks on full pay while it was being repaired. We couldn't do the job; specialists had to be flown out from London for that. We were towed to Singapore. Ten weeks of wine, women and song – and we didn't do much singing! The place was full of girls with plenty of nurses from the Highlands and Orkney. However, I decided I no longer wanted this way of life – the ship, I mean. Besides, I was now courting Ruby and about to start a family. I wanted to get on shore and get married.

One night the Chief Engineer invited me into his cabin for a drink. I was sitting there and he started asking me about my own sex life.

William (Bill) Gordon, b.1939. The Ben Line. Interviewed 2007.

Get a shore job!

Wood Street at that time was all fisher families. It was quite a hard life for us all. It was difficult out at sea. Twice my father contracted pneumonia and twice he was shipwrecked. All of this was accepted as part of the fisherman's job.

There were good times as well. Everybody co-operated; they got things done

John Main in his 80th year and long retired from his trade as a painter – and certainly not a fisherman.

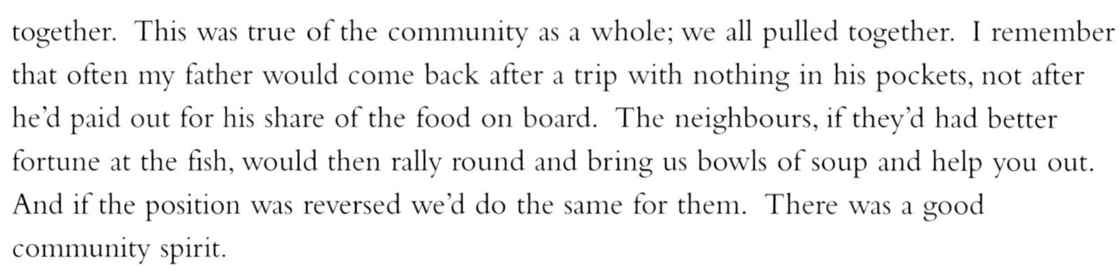

together. This was true of the community as a whole; we all pulled together. I remember that often my father would come back after a trip with nothing in his pockets, not after he'd paid out for his share of the food on board. The neighbours, if they'd had better fortune at the fish, would then rally round and bring us bowls of soup and help you out. And if the position was reversed we'd do the same for them. There was a good community spirit.

I myself wanted to become a fisherman but my father was against it: 'too hard a life, too risky – get a shore job.' Most of the time at home he was simply dog-tired. He would do his own gutting in the market; the boat might come in at four in the morning and he'd be there at the gutting till up to nine. He was so tired when he finally got home that as often as not he would go straight up to his bed. He would come home with his hands all hacked to bits and red where the salt had got at them. It was a terrible business. He would tell us that often on board they would all have to sit out at the pond – the deck place where they do the gutting – and just had to get on with the job while the seas were washing straight over them and they were freezing cold. It was for reasons like this that he warned me never to go to the sea.

John Main, b.1933. Wood Street, Torry. Interviewed 2003.

Harry Black at home, 2016.

The hardest job in the world

I served an apprenticeship with the Enterprise Ship Stores, a firm which offered services to fit out the boats for another session at sea. Our job was to see to all the metal work on a trawler – the stoves, the pipes, the galley stores. I often had to go onto a trawler for this work.

I had to go on board trawlers now and then and you wouldn't believe how cramped and primitive the crew's living conditions were. In their cabin there would be half-a-dozen bunks while the rest had to sleep on the foc'sle on straw mattresses. To begin with the boats were powered by coal and that made everything smelly.

The line boats led a pretty precarious existence. Sometimes they would dock and the catch was so small that the crew got nothing. But if they struck it rich then the rewards were high. I remember when I was 17 a line boat came in loaded with ling, halibut and cod; when the halibut was laid out it stretched halfway round the market. It was reckoned to be the biggest catch ever.

But the life on board was very hard. The boats would go right up north and sometimes it was so cold on deck that the water would freeze as soon as it came over. The crew would be constantly battered by this ice-cold water as they worked away. Sanitation was a bucket but often enough they would simply squat over the side.

The hardest job in the world. They had to keep going to make any money at all and sometimes might have to spend 48 hours on the deck, half asleep, with a sharp knife in their hand. Fishing was a 24-hour day business. You might drag the line for half-a-dozen

A great catch – but it wasn't always that way for the hard pressed fishermen.

hours and then the skipper would cry out 'Trawl-o!' and you had to pull in the line or the nets and this might be at three in the morning.

When they got back there were bills to be met – the grub bill for three weeks accommodation; they might have left a sub for the wife at the office and this would have to be repaid.

Yet people loved it; it was their way of life. Torry was nothing more than a large fishing village; when we were living in Grampian Road, some 75% of our neighbours were engaged in the fishing or in fishing related jobs.

Harry Black, b.1930. Grampian Road, Torry. Interviewed 2016.

The Navy was thoroughly good for me

I joined the Sea Cadets and was thoroughly enjoying it. There I got talking to a lad who told me all about the training ship HMS Ganges and life in the Royal Navy. I felt I was getting bogged down at home so I decided to get right away and join this HMS Ganges. I went to the recruiting office and passed the preliminary tests. Then I had to go down to Glasgow for the big medical. This I passed and then they sent the papers for my parents to sign. I was still very much a minor, no more than 15½.

My father simply looked at the papers and duly signed. And that was that.

This was the first time I had really been away from home; I'd never been further than a day trip to Edinburgh before but I wasn't nervous, rather excited in fact.

Despite its name HMS Ganges was a shore establishment. It closed in 1973 but when I joined up in the mid-Fifties the Royal Navy was still very much a huge and proud international affair, which maintained ships all over the globe, protecting British and

'My education at Ruthrieston had stood me in good stead'. Eddie Masson is second row, second right, 1954.

Empire interests. You were made to feel that you were privileged to be enlisting in such a famous and historical enterprise.

The first six weeks of training were passed in the annexe. This was square bashing, being kitted out and generally being knocked into shape. Straightaway you had to report to the barber for a neat short back and sides. One of the first things you had to do was to sew your name onto every article of uniform in red thread. We had to keep our kit in immaculate fashion. This consisted of two suits – a 'number one' and a 'number two' – working clothes, boots, socks. Everything was newly supplied. The clothes you had travelled down in were packed off into a suitcase and sent back to your home so that all contact with civilian life was severed.

Queuing for a cup of tea, Sports Day. Eddie is third from right.

Whenever you went ashore it had to be in your number one suit – you were representing Her Majesty's Royal Navy and you had better not forget it. All your badges had to be on display and your hat with the name of the ship on its band had to be worn. You would take a liberty boat across to Felixstowe and there you got six hours leave. We were too young to frequent any pubs but there was always the funfair and strolling about the streets and the chance to chat up any likely girls. Sunday was the day you paraded to a church service in the morning.

HMS Ganges, the class of 1955. Eddie is in the second row, at its right end.

Home leave came round three times in the year but I was never homesick. For me, that time on HMS Ganges was absolutely fantastic. I thrived on it all and was selected as Leading Boy from the very start. This meant I was in charge of the mess deck and its 42 other lads. Everything went well and I was further promoted to Petty Officer Boy.

I was in what was called the International Brigade: English, Scots, Irish, Welsh and Maltese all mixed together. We all got on well with each other, although I found the Yorkshire lads as difficult to understand as they did me. Discipline was the key and we quickly learned that we were all subject to it every minute of the day. If anyone stepped out of line even if only by an inch then the Chief Petty Officer would be down on him like a ton of bricks. This applied to any lad who failed to accept my leadership commands. He told me: 'You are in a position to give orders – but make sure they are the right orders.'

The Mess Hut, Drake 11 division: his responsibility was to keep it ship shape.

We were still at school. The days began at 6AM with a tidy up then fall in outside and march off to breakfast, then back to tidy up the mess deck, then off to school. We got the full range of academic subjects – English, Maths, Physics, Navigation and so on. Then with the morning session over, it was sport in the afternoon, followed by two more hours of lessons. I came out as a top boy and was given a certificate which announced that I 'was free from any further education'. The education I had received back home at Ruthrieston had stood me in good stead.

At night we all had beds in the mess deck though my bed, and that of the other Leading Boy, was at either end against the walls. We also had special blankets as a sign of our authority. Again tidiness was absolute; you had to leave the bed with everything so

Sunday Church Parade.

neatly tidied up that you could bounce a ball on the pile. Nobody was to leave before I could be certain that everything was spot on. And your boots had to be polished until you could see your reflection in them.

All this was thoroughly good for me. My year taught me discipline; it taught me leadership, how to give and how to take orders and also how to stand back and observe what was going on around me to see how the other lads were shaping up.

We were still of school age and so the cane was in use. One boy who tried to bunk off received six strokes on his backside from the Chief Petty Officer. Stealing was regarded as an absolutely heinous crime and called for the most severe punishment. Along the foreshore there was this steep rise called Laundry Hill and as a punishment you could be made to run up and down it. Once this Petty Officer, who had taken against a boy, forced him to run up and down; each time as they set off he would yell out: 'Rear boy to the front.' This meant that as soon as he reached the top of the hill he had to sprint as hard as he could to make his way to the front once more. In the end he collapsed and died. The Laundry Hill sessions were stopped after that.

I was never punished. I was a good recruit, one who took to everything the Navy could throw at me. My pay was £2.7.6d a week. Of this, two pounds was kept back into a savings account so you only actually had a few bob a week to spend. Out of this you had to pay for your own toiletries; the small amount left over I would usually blow on a bar of chocolate or an apple pie from the tuck shop.

I was seven years in the Navy. I saw the world, down to Gibraltar, then the Canaries and right down the African coast to Simonstown in South Africa. In the 1950s the Navy was still one of the most powerful in the world and had bases all over the globe: Hong Kong, Jamaica, Simonstown, Malta, Port Harcourt, Aden. This gave me the opportunity to visit some fascinating spots and also to meet some wonderful people.

But I realised that the Navy life, wonderful adventure though it was, had to come to an end. By this time I was going out with Dorothy and planned to get married; the Navy would be no life for a wife left at home. So at the age of 22 after seven years' service I came out, moved back up to Aberdeen and looked for a shore job.

For me those young days when I was Petty Officer Boy have marked me for life and for the better. Even now in my retirement the old ingrained habits of discipline and orderliness are still very much part of what I am. I can't bear to see anything out of place in the house. If I spot anything lying about I just have to tidy it away even if it's simply a stray leaf on the drive. Once a Navy man always a Navy man.

HMS Ganges and the ceremony of Manning the Mast.

Eddie Masson, b.1940. HMS Ganges. Interviewed 2016.

You could feel the platform swaying about

In the early 1970s I decided to try my luck in the burgeoning oil industry. For five years I was offshore doing logistics work. My main task was to ensure that ordered supplies did indeed arrive at the rigs and were in good order. In those pioneering days when the first fields were being opened up life was quite hectic. We regularly worked 15-hour shifts on a 6AM to 6PM basis and beyond.

These were the early days of the North Sea oil and things were still being built up more or less from scratch. They were drilling and this wasn't the straightforward task you might think. They had to go in all different directions so as to cover the whole field And you shouldn't imagine that the oil is lying there just waiting to be sucked up as if it's in some sort of pool. It's locked up in rock and has to be forced out under pressure through water injection.

Conditions could be very rough. You'd feel the platform swaying about in a gale and when the waves were running high. The accommodation rig is separate from the drilling rig so that there's the problem of transferring men from one to the other. This was usually done by lowering a big ring down into the water and then requiring the men to clamber on and off using rope holds. I've seen men falling full length because the ring was bobbing about so much. Occasionally this would be too rough to manage and then you'd call on a helicopter to do the transfer even though the distance was only 25 yards or so.

Fog could be a challenge too. Once it was so thick that going back and forth to the shore proved impossible for days on end. We were given the option of using the standby boat, which is constantly on patrol in case of anyone falling overboard. So we had to get into a dinghy then be hauled up by rope onto this standby boat, which happened to be a trawler. I couldn't resist going on deck, though told not to, so as to experience the conditions and I got my reward – the waves were as high as a house and we furiously bobbing up and down. Dangerous – but undoubtedly exciting.

Swaying about on the 'Billy Pugh', in transit between drilling and accommodation rigs.

But in those early pioneering times risks were all part of the enterprise. The approach was quite gung-ho and safety wasn't then the strict concern it has since become – especially after the Piper Alpha tragedy. They were then prepared to take on almost anyone; no medicals required. I simply signed up with an agency and got offered my various postings. Back then the rush was on to get in recruits.

I found the whole experience exciting; you were aware that you were part of a huge new enterprise. There you were, on a rig 150 miles out in the North Sea, and you could look around and spot all the other lights of other rigs twinkling away in the lonely distance.

Sanders Paterson, b.1942. The North Sea. Interviewed 2016.

The Britannia was one of the highlights

In my last two years in the Police I was in charge of the Harbour Division. I had my own Detective Sergeant and Detective Constable, and nine P.C.s. It was a busy unit down there; I enjoyed it. One of the highlights of the job was the SS Britannia coming in; we had a lot of work with the security for the Britannia. We had the divers out; they had to be searching the berths and, being Harbour Inspector, you're in charge of the Diving Team as part of your responsibility. The Chief Constable insisted that an Inspector went with the Diving Team wherever they went – and that was the Harbour Inspector.

There was one occasion – 1989 – the Britannia was coming into Aberdeen. For all the high-ranking officers aboard the Britannia, they still couldn't take the ship into Aberdeen without two of the Pilots going out to take the boat in. Well, on this particular occasion at about four o'clock in the morning the pilot masters were being transferred from their boat onto the Britannia and something happened, so that they were both injured. So, of course, they were taken to hospital and we were out that morning at six o'clock. The Deputy Chief Constable got in touch with me: 'Go to the Britannia and get a suitable press release.'

Her Britannia – but no longer. The Queen shows her emotion at its decommissioning, 1997.

So I went down there about half-past six but the Press Officer, Admiral So-and-so, wasn't available at that particular time but they said: 'If you care, you'd be welcome to have breakfast.' So I was on the Britannia for my breakfast – very posh and very nice indeed. High-powered stuff but very enjoyable. All the crew wore plimsolls so as not to mark the deck but I managed to keep my police shoes on. In due course the Admiral came down and together we made up a suitable press release. They were all right but the Queen was very concerned about the people being hurt, that something had happened on her Britannia.

Kenneth (Ken) Raitt, b.1939. SS Britannia. Interviewed 2016.

Deaths in the sea

My Mum's second oldest brother died in the Chinook accident off Sumburgh in 1986. He'd been in an earlier accident with a boat and he was a very strong swimmer and had survived that – but then died in the helicopter. My granda did lots of different jobs. He died in a drowning accident in the harbour. He was working on a fishing boat and he was getting catering supplies. He'd fallen off the gangway. They'd got him out but he died; it was put down as drowning.

Wendy Bradford, b.1972. Chinook helicopter. Interviewed 2016.

At last: Aileen's parents are married after their 16-year-long engagement.

The reluctant fisherman

Mum and Dad met when they were only 16 – but didn't marry till they were 32. And it was a continuous courtship too. One of the reasons it was so protracted is that they probably only actually met some 50 times during those 16 years. This was because of the nature of my father's work. His own father was a line-boat fisherman and he'd been brought up in Torry.

The family owned their own boat. They tended to look down on the trawler men, whom they regarded as mere crew, whereas they had shares as owners in their boat. They fished by lowering a thick rope into the sea from which spread out a network of smaller lines and that is how they hooked the cod and halibut, which they landed to sell at the mart. They would be away for 28 days at a time right the way up to Iceland but more than once they would return with little to show for their efforts except debt since the expenses of the trip mounted up and the cook and the engineer still had to be paid.

My father had shone at school and had been Dux at Victoria Road. He won a bursary to go to Robert Gordon's College but the family wouldn't hear of it. 'You're nae gaan ti Gordon's an become een o thon white-faced clerks!' was how my grandmother put it to him. 'You're gaan ti the sea jist like your ain faither.' That didn't suit him at all – he hated the very idea of the sea. The First World War broke out and, too young to enlist, he got a post at the recruiting office in Dee Street. He loved this work and revelled in meeting and working alongside so many different people.

On the day that peace was declared there was jumping and dancing in the office – but he found it difficult to join in because he knew what now awaited him. Sure enough, when he got home, there laid out for him was his sea kit; his mother had brought it out, just waiting for this moment when her son would follow the family destiny and prove himself to be a man by going off to be a true fisherman. He was 17 and ahead of him lay a life at sea. He was the oldest of three sons and he knew he had to go – and hated it. He never did manage to adapt.

The reluctant fisherman as a young man. Aileen Pettitt's father, James Lees, just before the First World War.

Eighteen months after the wedding I was born. Dad by now was aware that his own eyesight was fading. He knew he needed spectacles but also knew that he couldn't keep his skipper's ticket unless he had keen vision – don't forget, those were the days before radar so acute vision was thought to be a matter of life and death out on the sea. So what he did was to borrow his own father's ticket – they had the same name: 'James Lees' – and used that as his own. He had his share in what was the family boat along with two uncles and the grandfather.

I was four months old when the disaster happened. Dad was home from the sea and it was early morning and, as was his custom, was still in bed while Mum was busy making him a cup of tea. The paper boy delivered the 'P&J' so she took the paper through to him. Then all she heard from the bedroom was the cry: 'Ethel – something's happened – I can't see anything.' He had become practically blind. He was rushed to the hospital but there was nothing they could do for him – nowadays there would have been laser treatment but not back then in the 1930s. He lay in bed for several weeks and all they did was to rub green ointment over his body from time to time.

When he was released it was as a registered blind person. He was 34 and his career at sea was over. My auntie had married into a trawler family, the Robbs, and they had a fleet called the 'Viking' boats. They found a job for Dad in the fish market. When he was in his 70s he was admitted into Woodend Hospital to be treated for a blocked tear duct. I went in to visit him. The nurse told me: 'The doctor would like to have a word with you.' This is what he had to say: 'Do you realise your father is completely blind? How on earth he has been managing all this time I just can't tell you.' He was given a parcel which contained a white stick. After his death I came across it, still in its packaging.

So you can see, my father was a truly remarkable man. To say I absolutely adored him would be an understatement.

Aileen Pettitt, b.1937. Victoria Road, Torry. Interviewed 2014.

All she heard from the bedroom was the cry: 'Ethel – something's happened – I can't see anything.' He had become practically blind.

The SPORTING LIFE
Summer and All-Year Pursuits

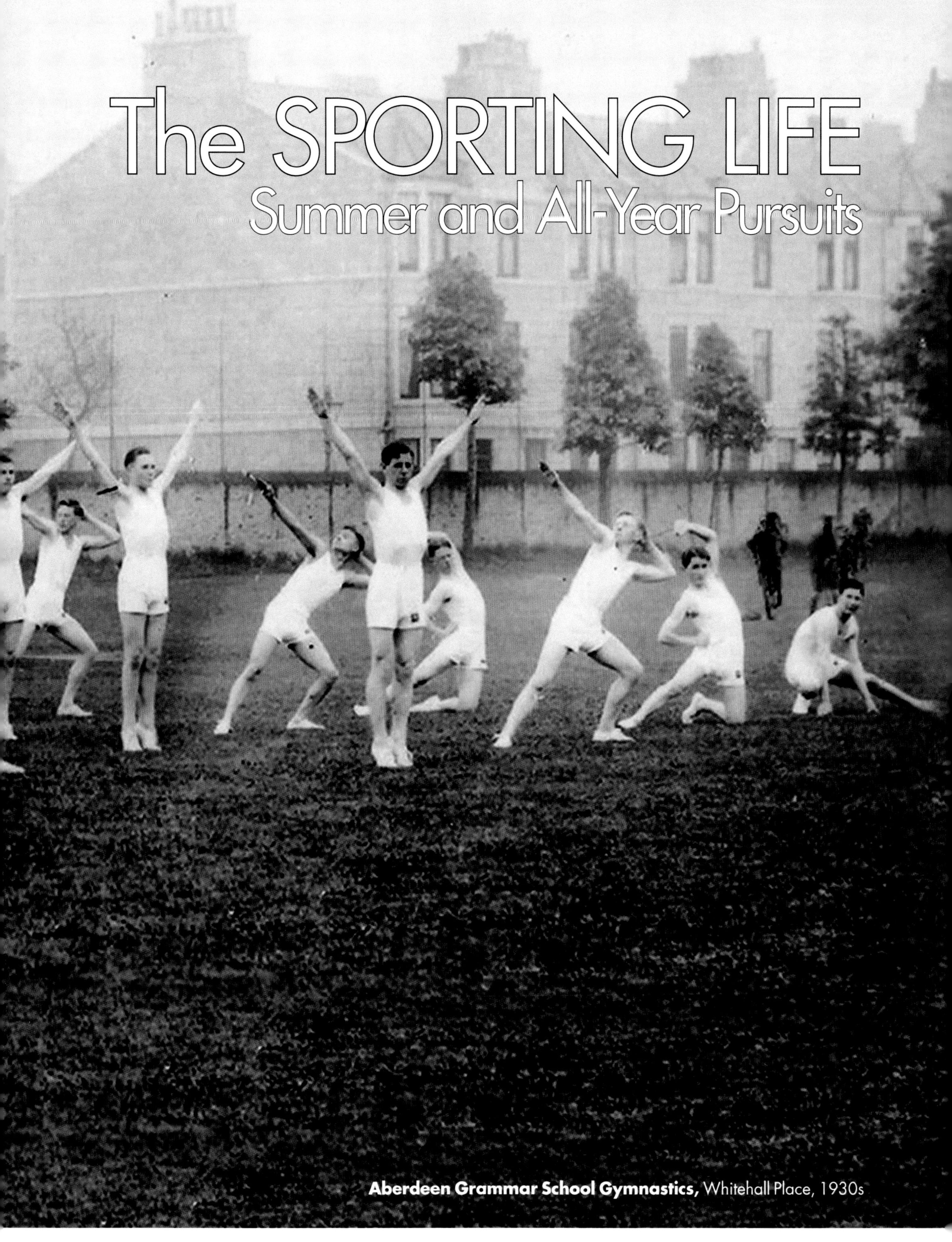

Aberdeen Grammar School Gymnastics, Whitehall Place, 1930s

SUMMER and ALL-YEAR PURSUITS

Cathy Gibson, aged 15, 1946. Two years later she won Bronze in the London Olympics. This is in addition to the three European Championship Medals she also won during her illustrious career.

The Swimmer: Swimming was big in Aberdeen

We were a swimming family. My father was president of the North of Scotland District and vice-president of the Scottish Amateur Swimming Association. I remember one year when my father was the convenor at the swimming gala and the local MP, Hector Hughes, was to open the event.

He informed my father that he hadn't prepared any speech but what he would do was to dive straight in – he was a famous swimmer and every day, winter and summer, when available he would take his dip in the North Sea. So there he was just in a dressing gown, which he threw off to reveal his trunks, calling out: 'I declare this gala well and truly open.' and dived right in. This went down very well.

I was brought up on the sport and became quite good at it. My father rose high in swimming circles as an administrator. Our preferred venue was the Bon Accord Swimming Baths in Justice Mill Lane. For years I was a regular there. I'd go for a training session before work at seven of a morning when you might well have the whole pool to yourself. But although I was a strong swimmer I never developed to the heights of my father's ambitions and eventually decided to give up on those lonely early morning sessions.

Before and just after the war swimming was pretty big in Aberdeen. The two Thistle Clubs – Ladies and Gents – the two Dee Clubs and the Bon Accord Club would each have their evening sessions, along with the common North District coaching session every Thursday evening.

Then there were the galas and the competitions. In one of these a competitor from England, Roy Romain, introduced the Butterfly stroke in the Breast stroke event and won by some distance. Thereafter Butterfly became a separate event.

In those days even international teams couldn't be expected to run to the expense of

The Bon Accord Baths in all their Art Deco glory, 1950s.

hotels so the practice was for members to be farmed out and be put up in the homes of the host club. I remember the famous Cathy Gibson coming to stay with us during the 1948 Scottish Championships held in Aberdeen. She was a formidable competitor but at the end of one race she had driven herself so hard that she passed out and had to be taken to our home to rest up in bed.

The next thing we knew was that there was a crowd of pressmen at our door the following morning. My father went to speak to them and his words made the front pages. The 'Sunday Post' ran the story: 'Robert Cooper says that Cathy Gibson will never swim again.' But what my father had actually said continued with the phrase: 'in these championships'. An early lesson in the art of newspaper sensationalism. She did make a recovery and did return to swimming though admittedly she was never quite the same again. But at her peak she had broken all the Scottish Freestyle records.

These Bon Accord Baths were a wonderful Mecca for all Aberdeen swimmers in those days. They had everything – well-appointed changing rooms, showers and a 10-metre diving board.

The Bon Accord Baths, however, were only completed in 1940. Up to then the Aberdeen public had only one baths open to it and that was the Beach Baths. They were very popular and swimmers travelled from all over the city to participate, many of them taking the tram which ran to it from the Castlegate.

In design they were typical of pre-war with changing cubicles offering a minimum of modesty, based along each side of the pool.

The recognised swimming clubs made good use of the pool for their own events: Thistle Gents on a Monday evening, Thistle Ladies on Tuesdays, the Dee Swimming Club on Wednesdays, Bon Accord on Fridays. The Thursdays were reserved for training

Hector Hughes MP, emerging from his daily dip off Aberdeen beach. [PHOTO: ABERDEEN JOURNALS]

purposes by the serious swimmers of these clubs under the direction of the Northern District Coaches.

Many high quality galas were held in these relatively simple settings. I can remember in 1939 my father bringing home the programme for a major event – a strong team from the USA performing under the name of 'Matt Mann and the Michigan Boys'.

When the Bon Accord Baths opened it was anticipated that the Beach Baths would close. But, no, Aberdeen enthusiasts continued to use both pools, some even preferring the salt water of the Beach Baths.

Robert (Bob) Cooper, b.1931. Bon Accord Baths. Interviewed 2014.

The Marathon Man: I'm down to 1,000 miles a year

My father was Freddy Edwards, a schoolteacher and accomplished amateur sportsman and coach. He was also a freelance sports journalist. Ever since I could remember he'd spent his Saturdays going to football venues in the city in the winter and cricket in the summer.

Most of his work was for Aberdeen Journals but he also did some work for the national Sundays. He would have to phone the results through; this was before the days of mobiles and laptops. He would rope me in to help. We didn't even have a phone at home so it would be a question of dashing off to look out the nearest empty red phone box and pray that it would be in working order. You'd have to gather your scripts together, take a pile of tuppenny coins with you, stack them up and feed them in as you read through the reports. Sometimes another member of the public would come to the box, wait a few minutes then start tapping at the glass to be given their turn. You had to do your best to ignore them.

So I certainly grew up in a sporting environment. Some of my sharpest memories are of the School Sports days at the Grammar, which would take place in June. You'd spend the whole of the previous month preparing: high- and long- jumps, shot put, relay races, the lot. I'd go in for as many events as possible so as to improve the chances of gaining the overall Champion award. The day itself was a huge event: flags, march past, parents coming along in their hundreds. Because of my total determination I usually did well. I'd come second most years but then in my Sixth I managed to become the Champion.

When I got into my Sixth year I decided that I simply had to make the most of my talents and began to train hard. I started out as a 440-yard runner but came to realise that I lacked the finishing kick to be able to emulate the middle distance heroes who were around at that time like Herb Elliot and Peter Snell so I switched to longer distances and ended up as marathon runner. I'd spend the whole winter training which was unheard of for a schoolboy in those days.

British athletics was going through an exciting phase then. It was the 1960 Rome

His first ever Marathon – and the winner. Mel Edwards romps home at Harlow, 1967.

Mel's father, Freddie Edwards, coaching Mannofield youngsters in 1979 when he was 76.

Olympics that got me going. I was just about to leave school and was able to follow events on TV. I also remember great races at the White City with British runners such as Brasher and Chris Chataway slugging it out against great European and Russian competitors like Zatopeck and Kutz. I've got a video of what was probably the greatest middle distance race of all time, which was held one evening at the White City. The world record was on the line: Kutz and Zatopeck had been invited to compete against Chataway. As they come into the final straight, neck and neck, the spotlight fixes on them. You can see how the sheer guts of Chataway just enables him to cling on and win by six inches.

They were heroes. There was also cricket at Mannofield. A memory is sharing a dressing room with the great West Indian batsman Rohan Kanhai while he was the professional there. I was appearing for a Mannofield XI and was to go in at number seven, one below Rohan. So we were both sitting in the dressing room, padded up, but our attitudes were somewhat different. While I was nervously waiting my turn Rohan was to be found fast asleep. When the wicket fell I gave him a nudge whereupon he woke up, strode to the crease and proceeded to knock up 50 runs in about 12 minutes before he threw his wicket away. I went in and scored a single not out. When I came off there was Rohan again, fast asleep on the bench.

I joined Aberdeen Athletic Club in 1962. There were some tremendous runners in the

'It's better in the early morning': Mel on his daily training run, Countesswells, 1990s.

city in those days. The leading long distance runner was Alistair Wood, who represented Scotland in the Perth Commonwealth Games. I started joining him on his morning training runs. He was a hard man and although he was 10 years older he really stretched me. You'd go along to King's for some training: 10 times 400, round and round the track – short strides one side, long strides the next. You'd be just coming up to the final one with him jogging along beside you and he would suddenly announce: 'OK, 600 yards flat out!' and he would beat me.

I enjoyed University. I took an Engineering degree. I was deeply into the Athletics Society and was doing all these duties as Captain. I was also beginning to edge my way into the national scene. In my final year I won the Scottish Junior Cross-Country Championship and was then selected as a Senior for the world championship in Dublin.

By now I was training 70 miles a week, which in those days was very high for a University student. But we weren't into dietetics then and knew nothing of hydration and nutrition and I don't remember doing anything special about my food. I just took whatever was served up for me at home. Mark you, I've never had any weight problems. I was 10½ stone then and I'm 10½ stone now.

Then came Cambridge. I represented the University in the annual cross-country match against Oxford. The rule was that if you got into the team you were awarded a Half Blue; if you finished in the first six that became a Full Blue. I came second so got the Full Cambridge Blue.

It was another three years before I finally got back to Aberdeen. During my time at Cambridge I'd got interested in concrete technology. Practical applications of that kind

Hare and Hounds, Aberdeen University, 1962. Back from left: J M Murray, W E Ewing, Mel Edwards, P T Barron, D I Crabb, J M Glennie. Front: R C F MacFarquhar, M Hewitt, D G Pyatt.

really appealed. As it happened, Newcastle was running just about the country's leading course in the topic, with Prof. Williams as one of the world's leading experts. I applied for a bursary and got it to go there. Then after a year Williams went down to Southampton and he took three of us with him, including me. When I returned to Aberdeen it was as a traffic engineer with Aberdeenshire County Council and later with Bear.

Come rain, shine or snow. Countesswells with son Myles, 2012.

While I was in Southampton I got involved in the British squad in 1968, I actually won the very first marathon I entered; this was in 1967 at Harlow in Essex, where I came home in my best ever time of 2hr 18min. This immediately catapulted me into the British rankings. I was one of those invited to take part in high altitude training in the French Alps.

The first evening there the coach gathered us all together and told us 'Look, high altitude is a tricky proposition. You'll need to acclimatise yourself gradually so take it easy for the first week.' Well, that kind of inactivity didn't appeal to me, nor to one or two of the others, so we just went straight out the first day for a good run. We were spotted and got a choking off but that didn't stop us. It was just as well because at the end of that first week there was a heavy fall of snow and the whole squad had to go home. As it was I benefited from my week's running and three weeks later I did a personal best. The 122 miles I'd done that week – my highest ever total – stood me in good stead.

I've been involved in running ever since I came back to Aberdeen. The centre of my activity has been Aberdeen Athletic Club. I did a lot of coaching and committee work in the 1970s and '80s. It's been good to put something back. I still do 25 miles or so a week. It's interesting that as you get older you don't need to do the same mileage to keep up your fitness levels. Now I find five miles a day does the same work as 12 did when I was younger.

Now my son, Myles, is into running. When I completed my 100,000th mile earlier this year [2005 – he's done plenty more since] he ran alongside me and was good enough to let me break the tape first. But I was averaging 1min 44sec per lap and he did one in 62 seconds.

The prospects for the 200,000th are pretty remote, I'm afraid. I'm now down to 1,000 a year. I tend to keep off the hard surfaces; I stick to the country, chiefly Countesswells Forest. I go out in the early mornings; there's nothing to compare with pounding through woodland at 6AM on a summer's morning, listening to the dawn chorus and seeing deer, rabbits and squirrels scurrying about. But I will also go out in other kinds of weather too, come rain, shine or snow, and always enjoy the experience. Running is just who I am.

Bringing him up to run. With 12-year-old, Myles, Linksfield, 2001.

Mel Edwards, b.1942. Aberdeen Amateur Athletic Club. Interviewed 2005.

Scotland v Australia, Mannofield, September 1948. The souvenir programme which sold for two shillings – and now fetches up to £400 as a collector's item.

The Young Sports Fan: An absorbing passion

Cricket has been an absorbing passion for me. The hours I've wasted poring over 'Wisden' or picking imaginary all-time teams. My father was a Surrey fan who had grown up on Hobbs and Sandham and the great wicket keeper, Herbert Strudwick. My elder sister also fed my fascination when she worked at the Public Library. She would bring me home cricket books and in that way I had an early introduction to the writings of Neville Cardus and Robertson-Glasgow – all quality stuff.

I would go along and watch Aberdeenshire at Mannofield where the professional, Alma Hunt, was a great hero. I would spend the morning of a match, anxiously scanning the sky to the west to look out for the gathering of any rain clouds that might sabotage the occasion. I can remember the agonies of having to hang around the ground waiting for resumption when the weather intervened.

I was in my last year at Robert Gordon's College when the Australians came to play Scotland at Mannofield in 1948 and Don Bradman made his final appearance on British soil. At that time the great local hero was George Youngson. In his youth he'd been very fast but as he matured he slowed down and could deliver these fastish off-cutters. Naturally he was in the team to play against Australia that day.

Well, Bradman won the toss and put Scotland in. By tea they were all out for 150 or so and the crowd could anticipate seeing the great man himself at the wicket. Australia opened up with two later order batsmen, McCool and Johnson, and the crowd expected to see Bradman come in at his usual number three position. But when McCool was dismissed we had to make do with Neil Harvey instead. It was obvious that the great man was saving himself for the next day and the big Saturday crowd.

When I turned up the next day there were 10,000 of us. After a decent interval Ian

He's in there somewhere. The 10,000 strong crowd which packed out Mannofield, among which was a young Buff Hardie.

The all-conquering 1948 Australian team, with captain Don Bradman centre which comfortably added Scotland to its tally, Mannofield, 1948.

Johnson surrendered his wicket and Bradman made his appearance, with our own George Youngson bowling. Now, during the Test series Bradman had had some trouble with the bowling of Alec Bedser and his ability to persuade him into lofting the ball round the corner to be caught by Hutton at backward short leg. Sure enough, after a ball or two, our own George Youngson got him to do the same – but there was no fielder placed there and the ball fell harmlessly to the ground. We all gasped but that was his one and only error. After this escape Bradman settled down and played with never a false stroke as he put his century together. I can still see the way he massacred the leg spin of the Scottish captain, W.K. Laidlaw; anything even the slightest bit short, he would just lean back and pull him through long on to the boundary.

If only... Don Bradman falls for Alec Bedser's leg trap, Second Test, 1948. Scotland bowler Youngson induced a similar false stroke, but had failed to post a fielder there.

Pittodrie also played a part in my upbringing. My father would take me there. I remember being present in season 1937/38 when we beat Rangers 2-0 and our goalie saved a penalty. The normal Aberdeen goalie of those days was George Johnstone, who had once been a baker so he was known to us all as just that: 'the Baker'. He was very adept at going up for the high ball so whenever we saw him safely clutching the ball in his hands after a jump up for it we would all cry out: 'A caker for the Baker!' But on this occasion he was injured and his place was taken by the reserve, a South African by the name of Pat Kelly. When Rangers were awarded their customary penalty we all feared the worst but the reserve goalie saved the day. Nor was that the only one of Pat Kelly's achievements: he married a Hilton girl who lived just round the corner from us. And this was the man who had saved a penalty against Rangers.

Buff Hardie, b.1931. Mannofield and Pittodrie. Interviewed 2006.

Still involved in the game. Joe Scott takes a breather from his umpiring duties, Methlick v Gordonians, 2008.

The Grades Cricketer:
There was cricket in the schools then

Raeburn Place was a good area to grow up in. We would play cricket and football in the street. We would chalk up a wicket on the wall or use a lamp-post; the boys would just use a piece of wood shaped like a bat and a tennis ball.

There was cricket in the schools then. I played for my Primary school at Skene Square. All the schools played at Harlaw in those days. Nowadays it's all football; the season seems to spread over the whole year but in our day the summer term was strictly cricket. In my time the teachers seemed to take a lot more interest in after-hours activities and a lot of schools had at least one master who knew the game and was playing in the Grades.

My father was associated with a city club, Balmoral, so it was natural for me to join them when I got to 14. I got a part time job in a shop when I was at school – holidays and Saturday mornings – up till 12 o'clock. After that it was cricket. We would play every Saturday from the last weekend in April till the middle of September. There were league games and friendly fixtures too, on the odd blank Saturday and on Sundays.

We would play at the Duthie Park, at the Links, Stewart Park and Westburn Park. The clubs were run by subscription helped out by the odd donation from businesses or individuals. And of course the schools played so there was no shortage of recruits into the clubs. There were works teams too: Hall Russell had a side and so did the paper mills at Mugiemoss and also Hall, the builders. Organisations like YMCA ran a team and there was the City Youth Club too.

I was always a medium pace bowler. The fact that I had a comfortable action and always ran straight through meant I could keep going right up to into the 1990s. I also got coaching at Mannofield. Rohan Kanhai used to take us and he would stick two stumps in the ground and encourage us to release the ball while we were level with them. This made us run straight through and look over the left shoulder.

I started early and continued till I was 60. I took more wickets for Balmoral than anyone else – mark you I played longer than anyone else as well. And I did once get Rohan Kanhai's wicket though he was on 94 at the time. I was playing for the Grades Select against Mannofield. He came prancing down the wicket but it was a good length ball and he got too far under it and skied it for a catch.

My father acted as an umpire. I did have my arguments with him. Once I was bowling against Dunecht. I appealed for a clear catch along with about half a dozen of the team and my father rightly gave it out. But the square leg umpire was an old Dunecht boy and he called out: 'Na, na, he niver hit it; the ball jist passed by the ootside o the bat.' The batsman stood his ground; I put the ball in my pocket and refused to bowl. Then my father said: 'Get on with the game. I've changed my mind – "Not out".' I had three balls left in the over and I hit the batsman with each one of them. Beamers. I bowled him out in the very next over; as he turned to leave the crease I called out to their umpire: 'Are you sure that one just didn't pass the outside of the stumps?' He said:

Lairds Cricket Ground, Methlick, 2008. A long shot of the match with Joe standing as umpire.

'Nae need to be cheeky, Joe.' My father didn't show me any favouritism, I can tell you.

I'd say standards have gone down since the time I started. There are still good players but the depth is no longer there. Another difference is that in our day families would come along and watch. It was common for the wives to go to the centre of town early on for the shops and then to come down to the park later with the children. Tea was always provided. In town the local baker would supply cakes and pies; in the country the usual thing was to take tea and sandwiches in the clubhouse with the wives serving it all up.

I retired when I was just on 60. I had to; I had a heart attack. It happened when we were playing Lads' Club at Woodside. We had a young Australian doctor in the side and he noticed that as I was going back to the start of my run up I was holding my chest. He came across and asked if I was all right. 'A bit of indigestion – that bradie at tea,' I told him. 'Well, just complete the over off a couple of paces and then go off and rest – and see your doctor first thing tomorrow.' Until then I'd never had any trouble; with my action and the fact that I was never a smoker meant I could bowl all day long. But it was a heart condition all right. I ended up in hospital; and that was the end of my playing career. I've continued as an umpire, of course.

Joseph (Joe) Scott, b.1933. Balmoral Cricket Club. Interviewed 2005.

The Highland Games Champion: I had this great will to win

We were a large family: eight brothers, two sisters. I came more or less in the middle. My father was a farmer. Our land was then right out in the country in the Newhills area but now the town has swallowed up most of it for housing.

It was a happy childhood; we weren't rich but we never wanted for anything. We were a close family with hardly any quarrelling or jealousies among us. Even now those of us

It was the farm work which laid the basis. A young Bill Anderson as part of the team on his father's farm, Newhills, 1950s.

who are left still get on and visit each other. None of my brothers ever showed any jealousy at my success.

My own introduction to the heavy lifting sports was as a young lad. My father was a strong man; he had thrown the hammer for the Home Guard during the war. Our farm acted as a meeting place on a Sunday afternoon for the farm workers from round about, mostly men who had worked on our farm and liked to come back for the social contact. And they would hold hammer throwing competitions.

I began to take an interest in the exploits of the Highland Games athletes. Every Thursday a paper called the 'Bon Accord' would appear and in the season this always carried all the details of what had been happening at the various Games of the preceding week. I began to follow the big names of the period like George Clark, Jack Hunter from Dunecht or Sandy Gray from Alford. From May to the middle of September there would be a Games somewhere or other for me to read about.

Undoubtedly the work around the farm, which we all had to do right from childhood, helped to develop our strength. But there was nothing special about our diet. We had the normal farm fare of the time with plenty of oatmeal and hardly any red meat – just the occasional chicken. But from an early age I would be helping in the dairy, lugging the 10 gallon churns about. The dairy lorry had an upper tier and I soon found I could hoist a churn up on to it unaided.

No question about it: all that lifting developed the muscles in my back in a way which was ideal preparation for my later career as a thrower and lifter at the Games. You need dedication to become a top class heavy athlete but I prepared mostly by practising the actual events. I didn't take up specialised weight training till I was 27 and that was only because Arthur Rowe, the British Olympic hammer thrower, had decided to enter the circuit. Up till then I'd things much my own way but Arthur gave me some real competition so I knew I had to up my game to keep ahead.

All of us Anderson men were strong and had much the same build – not especially tall but very compact and deep chested. When I was 18 I was six feet, half an inch in height and 15½ stone in weight and that remained the same right through my career.

Looking over the dyke. Family farm, 1950s.

My first appearance at Games was when I was 18 at Alford. I'd been out on the Friday with some pals for a drink at the Fourmile House at Kingwells and my brother, John, and his mate were urging me to give it a go. At first I was reluctant; I didn't believe I would be any good. But they kept telling me that I could throw better than some of those who were winning. Well, off I went; no kilt and a pair of football boots on my feet. I was successful in the heavy hammer, the shot put and the weight over the bar. I was astonished and so was everyone else. More than that, I came away with £10 10/- in prize money. This was 1956 and that was real cash then; I had never been so rich in my life.

Besides, I had enjoyed the thrill of the competition and the realisation that here was something I could be really good at. From that moment on I was hooked.

After my National Service and back home I did farm work. I had a job as a dairyman over at Tarves. This meant a 5.30 start to my day. I was still single and at the weekend I

would often come straight in from a dance, a swift change of clothes and out into the dairy.

In 1960 I got married and this was another important step. I reckon being married at quite a young age just as I was forging my career on the Highland Games circuit gave me stability and helped me to lead a disciplined and responsible life. If ever there was a danger of letting success go to my head Frances was always at hand to rein me in. I was brought up on family life and that is what has supported me all the way through. When I was on the farm with all those brothers and sisters there was never any scope to get above myself; one sign of it and I would be immediately slapped down. There's no question that this solid family background helped me greatly in my international career.

From 1959 to 1964 I was working on my brother's farm at Banchory-Devenick. One day I found myself out in the rain, driving a tractor without any cab, hauling a load of silage. Suddenly I was aware of a figure in a car, frantically waving at me: 'How would you like to go to the Bahamas?' I didn't need a second invitation.

This was David Webster who was involved in Highland Games sports. He had a link with J. Scott, who during the 1950s and the Sixties, promoted athletics in the Bahamas. I

Throwing the hammer: Hazlehead, late 1960s.

Tossing the caber: Hazlehead, late 1960s.

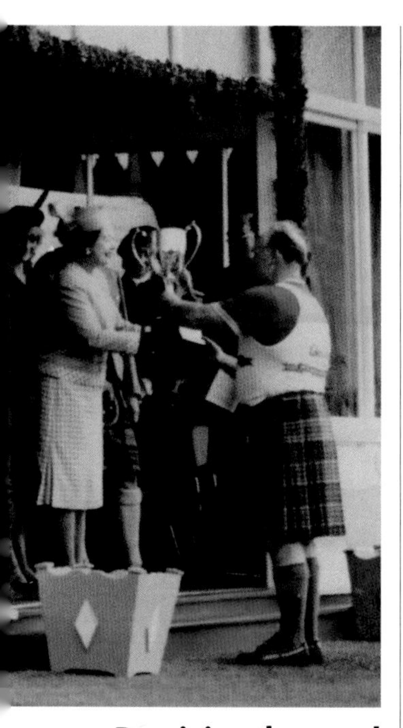

Receiving the royal congratulations, Braemar, late 1970s.

went over all right and it's a good job I did. Success in the Bahamas opened the door to appearances in Canada and the USA too.

I was there not to compete but to put on a show of strength demonstration. Each night I would have to toss the caber, shot put, throw weights over the bar and, the climax, to lift the Manhood Stone. This was the famous trial of strength, weighing some 265 pounds. The original stone was at Braemar but a replica had been made and this is what I was challenged to lift each night. I reckon that by the end of my stay my right arm was longer than my left.

This led the way to many appearances all along the East Coast, to Washington, Baltimore, up to Montreal and Toronto. The money was superb and the accommodation first class.

My career has taken me all over the world. Even though it's years since I retired I am still remembered. Last year I was invited over to California, to Santa Rosa, where I had been the champion five times. The Americans are really only interested in winners but if you are one then they will raise the roof to celebrate you. So when they came to hold the 150th anniversary of their Highland Games they invited me to share in it all; they treated me as a hero.

I also appeared before the Royal Family quite often. In the old days they would come to the Braemar Games and then come out onto the field to chat with you about your technique and so on. Now security concerns mean they have to stay in their seats. I also got presented with an MBE by the Queen Mother.

Just some of his trophies. Taken at Braemar, 2008.

When I was competing I was never bothered by nerves. I had this great will to win and could keep very cool even in a crisis. I knew that as long as I was lying no worse than second with the final round of throwing to go I was certain to pull out the throw which would ensure victory. Actually I was a terrible loser; I just hated to be bettered and that drove me on. But I was careful never to display it; if I lost I would be gracious about it, even though I'd be seething inside.

Arthur Rowe and I were great rivals from the late 1950s over the next 10 years. The media liked to build us up as great foes but actually we got on pretty well with plenty of joking and banter between us. I never resented this Yorkshireman coming up from his home in Barnsley to participate on the Highland Games circuit. For me it was welcome competition; I had had it all my own way till then so his presence helped me to improve. At last I was

A visit to Buckingham Palace in 1977 to receive his MBE. With wife Frances, son Kenneth and daughter Rosemary.

getting some real competition.

At home I made a point of never messing about. I'd get back from a trip in the evening and I'd be away at work the next day, bright and early. It was never my way to sit about the house even though, with my winnings, I could afford to take it a bit easy. I trained and trained, at least three evenings a week. When I moved into Aberdeen I would still return to the farm for a spot of practice and later I had the garage here with weights as my own gym. To build up the legs I would go off for running in Hazlehead, rain or shine, snow or dry.

But I didn't bother with any special diets; I just ate the everyday stuff that anyone had. I didn't refuse the odd dram either though I never overdid it. Nor did I have any special pre-match routines: I just used to jump in the car and away.

Nor was I ever one for the bright lights. I saw myself as a dedicated competitor; my job was to go out and win and not to play the big personality. Give me a hammer in my hand and I knew what I was doing; put a microphone in front of my mouth and I never felt at home with it. Of course I sometimes had to say a few words and I always hated it. I remember once I was at Denver in front of a crowd of 30,000 and had to make a speech. I got through it and afterwards the Pipe Major came up to me and said: 'Well, that's the best speech we've ever had.' 'How so?' I asked him. 'It wasn't too long.' was

I was never a full-time athlete. I got a job in the building trade and started as a labourer but later got promoted to ganger.

the answer.

I competed right up till I reached 50. I reckon that even when I was in my mid-40s I was as good as ever I had been. But age did eventually begin to catch up with me. Then there came a tour to Australia and I took Frances with me. Suddenly I just knew I didn't want to carry on any more. I'd had enough and so I retired.

But I was never a full-time athlete. Although I quit farm work I got a job in the building trade. I started as a labourer but later got promoted to ganger. After I retired from athletics, I settled down to my work in the building trade. For the last 15 years of my working life I was with Stewart Milne's firm, laying the foundations, putting down slabs, and setting up the fencing at Kingswells.

All went well with me till two years ago. One night we were at Banchory at the dancing, which has always been an enthusiasm of ours; I came home and realised I didn't feel well. I got up in the middle of the night, came downstairs and that's where Frances found me. I was taken to ARI and spent 42 days in a hospital bed. It was double pneumonia. At one point it was reckoned that I was a goner but my usual will to win helped to pull me through.

So from a man who'd never had a day's illness in his life I have become one who has to take care. We still go out dancing but I have to stick to strict limits. I'm no longer allowed to do any lifting – I who had once been the best in the world at it.

William (Bill) Anderson, b.1937. Highland Games Circuit. Interviewed 2016.

The Hill Walker:
Away to the hills on Strachan's bus

Everybody at Aberdeen University Press went hill climbing and rock climbing. We all went away on a Friday night on a Strachan's Bus up to Braemar and on to Bob Scott's Bothy and Glen Derry; we created mayhem from then until Sunday. They must have breathed a sigh of relief in Braemar when they got rid of us on a Sunday night.

On the Monday we all spoke about it and every Thursday we went to the Stewart Lounge in Back Wynd and discussed in great detail what we were going to do the coming weekend. By Friday night away we went on Strachan's bus again. I had many years of that.

We came home from Braemar late on the bus on a Sunday night and as my pals, Davie Reid and Derek Pyper, were telling me, if they'd been held up on a climb and didn't get back until late, they were so worried that anything could hurt their apprenticeship, like if they came in late and the foreman said: 'Far the hell wis you?' So they slept outside on the doorstep of the University Press, then worked all the next day in their climbing gear and went home on Monday night.

Alexander (Alex) Rae, b.1947 Glen Derry. Interviewed 2016.

Alex Rae at the head of Glen Eye with fellow climber Mick McKie.

The Novice Swimmer: I nearly drowned in the Beach Baths

We went to the Beach Baths; I nearly drowned in there. One of my chums said 'I'll teach you to swim,' so he took me there. They used to have the inner tubes of car tyres there, things you could play on, sit in, and paddle round at the shallow end.

I couldn't swim a stroke. This chum said: 'I'll take you up to the deep end on the tube,' and I thought: yes, that'll be good fun. The deep end was seven feet deep and it was packed with kids so nobody saw what we were doing. He pushed me up to the deep end right up to the very end to the diving platform place and he said: 'Now I'm going for a dive; I'll dive off the platforms then I'll push you back again to the shallow end.' I said: 'Yes, OK'.

I couldn't even see the bottom; the water was very salty; it was like being in the middle of the ocean. This is great, I'm thinking. So away he went to have a dive and I was paddling away there when all of a sudden the lifebelt was pulled away from me by some kid saying: 'That's for the kiddies at the shallow end.' I suppose he assumed I could swim.

I was going down and up and down – and while I was doing that my chum Lawrence was already up on the boards and there's kids all over the place splashing about. He told me later that he looked down and saw no life belt, nothing, and kids were all diving in at the time and he didn't know what to do. Then he spotted me, struggling in the water. He told me that he dived in and tried to hit me on the chin to knock me out so I'd be unconscious and he could pull me to the side.

I remember my arms and his arms flapping about and of course he didn't succeed in

When I was half way through this process of drowning I felt the water coming up inside my belly.

doing anything as regards trying to save me. I remember going up and down. I didn't panic; I was so young, I didn't know what was happening really. When you come up you breathe and also you take in water at the same time; that's what happens to you when you're drowning. When I was half way through this process of drowning I felt the water coming up inside my belly, the colder water rising up, and remember saying to myself: 'Gee whizz, that's funny that.' When it reaches up to your epiglottis, over the top, that's you, you've had it. And while that was happening, I don't know who tried to save me but then I woke up at the side of the pool. I was lying flat on my belly, and the guy was still on top of me, doing the Holger-Nielsen, pumping away on me. My mouth was closed and all of a sudden I woke up and my breakfast and my dinner were all over the place. I remember I sat up and the guy in charge – he was a little man with a red face – was looking down at me with his face like a tomato; he was really worried.

I soon learned to swim and loved it. I swam for the school at Ferryhill Primary. We used to go to a school in the Gallowgate, near Marischal College, up towards what's now a car park. Well, there used to be a school there called the Middle School and there was a swimming pool there and that's where we went for practice and we swam the races. It was an awful small pool but it was good fun.

James (Jim) Butler, b.1923. Beach Baths. Interviewed 2015.

The International Cricketer: Not bad for a lad from Mannofield!

Both my parents came from strong sporting backgrounds; my father was well known in Aberdeen cricket, national league hockey and like my mother was also a capable tennis player. But Mum also had cricket in her blood as her father, my grandfather, had also played for Scotland.

I was fortunate to go to Robert Gordon's College as my father had before me and that's a school where you get enormous opportunities to play a range of sports. But cricket was my first and greatest love. Right from the start I realised I had a talent for the game. At Primary school when we played rounders I could see that my hand-eye co-ordination was better than most.

I joined the Mannofield club. Every Sunday morning through the winter months whatever the weather I would go up to the nets there. There were about a dozen of us who were regulars, some of them first team guys. One of the faithful was this old chap, Alec Holgate, who must have been nearly 70, a slow bowler. He would be there, smothered in half a dozen sweaters, clad in whites, wearing an old flannel shirt and with a scarf wrapped round his neck. Fantastic.

And these were proper hard sessions, with the best of coaching from George Murray and Stuart Grant. They'd work away at my technique with the result that when the season came round I could get off to flying start and not have to fuss around at any little

Batting against the might of Australia, with Adam Gilchrist behind the stumps.

weaknesses and sloppy habits that might have set in during the off season.

At home I also seized every opportunity to get hold of a ball and used the garden as an opportunity to hone my fast bowling and my stroke play. Once when executing a lovely square cut I smashed a ball through the neighbour's greenhouse and on another while I was imagining myself to be a fast bowler, I ran in, let fly, the ball hit a ridge on the lawn and sheered up through the sitting room window. I would also engage in imaginary Test matches against the neighbour's son: he would be England and I naturally represented Scotland.

I had a close friend from Robert Gordon's College days in Neil MacRae who was very committed to building up a career in sport, especially cricket. He attended Loughborough University, the top educational sports establishment in Britain. Then entirely off his own bat he went out to South Africa for the winter.

When he left school Neil was by no means an outstanding talent but mentally he is very strong and determined. That temperament, combined with all the opportunities he was getting both at Loughborough and in Cape Town, transformed his game. When he returned he was a completely different proposition, someone who now knew his game and how to construct a good score even against first-class opposition. I was impressed; I wanted some of what Neil had got.

To do that I realised I would have to be prepared to spend my winters somewhere in the southern hemisphere. At Mannofield you get the odd young Australian coming our

Another Smith victim. Celebrating the capture of Shahid Afridi, with Craig White, Scotland v Pakistan, 2007.

way, as like as not someone backpacking his way across Europe, before settling down to his adult life back home. I contacted one of them and asked him if he could possibly help me. He invited me out to his home town, Perth, Western Australia.

One September I got all the cash I could, packed my equipment together and on a wing and a prayer made my way out to Perth. I remember sitting in the plane as it made its approach and gazing down at the vast stretch of lights beneath me. 'God', I thought: 'this place is huge. What the hell am I doing coming out here?' I had no more than £200 in my wallet and a relative stranger about to pick me up and whisk me to his home. What if he wasn't there at the airport?

But true to his word he was and willing to do what he could for me. Over that Australian summer I stayed with him and tried to make my way as a cricketer. This meant getting to grips with the Aussie club system, which is so much tougher than anything I'd faced previously. Unlike here, the top players still keep contact with their home clubs and practise and even turn out for their home teams at a weekend match. You'd go along to the nets at Scarborough and see Justin Langer there or at Perth and bump into Adam Gilchrist – two of the very greatest cricketers ever to play for Australia. And no quarter would be given – these players would come at you as hard as if they'd been playing in a state match. You'd find yourself facing a first-class fast bowler in nets and realise that he was trying to put this young Scots upstart in his place.

I went out over six successive winters. For me those spells in Australia made up a marvellous experience, one which brought on my game enormously. But after my first month I was skint. So my club fixed me up with a job and a car. The job – oh my God. – was awful but it paid enough to cover my living expenses. It was in a sheet metal factory, which specialised in the fabrication of rain gutters. My role was to feed these huge coils of steel into rollers. For this I was given a pair of fabric gloves but the metal was razor sharp and I would go home at night with gashes all down my legs. The lubricant used was kerosene and, despite the gloves I got soaked with the stuff and developed blisters all over my hands.

It was gruelling but, as they say, character forming. So I improved massively. But how to get into the Scotland set up? It did help that I took up wicket keeping though I had played purely as batsman till I was in my late teens. Roddy Smith was the incumbent at Mannofield and had represented Scotland but he wasn't really enjoying it so he decided to hand the gloves over to me, with these words: 'It's over to you – but don't fuck it up.' That's always been the sort of challenge I thrive on so I took the field with his words ringing in my ears. From the very first game I took to it; I held on to a couple of blinders and really never looked back from that point on.

It was still tricky making that breakthrough to the full national team. But I had a sense of my own worth and would happily have committed my life to full-time professional cricket for an English county. I wrote to one or two asking for a trial and a couple did come calling, including Warwickshire and Sussex. John Edrich, the old England Test batsman, was now living in his retirement in Ballater and for a season he came along to

Mannofield to give us some coaching. He knew what I was capable of and had a word with his old England mate, John Snow, the ex-Sussex and England fast bowler. So, I was invited down. I had a hell of a train journey to reach Hove because there were strikes. I arrived after 24 hours having had hardly any sleep. I was playing for their second 11 against a strong Surrey side and got a duck. But I kept well and this was on a tricky wicket. In the second innings I batted so well that I got a 90 and helped us to a victory.

Well, I thought, I must be in with a real chance here. But it never came. What I hadn't known was that Sussex had two young 19-year olds waiting in the wings who were obviously tremendous prospects. One was Matt Prior, who went on the play 79 Tests, and Tim Ambrose, who also gained England recognition. I had gone to the wrong county and at the wrong time.

But I was now approaching 30, without a fixed employment, married and expecting a baby. I realised that I could no longer sit around, waiting for a call that was probably never now going to come. I had to settle down. So that was the end of my hopes of becoming a county professional down in England.

In 2002 I joined the Police Force and this has proved to be an excellent decision. The Force was always supportive of my cricket and never once stood in the way of releasing me to play for Scotland. I also had time to practise and to train.

But despite disappointments I have enjoyed some wonderful experiences, achieving my goal of representing my country and appearing over 180 times for Scotland, including three World Cup tournaments.

One of them was in the West Indies in 2006. A high spot was when I went in with our score at something like 40 for 5 against Australia and Glen McGrath, just about the

All the shots: Executing the perfect reverse sweep, Scotland v England, 2009.

Facing Shaoib Akhtar – the fastest bowler ever – was the one time in my career that I felt I was going to end up in hospital.

world's leading pace bowler, was in action. I managed to see out his over and then came up against Shaun Tait who, if less skilful, was much faster. But he sent down a couple of half volleys, which I sent to the boundary and suddenly the crowd was on my side, I was relaxed and away. I managed to get a half century that day and that against the world's best side. Although it was in a losing cause it gave me great satisfaction.

I was having the chance to perform against the world's best and that was a huge thrill. Batting against the Aussies in a competitive match was miles away from the old Mannofield days of course. It's not a transition you can make just like that. I had to work my way up by dint of application and self-analysis.

The first real test I had as a batsman was a match against Durham when I found myself facing the England journeyman fast bowler, Martin Saggers. At that time my thought was, he was so quick. But you stick in, you learn to move your feet and to concentrate and eventually you do begin to see the ball. Experience and the right attitude can work wonders. You do adjust to the higher challenge. I learned to work on my trigger movement as the ball was coming towards me, to get behind the ball. You adjust and it does become easier – and that sort of adjustment had to be made every time you stepped up a class.

Even facing the fastest bowler I, or anyone else has ever faced, Shaoib Akhtar in 2003 in a Sunday League match against Durham – he was the first to be clocked at over 100 mph – you realise that there's still something you can do about it. He was an incredible presence at the wicket, running in like a streak of lightning and then bending that supple body of his into a delivery. He had the amazing, even freakish, ability of arching his whole body back to appear like an elastic band that could lengthen out and then snap shut. I admit to being physically nervous; it was the one time in my career that I felt I was going to end up in hospital. The Durham players later stated that in all the years he was with them this was the quickest he had ever bowled. I still remember them smiling at me, not mockingly but just pleased it was me and not them.

When I got to the crease he'd already taken four wickets for one run and our world class professional, Rahul Dravid, had been dismissed by a trundler at the other end. We were five for zip. He was clearly sniffing the possibility of an early finish and then a night out at the Edinburgh night clubs so he was really tearing in. And when he didn't immediately add me to his victims he went round the wicket and started to direct the ball at my body. 'God, he's trying to hit me; he might even kill me.' But somehow I survived, evaded injury and after a couple of overs more he was taken off for a rest. He had become so pre-occupied with hostile short pitch bowling that he forgot to get me out. And then the following year when I faced him once more he didn't seem the same bowler; I played probably my best innings for Scotland, ending up with 78 not out in a successful run chase for victory.

Fortunately, self-discipline has never been a problem. I was never much of a drinker and even after a successful match it would usually be a case of the one shandy – though those two to six hour drives home might have had something to do with that. At tournaments I made a point of never having alcohol till after it was all over. I reckoned that even a small amount couldn't be anything but a threat to your general fitness. Looking back, I overdid the intensity and maybe it would have been better if I'd learned to let go a bit more, as opposed to sitting in a hotel room, becoming more and more wound up, but that was not my nature. For me there was always so much at stake that I wouldn't do even the slightest thing to jeopardise it.

Although I would have loved a career as a professional in English county cricket I've always been happy to stay in Aberdeen. For me it acts as a big village, a friendly place where you will always bump into someone you know whether it's on the streets or in the shops. And I can't complain either about any lack of cricketing opportunity. Of course it would have been nice if the temperatures had been a few degrees warmer and the wickets a bit harder but Mannofield has always done its best for me and is a fantastic facility.

I know that I am blessed to have been able to play against most of the world's leading performers of my time and on the most famous grounds in the world, that my days in the sun were so rich and so satisfying. Facing Glen McGrath, Mattiah Murallitheran, Flintoff, Anderson, and the rest – and even Shoaib Akhtar – not too bad for a lad from Mannofield!

Colin Smith, b.1972. Aberdeenshire CC and Scotland. Interviewed 2015.

Between 1999 and 2009, Colin Smith represented Scotland at cricket 182 times. With his friend and business partner, Neil MacRae, he runs 'Legends', a firm which specialises in cricket equipment, most notably the manufacture and distribution of 'Katchet', a fielding practice aid.

The Middle-Distance Runner: Running in the family

My father, Mel Edwards, is a road safety engineer and he has also run his own sports consultancy, specialising in motivation, coaching, and the organisation of races. He has been a notable athlete not just in local but also national terms. He is a long-distance runner and his personal best for the marathon stands at 2hr, 18min, 24sec. In 1968 he was a second reserve for the British Olympic team for Mexico.

He has always been a great inspiration for me, not just his record but in his attitude and undying enthusiasm. I have been raised in an athletic environment. On the very day I was taken home from the maternity ward he took me on a detour to be present at a cross country meeting at Balgownie – all this before I actually entered my own home. You could say I have been destined to follow in his racing footsteps but he has never put pressure on me; for him athletics has always been about enjoyment and he's made sure that it has been that way for me too.

I love all aspects of the sport – even the dieting and the hard training. In this respect I am lucky in my coach, Lewis Walker, who keeps things simple and tries to help my enjoyment and not just act as the hard taskmaster. He has helped me to see that keeping

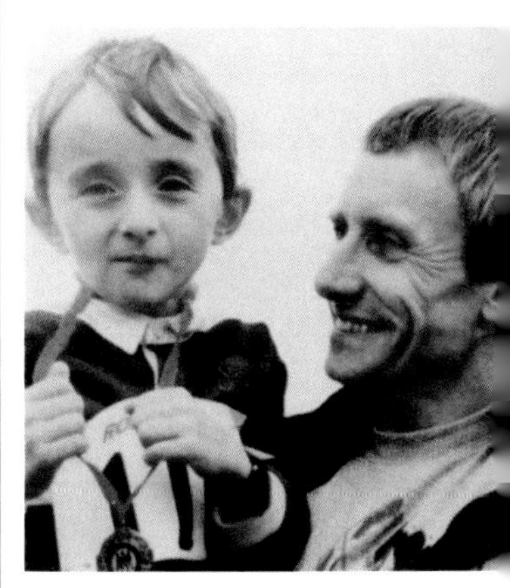

A pair of medal winners, present and future. With father Mel, 1992.

Running in the family: With cousin Erin Northcroft, holding a back garden race, 2008.

to a strict regime gives its reward in terms of better performances and so leads to greater satisfaction and pleasure.

I can't remember a time when running hasn't been part of my life. I must have entered my first fun run when I was no more than three years of age. I remember how proud I was to receive my medal for completing the run and then wearing it round my neck. I used to love those fun runs in the Aberdeen parks and knew that winning any of them would make my dad so proud. I can remember being taken along to stand at the courses, all wrapped up, so as to see my father in action. I also remember thinking to myself: 'I want to be part of this when I'm older.'

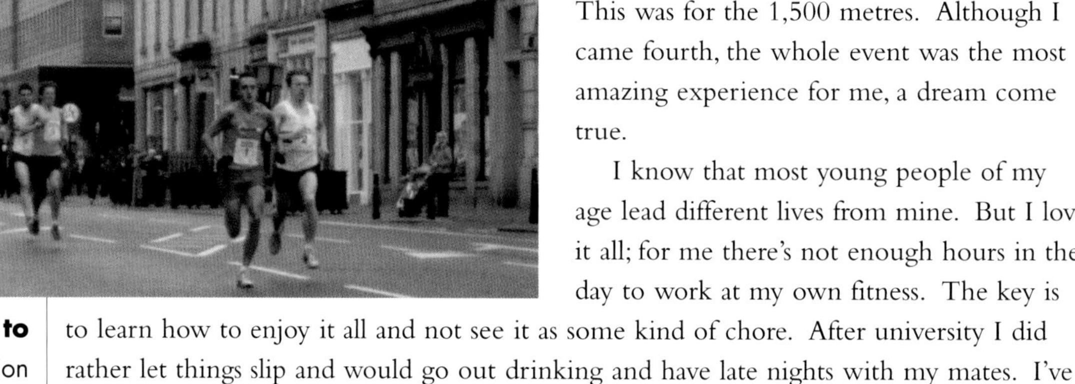

Powering to victory in the Union Street Mile, 2012.

The culmination has come this year with my selection to represent Scotland in the four-way international meet in Glasgow. This was for the 1,500 metres. Although I came fourth, the whole event was the most amazing experience for me, a dream come true.

I know that most young people of my age lead different lives from mine. But I love it all; for me there's not enough hours in the day to work at my own fitness. The key is to learn how to enjoy it all and not see it as some kind of chore. After university I did rather let things slip and would go out drinking and have late nights with my mates. I've had to find out the hard way that rolling home at 3 a.m. is not conducive to athletic success. Early nights, no alcohol, a watchful diet – these might have once been sacrifices but are now just part of what I am.

A typical week for me will be, on Sunday, one easy paced long run in Hazlehead Park of 60 minutes, on the Monday, Wednesday and Friday, two runs each day, really to keep things ticking over. But Tuesdays and Thursdays and Saturdays are the intensive sessions of track work down at the Sports Village. In the morning the run will be slow and easy, followed by hard sessions later in the day. I also try to get eight hours sleep minimum at night.

A Beach prom run with his Kenyan friend and world-class athlete, Gideon Gathimba, 2015.

As for my diet, it will be porridge and a smoothie in the morning, maybe scrambled eggs and soup at lunch and for the evening meal, chicken and vegetables. Snacking is strictly forbidden; I can't remember the last time I had a packet of crisps or sweeties. If I find myself drifting over to the biscuit cupboard, I'll stop and ask myself: 'And how exactly will this help you go faster?'

I've had my heroes in sport but the chief one has always been my dad. His enthusiasm and example have been a true source of inspiration. The way he has kept going through the years, and now through his cancer and treatment, is always there before me. He goes out each day and is now up to 105,000 miles in his career – that's four and a half times round the earth. Each morning the year round, he will be out of the door at 6AM, 72

years of age and suffering from a serious form of cancer. He will look for me to be doing the same and if when he's about to leave he sees my training shoes lying at the door, he'll take a photo of them and send it to me with the message: 'Not up yet?'

Early morning training run, Kenya, 2015.

Aberdeen is where I've grown up in the sport but since 2011 there has been another setting in which to pursue it – Kenya. I have now had seven trips out there and aim to return twice a year. The spectacle of dozen of runners appearing each morning at six o'clock, almost in a stampede of dust and energy, is amazing.

European visitors to other parts of Kenya have become quite common not just for tourism and safari but now for athletics. They come out to train, to rub shoulders with the many local high class performers and to chase the secret of Kenyan success. That is something the Kenyans find quite amusing because for them the answer is obvious: train and train, sleep well, eat well. They will kid outsiders – known as *mzungu* – by claiming it is all down to eating ugali, which is the local diet of maize and water.

For me I feel doubly blessed in what my own running has brought me. I love my sport and will continue to do my best to make the very best of whatever potential I have; but I also love the work in Kenya helping children there which my athletics has brought me. When you see children, skipping off in their excitement to go to school because of the funding we've brought and then compare it to the apathy of many kids back here, you realise just how, in more ways than one, rewarding my life in athletics has become.

Myles Edwards, b.1988. Aberdeen Amateur Athletic Club and Iten, Kenya. Interviewed 2015

In addition to his athletics, Myles Edwards has established a charitable foundation, along with his Kenyan athletic friend, Gideon Gathimba, the aim of which is to support the work of an orphanage in Karatina, the Pavilion Children's Village. He now divides his time between his athletic career and his work for the Gathimba Edwards Foundation. He is grateful to the Aberdeen IT firm 'prosource.it' whose sponsorship has made this work possible.

Jimmy Wood, winner of the British Veterans, 1994.

A game with a grace all of its own

Tennis didn't run in the family but in those days when I was growing up the game got plenty of attention in Aberdeen. This was just after the war and people were hungry for almost any sporting attraction so when tournaments were held on the lawn tennis courts at Westburn Park hundreds would turn up just to watch. There were no stands or real seating; the crowds simply stood, separated by ropes from the courts.

So it was quite natural for me as a young lad to go along and try the game for myself. When I was eight my pal, Dave McColl, and I decided to go along to the Westburn courts, borrow some racquets and balls and give the game a go. We both took to it straightaway. I simply fell in love with tennis; not only did I appear to have a natural aptitude for the game but its elegance appealed to me. It was the beginning of a lifetime enthusiasm for this most graceful of all sports.

Tennis was quite a different proposition when I took it up. Although there was a great interest in it there was little in the way of coaching or training regimes. Most played for the sheer enjoyment of the game and the companionship that it brought. That's the way it was for me. I never received any organised coaching, never felt any pressure – I was left alone to play the game for fun and that's the way it has always remained for me.

However, there was some organisation of the game in Aberdeen. The Westburn Park was home to some dozen clubs and there were regular leagues and tournaments. The best juniors did get noticed and when I was 16 I got invited to join the Forecourts Club, which was based at Devannha Gardens. This was reckoned to be the leading club in the city and the place to meet the very best and to hone your game against them. At that time just about the leading player was Vic Garland, a fine athlete and a colourful character. So it was a great thrill to move up into the Forecourts team and to appear alongside him.

But still no real coaching: Vic Garland did give me advice – with him concentration was imperative. He preached always to fight hard for each and every point, to give nothing away and to develop a killer instinct. I took that all in but would still regard my tennis as, first and foremost, fun.

En route to winning the 1962 Scottish Championships.

But on the whole I was left to develop naturally. After all, these were the days before television in every home so there were no models for me to follow except the local ones. Just about the only glimpse I ever got as a boy of the world's best was once a year, when you could go along to McMillan's shop on Union Street and catch a film of the Wimbledon finals.

My National Service did give me the chance to develop my game. I was in the RAF and got into its team. This gave me some wonderful experiences; we would jump onto a plane and go over to Cyprus, to Malta and to Gibraltar and play matches there.

Back in Aberdeen I developed my career as an Art teacher. After Robert Gordon's College came six years at the Art School, followed by thirty years as a lecturer at Aberdeen College. Tennis had to remain a spare time pursuit.

The game was still amateur – it didn't become professionalised till the late 1960s when I was nearing 40. There were very few coaches employed by the LTA; Scotland had only

one and he was based in the Central Belt – in those pre-motorway days a four-hour drive away.

So my own opportunities were limited but I've never regretted that. I still enjoyed many wonderful times. I've had a very long career; I was able to continue it up to my 80th year. I have been Scottish Champion on two occasions – 1962 and 1964. As a veteran, I've represented Britain many times and have travelled to Spain, to Germany, to New Zealand and Australia to do so. I was ranked number two in the world in the over-60s age group. I've played against the leading British players of my time, especially as a veteran. I beat Roger Becker, the old Davis Cup man, for the British Veterans' title and often emerged on top against guys who had qualified for Wimbledon.

As a player I have been blessed with a good physique and lots of natural power. I wouldn't describe myself as a fine touch player. For many years I had, as a partner for the doubles, George Kelly, who played football for the Dons and was a fine natural sportsman. He would perform the subtle shots and the angled drop shots and so on; I just supplied the power. I had a strong serve, an effective back hand and volleying power and could bash the ball about the court all right – and that was my game.

So I've had my moments. But I've always been realistic and never wasted time wondering whether I could have got to the top. You've got to remember that I was brought up in the amateur era in the days before intensive coaching, before teams of dieticians, and sports psychologists and all the rest of it. When I see Andy Murray being followed around with his team of 10 advisers I've never felt I was missing out. Tennis has now become so much more sharp edged and demanding, a full-time pressurised commitment rather than the six or eight hours a week recreation it has remained for me. For me I have been able to retain my enthusiasm for it largely because it has never been more than an enjoyment.

James (Jimmy) Wood, b.1934. Cults Tennis Club. Interviewed 2017

Not like it was in his young day: Tennis Aberdeen organising a session for youngsters, Westburn Park, 2016.

Music Hall Show, 1967. A young Michael Main is on the right.

The Pigeon Fancier: One of nature's mysteries

I've always had pigeons. It started off when I was just a boy and my father was away for anything up to two weeks at a time, working on the hydro dams. My mother would take me down to Blackfriar's Street to meet him off the bus on his return home. One day he appeared carrying a cage. It had a pair of white fantail doves; he'd been working at Candacraig where they'd been demolishing an old dove-cot and he had acquired these birds. He himself had enjoyed keeping pigeons when he was a boy; he knew I loved animals and so he reckoned I would take to them. He was right; I was immediately hooked and have kept pigeons ever since.

I joined the local pigeon club. When I was a boy pigeon fancying was very big in Aberdeen. Just about every other one of the old air raid shelters had a loft built into it. There were lofts at all the allotments too. The ones at Froghall were a great centre for the sport. People then kept dogs and chickens and rabbits, and pigeons were part of that general interest in home reared animals.

Back then we sent off our birds by British Rail. My father and I would take the bus down to Union Street with a basket of pigeons, go down the steps to the Green and across to the Joint Station. It was treated as a big event; men would dress up in collar and tie and suits. At the other end the station master would send off a telegram to tell you exactly when the birds had been released. And the clock at Froghall would be set. There was nothing wrong with my maths so I would be given the task of working out the precise velocities as the birds arrived home and were clocked in. Then on the Sunday I would jump on my bike and do a tour of the best birds and chat with the owners.

I love everything about racing pigeons. I love preparing them for a race. They are true athletes and you train them up as such. You start off with small distances, maybe take them to Stonehaven to begin with, and then there will eventually come the day when you can sit, waiting in your back garden after they've been set the task of flying hundreds of miles and suddenly hear the whir of the wings and see them plop back into their coop. The excitement of that moment is amazing.

A lot of money is involved. A pigeon with a good pedigree and a race record can fetch thousands of pounds. One has gone for £125,000. That's the kind of sum rich Arabs are prepared to fork out. When you buy a pigeon you also buy its record with it and that includes any trophy it might have won. So a lot of prestige is to be bought along with the bird.

A racing pigeon is a remarkable bird, one of nature's true wonders. They are so tough and so brave. They played a noble part in both the World Wars, carrying vital messages. Many of Aberdeen's best pigeons were taken by air from Dyce for the armed services. They would be taken onto planes so that if the plane was shot down the bird could take back details of where and when in a canister on its leg. A lot of lives were saved that way. Some have been awarded medals – the Dickin Medal – for their work in the Front line.

Not a granny flat after all: Michael's self-built pigeon loft.

I've built my own pigeon lofts here in my back garden. When it was going up my

Froghall allotments: the regular 'Sunday School' for pigeon fanciers, 1950s.

mother-in-law was convinced it was a granny flat for her, the building was so large and so carefully put together. I now keep some 100 birds in it and I can tell you the pedigree of each one of them. Some can be traced back to the 1940s.

Pigeons are quite individual characters. Just like humans you have ones which are alert or dozy, ones which are highly strung or dominant or placid or vicious. They are tough and that is just as well when you consider the dangers and hardships they have to put up with during a flight home: people shoot at them, birds of prey attack them, telephone wires slice into them and they get buffeted by the wind.

But they are hardy, brave birds. Three weeks ago I had one which had come back all the way from Ypres in northern France and he had a three-inch cut right along his chest and some of his flights missing. He had evidently hit into a wire – yet he still got home.

What I'm really interested in is the breeding side. I've taken half a dozen from Belgium this year so as to build up my stock. It's the same with my budgerigars – I breed and show them at championships, often with a fair amount of success. With my pigeons I've won just about every trophy there is locally and further afield. There are five clubs in Aberdeen and I am attached to the Silver City Racing Pigeon Club. We employ drivers to take the birds to the various departure points. Everything has to be precise, the exact latitude and longitude plotted on the map. The birds are electronically tagged so that when they return they pass over a pad and their exact time is recorded.

Pigeons can cover hundreds of miles with unerring accuracy. Last Saturday my bird covered 73 miles plus 1,407 yards – distances are worked out to the last decimal point – in one hour 27 minutes. They travel at an average speed of 50 mph and can get up to 60. In 1967 a pigeon of mine was liberated at Rennes in France and got back here in 15 hours of nonstop flying. That was a distance of 627 miles although, given the weather and wind conditions, it probably did more like 800. My Bon Accord Blue held the record for that race and it stood for 21 years.

How they navigate their way is one of nature's most amazing mysteries. Various theories are advanced: could it be the pull of the earth by the moon? sense of gravity? smell? the stars? the earth's magnetic field? Nobody has really been able to explain it. What I know is that when you are sitting at home and suddenly hear the plop and the rustle of wings as your bird arrives safely home after a 500 mile plus flight – well, the tension of the waiting and then the thrill of the moment of success beats anything.

Michael Main, b.1948. Silver City Pigeon Racing Club. Interviewed 2016.

The Main-Jenkins budgerigar gains the Grey Green class certificate, World Championships, Doncaster – and the cover of the 'Scottish Budgerigar'.

The Professional Golfer: I was always a ferocious practiser

I am one of a set of triplets. I realise that triplets are something of a rarity but having been one all my life and never knowing anything different I think of myself as quite normal. However, I also realise that we were treated rather differently: right up till the age of 11 we were always dressed alike. And I was always known simply as 'one of the triplets' never as 'Muriel.' I didn't really have my own identity.

Maybe that's why I became a professional golfer. Up until we reached 14 we all three of us played golf and all three of us were similarly talented at it. Each summer the family would rent a house out at Aboyne for a couple of months during the school holidays and this went on for 10 years between the ages of five and 15. We would all play golf together out there but then when we reached 14 or so my sisters began to lose interest and wanted to devote more time to discos and other pursuits. Although I wasn't aware of it at the time I now sometimes wonder if my reason for sticking with the golf was to strike out with my own identity. Even so this often simply meant: 'Oh, so you're the golfing triplet!'

We have settled out on our own paths through life. They are both married and both have two children whereas I have remained unmarried and enjoy the freedom that gives me. But we remain close: recently we spent our 60th birthday celebrations together in Venice.

As children we lived in the city, in Fountainhall Road, but I wanted nothing more than to be out of doors, throwing myself into something active. That's why I loved our summer holiday times out at Aboyne, not just the golf but tramping the hills, going down to the Dee with a rod we'd fashioned out of a rowan tree branch, cycling, just running about; anything that involved outdoor activity.

I started golf when I reached the age of nine. My father was a very good amateur player with a handicap of two and I suppose I've inherited some of his talent. As my enthusiasm for the game grew he would take a close interest in my progress. He would encourage me to do better and better. This could be a bit irksome at times as when we played together he would offer a running commentary on my skills. Stuff like: 'You weren't using the right club; you should have run it up with a five-iron.' I found that hard

going at times – and not necessarily made better by the fact that he was usually right.

I felt that however well I might consider I was performing, it was never quite good enough to meet his standards; but his drive and his criticisms helped to push me on and never to settle for second best.

But how I really began goes back to those summer holidays at Aboyne. When my sisters and I were out there the three of us got into the habit of going along to the village green and playing on its open spaces as well as visiting the swing park. There was also a set of local lads who would go along and play football and cricket and we would watch and listen to them. One day this boy wasn't having much success at his cricket and he was swearing away quite loudly. Now, we were quite innocent, well brought up young ladies, so some of his vocabulary was quite strange to us. When we got home the first thing we did was to go up to Mum and ask: 'What does f——! mean? She was absolutely shocked and when our father got in she related the story to him. His response was: 'We're going to have to get the girls out of that park.'

The next week when he got home it was to load up the car with three sets of golf clubs, shoes, bags and balls for us all – just cut down hickory sticks, nothing fancy. Then he drove us along to Aboyne Golf Club. That soon became our daily routine. We'd get up, have our breakfast, and then walk along to the club; Mum would come along with her trolley, which was loaded up with clubs and, on the handle, baskets full of tea and biscuits. We'd play our 18 holes with a refreshment break at the 12th. That was our morning; in the afternoon we'd return to the course and play another 18 holes and then, after the evening meal, maybe a further 12 holes or so.

So that's how my golf got going. I was absolutely gripped by the game. When I

A proud moment: The Curtis Cup line up, 1978 – and Muriel is second right.

An early triumph: Aboyne, 1960s .

reached 14, I decided that I wanted to play through the winter as well so I joined Murcar. People at the club saw I had some talent and suggested I enter competitions, so the following year I went down to Edzell to play in the Scottish Girls' Championship. I met some super girls there and had a great time of it. That was me hooked. From that point onwards all I ever wanted to do was to devote my time to golf. It became my life.

I was a ferocious practiser, a real perfectionist. But I had a problem: I used to hold the club in a cack-handed way, right hand above left, in a sort of baseball grip. For a child that's the grip that often comes naturally and that's the way I was doing it.

At the age of 15, I got selected for the Scottish team in the Junior internationals. It was a wonderful experience at that age to travel all the way down to Wales by train, along with Mary Kirk from Inverness, who'd also been selected. I can still picture the two of us, clattering over the footbridges, all laden with our clubs, our holdalls and our trolleys. But I was still using my cack-handed grip and, when I went to warm up on the first tee my Welsh opponent just stood there, staring at my grip and trying hard not to let out a superior giggle or two. But I had the last laugh – by beating her six and five.

None of this stopped me from making good progress. I got into the Scottish Girls' Team and that meant I qualified for a £5 voucher for golf lessons. In those days £5 went a long way, enough to trade in for a dozen whole sessions. But the gift came with a stipulation: I was told that it was conditional on my working to change my grip to the orthodox left over right. To begin with I resisted but when the following year the same thing happened, I decided that the time had finally come to change my grip.

I went to Jock Lawson at Murcar and together we worked on the problem. To begin with it was very tricky. For many months after that, I could only top the ball along the ground; sometimes I would go off by myself and have a sneaky shot using my old grip – and then it got to the stage where I couldn't hit the ball cleanly either way. But I knew that I had potential; after all I had achieved a three handicap playing cack-handed and was anxious to see how far I could go in the game. So I was determined to conquer the problem and over the winter I did a lot of hard work. By the late spring I finally was managing to get along with my new grip.

Although it was tough at the time I realise that if I hadn't taken that step I would never have been more than a very good amateur. My ambition was simply to be as good as I possibly could, to get a place in the Scottish team. I made steady progress. I did well at the Scottish Girls' level and got into the Scottish Girls' Final.

In the meantime I also had to earn some money, to get a job. At school my mind had been increasingly taken up with golf. When I left school I went to college to do an accounting course. Then I got a position with the Clydesdale Bank. I owed my opportunity to join the bank to Sir Robert Fairbairn, who was a director of the bank and also of the Scottish Amicable Society. My father, being with Scottish Amicable, knew him and when they met they chatted about me. He asked: 'And how's your daughter, the golfer, getting on these days?' He then told my dad that if I were to apply to his bank I would be given as much time off as I needed for my golf.

Off to represent Britain and Ireland in the Curtis Cup, 1978.

The appointment as Portlethen professional, 1990.

The bank was very generous towards me; in my final year with them I was away for as many as 12 weeks – to participate in the Scottish Ladies, in the British Ladies, the Scottish Stroke Play, the County Cup, the Curtis Cup – and that in the States – followed by the American and Canadian Opens. Finally I flew off to Fiji for the World Cup. But at least the bank was able to regard my golf as being good for its image; there were press photos of me behind the counter, counting out pound notes. The bank regarded the whole exercise as good for its image with the public.

But I was never going to make a banker. My sole ambition was to develop into a top-class golfer. Things went well: I made it into the Curtis Cup, then the World Cup. But I came to realise that to advance even further I would need to turn pro. I was very fortunate that one day a businessman friend of my father phoned me up with 'Do you want to become a professional? If you do, I'll sponsor you.'

European Order of Merit, 1980.

So I turned pro in May 1979. The European Ladies Tour started up so it made sense to join that. I won the Order of Merit in both 1980 and 1983. Looking back though, I can see that my approach was somewhat amateurish still. But in those days so was everyone else's: there wasn't the whole battery of backroom advice that you take for granted nowadays – no dieticians, no sports psychologists, no specialised fitness training. My approach was the same as what had served me well enough during my early days – practice, practice, practice. My preparation was simply to hit as many balls as I could at practice, working to perfect my game by actually doing it.

There were no big driving ranges then so I would go out onto the practice ground with my caddy, send him off into the distance, take a bucket of balls and fire them off at him, one by one. He would pick them up and then return them to me so we could go again – and again and again. He wore a big baseball mitt and would try to catch the balls as they came sailing towards him. Whenever he succeeded you would hear the ball landing in that glove with a satisfying thud.

But even he would tire eventually so the conversation would then go: 'Just another bucket, John, just one more,' and he would say: 'But Muriel, everyone else has gone home.' And I would reply: 'Never mind them – just one more bucket.' You'd hit a good one and immediately think to yourself: 'I must repeat that – now.' and if it was a bad one: 'I must do better – let's try another one.' Either way, I kept on hitting ball after ball; perfection was my aim.

When I came to a tournament I wouldn't say I was ever shaking with nerves but I definitely felt an adrenalin rush and that could become quite addictive. That's why in the end I gave up serious tournament golf. I was beginning to find that that sense of excited anticipation had ebbed away. By the time I got into my mid-30s I found myself simply going through the motions. The inner spark had gone; I had burnt myself out. I had been playing competitively since the age of 15 without a break. Back then I just had myself to rely upon; there was no sports psychologist to come to my aid. I was on my own and ultimately that wasn't enough.

The job at Portlethen came up at the right time for me just when I had decided I'd had enough of the tour, back in 1989. I saw the advert and knew that I had to go for it – I love a new challenge. So I became the very first female pro attached to a club ever to be appointed in Scotland – even now there's only ever been one other.

I've loved every minute of it. It's been a privilege to be at the very beginning of a brand new club and see it go from strength to strength. The members have been marvellous through all that time. In fact I still wake up in the morning, pinching myself at the prospect of going off to a

The perfect swing: Muriel in action.

Her other passion: With the children of St Joseph's Chennai, 2010.

job which has never seemed like a job at all but simply a lot of fun.

But on my way to settling down as a club pro I did have some great times. There were those two Order of Merit successes in 1980 and 1983. I also had some great amateur highlights, the Curtis Cup in America being one of them. I would regard that as the pinnacle of my amateur career. To be lined up with the rest of the team on that opening morning and hear the national anthems being played and watch the flags being raised up and feel a shiver go down your spine and the legs beginning to shake, well that was real excitement. I remember standing there and thinking to myself that this is what I'd been working for, that this was how my hours and hours of practice were paying off.

And the comradeship with the other women was quite wonderful too. I thoroughly enjoyed the lifestyle, seeing new places, the banter with the others. At the beginning of the Tour there was a great sense of togetherness. We were all anxious to show that the women's game was a serious proposition so that whenever one of us handed in a top score the rest of us would rejoice in it too. Everyone was rooting for everyone else.

I mean, what could be better than playing the game you loved, being paid for it, living alongside others doing the same and travelling the world? I am very lucky to have been there to do all that. Looking back I can honestly say to myself that I have enjoyed a wonderful life. I know that I won't die saying 'If only…' Nor have I ever had to get up and think 'Oh no, another day of work.'

Golf in the North-east is in a good place. I maintain that it's a great game for any

I remember going to Royal Burgess in Edinburgh to take part in a pro-am and seeing a large sign outside which proclaimed: 'No dogs or women allowed.' Note the ordering of those words.

youngster to take up. It's not just the sport itself and the open air but the values it instils in you: discipline, etiquette, sportsmanship, adherence to rules and, above all, proper effort. It's such a precise game that nothing but the most meticulous care and attention to detail will do. It's been a pleasure to see how a youngster can come to the club, all rough edges and awkward behaviour, and grow up through the game. It's a real character builder.

And the role of women has improved out of all recognition too. That isn't to say that there haven't been one or two amusing incidents during my career on account of my gender. I remember playing down at Elie and having to have the layout of the clubhouse carefully explained to me. The ladies' changing room was situated on the right hand side but I was told that on no account must I go straight to it, round in front of the clubhouse, since the gentlemen's lounge was there and it simply would not do for any male member to look up and get a glimpse of a female passing by his window.

I also remember going to Royal Burgess in Edinburgh to take part in a pro-am and seeing a large sign outside which proclaimed: 'No dogs or women allowed.' Note the ordering of those words – they had to get their priorities right.

Now of course the Royal and Ancient at St Andrews has finally removed its rule banning women from their clubhouse. But when I was appearing in the Scottish and the British Ladies tournaments there they were quite happy to waive that restriction for the week. So I'm fairly relaxed about that sort of thing. If you don't like the way any one club is run then there are plenty of others you can go to.

And now I'm fast approaching the moment when at the end of this year I will have to hand over the reins to someone else. Of course I'll miss it but I feel it is the right time to go. I know I am leaving the club in good order, with a mature championship standard course, a brilliant green keeping team, a friendly atmosphere and a waiting list. It's time for me to take the time to explore my own country, to visit all those places I have been too busy to go to – Aberdeen Art Gallery, Castle Fraser, the Maritime Museum, the hills and the river valleys. And, of course, I'll be able to spend even more time in the place I've come to regard as my second home: the St Joseph's Centre in Chennai.

Muriel Thomson, b.1954. Portlethen Golf Club. Interviewed 2014.

In addition to her illustrious career in golf, Muriel Thomson has devoted herself to working with, and raising funds for, the St Joseph's Centre in Chennai, India. This is a Franciscan enterprise which cares for some 120 orphans and semi-orphans.